BOOK OF JEREMIAH

A Commentary

THIS VOLUME WAS MADE POSSIBLE THROUGH THE EISENDRATH

PUBLICATION FUND, INSTITUTED ON THE TWENTY-FIFTH ANNIVERSARY

OF RABBI MAURICE N. EISENDRATH AS PRESIDENT OF

THE UNION OF AMERICAN HEBREW CONGREGATIONS

THE JEWISH COMMENTARY FOR BIBLE READERS

BOOK OF
JEREMIAH

A Commentary by Solomon B. Freehof, *D.D.*

UNION OF AMERICAN HEBREW CONGREGATIONS

NEW YORK · MCMLXXVII

LIBRARY OF CONGRESS CATALOGING IN PUBLICATION DATA

FREEHOF, SOLOMON BENNETT, 1892–
  Book of Jeremiah.

  (The Jewish commentary for Bible readers)

        Bibliography: p.
        1. Bible. O. T. Jeremiah—Commentaries. I. Bible.
  O. T. Jeremiah. English. Jewish Publication Society.
  1977. II. Title. III. Series: Commission on Jewish Edu-
  cation of the Union of American Hebrew Congregations
  and the Central Conference of American Rabbis. The
  Jewish commentary for Bible readers.
  BS1525.3.F73   224'.2'077   77–8259
  ISBN 0–8074–0008–4

WITH PRAYERS FOR A LONG AND CREATIVE CAREER,

THIS BOOK IS DEDICATED TO MY HONORED COLLEAGUE

AND SUCCESSOR, WALTER JACOB

EDITOR'S INTRODUCTION

IN EVERY GENERATION, there are a few select individuals who become legends in their own time. Some prodigious accomplishment, some exemplary achievement, elevates them and sets them as models to be admired and emulated by others.

In our generation, especially in the realm of Jewish scholarship and Jewish education, Solomon Freehof is one of those rare and special human beings. This superb commentary on the Book of Jeremiah is only the latest in a seemingly endless list of books and articles that have opened the eyes of our people to the precious heritage that is their inheritance from the past.

On the occasion of Rabbi Freehof's eighty-fifth birthday, we are pleased and honored to share this gift of learning from him to our Jewish community. I know that high school, college, and adult students will find this volume an invaluable tool in their pursuit of Jewish literacy and understanding.

We extend to Rabbi Freehof our best wishes for many more years of creative endeavor—and our thanks for his lifetime of service to Reform Judaism.

Daniel B. Syme

BOOK OF JEREMIAH

A Commentary

Introduction

1. The Jeremiah Literature

THE BOOK of Jeremiah is one of the larger biblical books. Yet its fifty-two chapters are in all probability only the remnant of a much larger literature containing sermons by Jeremiah and narratives about him. Duhm, in his commentary on Jeremiah, presents the reasons for his belief that there was once much more Jeremiah literature than we have now. In the biblical Book of Daniel (9:2), we read: "I, Daniel, meditated . . . on the word of the Lord which came to Jeremiah the Prophet that He would accomplish for the desolation of Jerusalem seventy years." Also in II Chronicles 36:21: "To fulfill the word of the Lord by the mouth of Jeremiah, until the land hath been paid her sabbaths; for as long as she lay desolate, she kept sabbath, to fulfill three score and ten years." He states that neither of these statements makes a reference to anything found in our present Book of Jeremiah. Evidently, then, they were taken from other "Jeremiah" writers. Actually there is a verse in Jeremiah (25:11) which speaks of the Bablyonian exile lasting for seventy years. But Duhm considers this verse to be postexilic.

There is some indication in the present Book of Jeremiah that there was other Jeremiah literature. In chapter 36:17 and 18, Baruch, the friend and secretary of Jeremiah, tells how he copied the sermons of Jeremiah. "And they asked Baruch, 'Tell us now: How did you write all these words?' Then Baruch answered them: 'He pronounced all these words unto me with his mouth, and I wrote them with ink in the book.'" Then in verse 23, we are told that the king burned that book and Jeremiah dictated again to Baruch, and verse 32 says that in addition, "And there were added besides unto them many like words. These "many like words" may well be found in our present text of the book.

That there must have been differing texts of Jeremiah in circulation is evident from the fact that the Greek translation (the Septuagint) is so markedly different from our Hebrew text. Cornill, in his introduction, p. 312, calls attention to the fact that there are twenty-seven hundred words in the Hebrew text which are missing in the Greek version. Besides, the order of many chapters varies considerably from the Hebrew version of the book.

According to tradition, Jeremiah was the author of the biblical Book of Lamentations, which is deemed to be virtually part of his book. In fact, the Talmud (Baba Bathra 15a) says that Jeremiah was the author of his own book, the Book of Lamentations, and the Book of Kings. Also in the Apocrypha, in the Book of Baruch, there is a letter of Jeremiah to the Exile.

The prophet and his writing remained a living part of Jewish tradition. The somber mood of most of Jeremiah's preachments made them appropriate readings for times of sorrow. The Book of Lamentations—deemed, of course, to be of Jeremiah's authorship— was the main reading on the anniversary of the destruction of the Temple (the ninth of Av), and on that day the Haftarah was also from Jeremiah (8:13-9:23). Moreover, in times of personal grief, the writings of Jeremiah were deemed to be appropriate for private devotion. A mourner in the seven days of his mourning may not study Scripture in general, or the Talmud, but the Talmud in *Taanit* 30a says that he may read the Book of Job, the sad parts of the Book of Jeremiah, and the Book of Lamentations, which was, of course, taken to be of Jeremiah's authorship. This talmudic statement has become an established practice and as such is recorded in the *Shulchan Aruch*, Yore Deah 385:4. There are also the eight prophetical readings in the synagogue taken from the Book of Jeremiah; these passages were well known to every Jewish worshiper.

2. The Historical Background

Jeremiah was the last major prophet before the destruction of the Jewish state in 586 B.C.E., and since he lived in such eventful times, it is to be expected that he would have a strong sense of history. It is understandable, too, that the Talmud should consider him to be the author of the Book of Kings. As for the biblical Book of Jeremiah, it seems to contain more historical material than the other prophetic books. For example, Jeremiah 1:2 begins, ". . . in the thirteenth year of king Josiah," and verse 3, ". . . in the days of Jehoiakim the son of Josiah, king of Judah, unto the end of the eleventh year of Zedekiah the son of Josiah, king of Judah, unto the carrying away of Jerusalem captive in the fifth month." There are datings in Jeremiah 3:6, 21:1, 25:1, 26:1, etc., etc.; 34:1 and 6 are described as taking place during the siege of Jerusalem by the Babylonians; and 37:1 begins with a clear historical reference: "And Zedekiah the son of Josiah reigned as king, instead of Coniah the son of Jehoiakim, whom Nebuchadrezzar king of Babylon made king in the land of Judah." What is perhaps even more important, these various datings are correlated in a number of places in the book with the datings of the Babylonian kings. Thus 32:1: "The word that came to Jeremiah from the Lord in the tenth year of Zedekiah king of Judah, which was the eighteenth year of Nebuchadrezzar."

Since the dates of the Babylonian and Assyrian kings are known to us exactly from inscriptions and other sources, the book serves as a valuable check for the dating of events in Jewish history. And because of that fact, it is possible to give an exact date for Jeremiah's preaching. Thus John Bright, in the introduction of his *Jeremiah* (p. xxviii), dates Jeremiah's preaching career as beginning in the year 627 before the common era and ending after the year 587 (in Egypt). (See also Cornill, p. 296.)

Jeremiah's career can be understood best if studied against the background of the kings of Judea in whose time and presence he preached. His great predecessor Isaiah preached "in the days of Uzziah, Jotham, Ahaz, and Hezekiah, kings of Judah" (Isaiah 1:1). Hezekiah, in whose reign most of the preachings of Isaiah took place, was followed by his evil son Manasseh. Manasseh was followed by his son Amon. Amon was murdered in a palace insurrection, and he was followed by his infant son Josiah, in whose reign Jeremiah began to preach. Josiah was the righteous king in whose reign the religious reformation known as the Deuteronomic reformation took place. Josiah was slain by Pharaoh-necoh, who was marching north to battle with the Babylonians. He was succeeded by his son Jehoahaz who was taken captive by the Egyptians and was succeeded on the throne by his brother Jehoiakim. He was succeeded by his son Jehoiachin who was exiled to Babylon in the first Babylonian conquest of Jerusalem. He was followed by Zedekiah, the third son of Josiah, who was king in Jerusalem at the time of the final destruction in 586. After the destruction of Jerusalem and the assassination of Gedaliah, Jeremiah was forcibly taken to Egypt by the remnants of the Jewish community, which fled to Egypt for safety. He preached one sermon there which is recorded and then we hear no more about him.

The reigns of these various kings of Judea, while central in Jewish history, were somewhat peripheral to the larger history of the Near East. Actually the fate of both the northern and southern kingdoms depended upon world events. Their special geographical location made it impossible for the Jewish kingdoms to isolate themselves from the larger historical movements of the era. The Jewish kingdoms lay exactly in the path of the conquering armies that constantly swept over the Near East. The main historical struggle for dominance was between the Nile and Mesopotamia. On the Nile were the various dynasties of Egypt; in the Mesopotamian area, first Babylon, then Assyria, then Babylon again, and finally Persia, struggled for dominance of West Asia. Whether it was the Egyptians marching north and east or the Mesopotamian armies marching west and south, the main line of march crossed the lands of the small Jewish kingdoms, which were weak and fragile compared to the warring giants. Thus, what happened to the kings of Judea and to Jerusalem was only in a minor degree the result of the political or military actions of the Jewish monarchy.

In the time of the Prophet Isaiah (chiefly in the reign of King Hezekiah), the two contestants were Egypt and Assyria. During Jeremiah's career, in the early part of his ministry, the Mesopotamian power was still Assyria. But in the latter half of his ministry, Babylonia had taken its place as the Mesopotamian contestant with Egypt for world control.

In addition to this endless military seesaw, there seems to have been, in Jeremiah's time, an irruption of a barbaric people from beyond the borders of the Near East. According to the Greek historian Herodotus, the Scythians (who dwelt around the Black Sea and the eastern Carpathians) suddenly burst into the Near East, marching southward, devastating the land until they reached Egypt, where Egypt bought them off and bribed them to return to the north. Many biblical scholars believe that it is to this invasion from the north that Jeremiah has reference in his sermon beginning with chapter 4 (see verses 6 and 7): "For I will bring evil from the north, and a great destruction. A lion is gone up from his thicket, and a destroyer of nations is set out, gone forth from his place; to make thy land desolate, that thy cities be laid waste, without inhabitant."

Yet the incursion of the Scythians from the north was a calamity that occurred only once, whereas the struggle between the Nile and Mesopotamia was a never-ending danger. Actually nothing could save the two Jewish kingdoms and preserve them for any length of time. There were always patriotic groups arising to free the country from its overlord, whichever it was at the time. A freedom campaign usually involved an attempt to make alliances with one group or another. Generally it was an alliance of the small neighboring countries, and with Egypt against the Mesopotamian powers. The Prophet Isaiah, for example, advised against such foreign alliances. Whatever type of resistance was organized, nothing actually helped. The two little kingdoms, Israel and Judah, were simply in the way; and whichever of the two powers was the more powerful in a given era, that power became the overlord of the Jewish kingdoms.

During the long ministry of Jeremiah there were radical changes in the world picture. In the early days of his ministry, when Pharaoh-necoh marched north to aid Assyria against the Babylonians, King Josiah had the foolhardy belief that he could stop the Egyptians. But in that ill-considered attempt he was killed. As for Assyria, its capital city, Nineveh (which, during the century of Assyrian dominance, was of course the capital of the Near East), was finally destroyed in the year 607 by an army of Medes from the north. This meant that the Babylonian kingdom, which was gradually reviving, now became master of the Near East and the eastern opponent in the struggle with Egypt. In the year 605 (i.e., two years after the destruction of Nineveh) Pharaoh-necoh II was defeated by the Babylonians under Nebuchadnezzar at Carchemish on the Euphrates River, in one of the decisive battles of human history. It is to this that Jeremiah refers in 46:2 ff.: "Of Egypt: concerning

the army of Pharaoh-necoh king of Egypt, which was by the river
Euphrates in Carchemish, which Nebuchadnezzar king of Babylon
smote in the fourth year of Jehoiakim the son of Josiah, king of
Judah."

Thereafter Babylon was the dominant power in the Near
East. It was Assyria that had destroyed the northern kingdom of
Israel, and its capital city of Samaria, in the year 722 B.C.E., and it
was Babylon that destroyed the southern kingdom of Judea, and its
capital city of Jerusalem, one hundred and thirty-six years later (in
the year 586 B.C.E.).

In the time of the Prophet Isaiah, when Jerusalem was besieged by the Assyrians, the city was saved perhaps because the
northern kingdom still existed. It had made its own alliances and
acted as a buffer state, a fact which for a while at least diminished
the strength of the invading Assyrian armies. But in the early years
of Jeremiah's career, Assyria was already a fading power. Now
Babylon, resurgent, took over the dominance of the Mesopotamian
lands. The northern kingdom had been destroyed for over a century
and there was nothing to impede the onward march of the Babylonian invaders. Therefore the sense of an inevitable doom hovered
over the people of the small kingdom and shadowed all of Jeremiah's prophecy. Of all the prophetic books, the Book of Jeremiah
gives the darkest mood of inescapable tragedy.

3. The Personality of the Prophet

SHELDON BLANK has written a book-length biography of the Prophet
Jeremiah. Deeply understanding and warmly appreciative of the
prophet's personality, it is based chiefly upon actual records in
the biblical Book of Jeremiah. We mention this biography not only
for its own merits, but because it throws light on the unique character of the biblical book.

It is doubtful whether such a full-length biography could
be written today about any other of the biblical prophets—that is
to say, without the biographer needing to fill large gaps with material drawn from his own imagination. The Book of Jeremiah is
by far the richest of all biblical books in biographical material of

the author. First of all, there is a record of the actual events as they occurred: Jeremiah put into the stocks, put into a cell, put into a muddy pit; Jeremiah dictating his sermons to his friend and secretary, Baruch; the text of the scroll, cut up and burned in the presence of the king; Jeremiah dictating a larger text of his prophecy; Jeremiah buying some land in his hometown of Anathoth; the method by which he preserved the legal papers involved; his conversation with the general of the conquering Babylonian army; his being virtually kidnapped and taken away by the Judean refugees to Egypt.

All these and many other biographical data (many more than we have of any other prophet) are recorded. But perhaps of greater importance than these biographical facts is the extraordinary amount of emotional self-expression. There are about a dozen passages of frank self-revelation. Jeremiah frequently speaks about his own feelings, his shrinking from the prophetic task, his reluctant acceptance of it at God's command, his lonely unmarried life, the dislike and hatred which his sermons aroused in his contemporaries and his bitterness against them, his sadness at the very fact that he lives in such a time of tragedy, and even his Job-like arguments with God Himself. In some of these emotional outbursts, the prophet pleads with God for help and even cries out for vengeance against his enemies. Twice he finds his life so bitter that he wishes (in almost the same language later used in the Book of Job) that he had never been born: "Woe is me, my mother, that thou hast borne me, a man of strife and contention to the whole earth! . . . Every one of them doth curse me" (15:10 ff.). So too in 20:14: "Cursed be the day wherein I was born . . . ." He ascribes his sorrows and his suffering to the fact that God had "enticed" him into prophecy and put him into a position where he must denounce people and awaken their enmity or mockery. "O Lord, Thou hast enticed me . . . and hast prevailed. I have become a laughing-stock all the day, everyone mocketh me. I cry: 'Violence and spoil,' because the word of the Lord is . . . a reproach to me" (20:7 ff.).

These tragic passages of self-expression are generally called by commentators "Jeremiah's confessions." The term is hardly exact. "Confession" gives the connotation of an admission of guilt. There is no such thing in these passages. Jeremiah accepts the mission assigned him by God. Though he complains to God Himself of the misery which the task has brought him, he yet says he has willingly and at times even gladly accepted the task, even though it meant loneliness and pain. "Thy words were unto me a joy and the rejoicing of my heart; because Thy name was called on me" (15:16). "As for me, I have not hastened from being a shepherd after Thee" (17:16). These, then, are not "confessions" of guilt. They are self-revelations, outpourings of the inner life, the story of his inner sorrow and the discovery of his inner strength.

Pfeiffer, in his *Introduction to the Old Testament*, p. 498, describes Jeremiah as follows: "Jeremiah is the first in the line of mystics who have recorded their inner experiences; the first to argue thus with God and to have ascended *de profundis* from the slough of despond to a glorious and triumphant faith."

There is no such self-revelation, at least not to such a degree, in any of the other prophets. Here at least one prophet reveals his inner life without reserve. Perhaps Isaiah and Amos and Hosea had felt similar inner loneliness and pain, but we do not know that because they do not tell us. Perhaps Jeremiah has revealed a tragedy which the other great prophets kept concealed within their hearts. But perhaps this is the special tragedy of a unique individual, a priest who became a prophet at God's inescapable orders, a priest who never married and had no family to strengthen and console him; who had one comrade at least, Baruch, and an Ethiopian palace-servant who took pity on him. Perhaps Jeremiah was unique in his tragedy, yet his is a human tragedy, one which might come to any sensitive soul with an inescapable mission in a tragic age.

4. The Career of Jeremiah

OF COURSE much of Jeremiah's inner sorrow was the reflection of his outer miseries; and much that made his life miserable might never have happened to him in another period of history. He was charged with being a traitor because of his opposition to what he considered a futile revolt against the mighty military powers. He was hated. He was imprisoned. He was saved. His works were burned and written again and preserved. The last king of Judah, Zedekiah, summoned him to seek his help and sought to protect him

against his enemies. He was befriended by the Babylonian conquerors when Jerusalem was destroyed in 586. Then there was a
murderous revolt among the remnant left in Judea, and he was taken
by the refugees into Egypt, where apparently he died and vanished
from history.

Besides the world events and the tension which they aroused
among the people, a major religio-social event, which changed the
nation's mode of worship, also had an impact on the life of Jeremiah. This event described in II Kings 23, took place in the early
days of Jeremiah's career. A book was discovered in the Temple,
and because of it, a new solemn covenant, in a ceremony conducted
by the king, was made between God and the people. This led to a
religious revolution. All the shrines in the country were abolished,
and henceforth only the Temple in Jerusalem was deemed sacred.
The idolatrous worship was cleaned away, and there was a sense
of a new religious dedication on the part of the people. The book
which led to this rededication is generally understood to be
(chiefly) our present fifth book of the Torah, the Book of Deuteronomy. Beside the new religious life for the people which the book
was meant to create, it started a new literary impulse affecting
much of the Bible. It seems hardly possible that such a great religious revival would not have had a profound influence upon a
young prophet whose concerns were concentrated upon cleansing
the hearts of the people and moving them away from idolatry.

Yet many modern scholars have insisted that Jeremiah was
opposed to the Deuteronomic reformation. The root of their ob-
jection is their general doctrine that Jeremiah, together with the
other great prophets, was completely opposed to "ritual and cult."
The Book of Deuteronomy is full of ritual and "cultic" commandments. Hence Jeremiah must have been opposed to it. However,
these scholars are confronted with the astonishing fact that there
is a strange identity in language between the Book of Jeremiah and
the biblical Book of Deuteronomy. Many unique and original
phrases are found in both. As a matter of fact, the modern Israeli
biblical scholar Yehezkel Kaufmann records, in volume 8 of *The
Religion of Israel*, more or less two hundred phrases found only
in both books.

Those scholars who insist that Jeremiah opposed the reformation must explain away the similarity of language, and must also

find a reason why there is no clear denunciation of the reformation in Jeremiah, since they say that Jeremiah was opposed to it. They explain this by saying that the Book of Jeremiah was edited by Deuteronomic editors who removed whatever denunciations of the reformation were made by the prophet and who also rephrased the book to fit the Deuteronomic literary style. But a recent scholar (Bright, p. xci) expresses a much more moderate view of the relationship of Jeremiah to the Deuteronomic reformation: "At the same time it was almost unthinkable that Jeremiah could have opposed Josiah's effort to rid the land of the very paganism against which he had preached with such vehemence, or that the king's attempt to revive the theology of the ancient Mosaic covenant . . . the plausible supposition is that Jeremiah . . . though not necessarily approving of all of its features, was initially in favor of its essential aims." A reasonable view of the subject would seem to be this: Jeremiah was deeply impressed by the reformation; therefore his book showed the influence of the Deuteronomic style. However, when the people reverted to their old sins, he saw that the spiritual purification which he and many others had hoped for had proved to be a delusion. Now he felt that another rededication of the people to God would have to be much more sincere than this one had proved to be and must be more truly a "covenant written in the heart" (Jeremiah 31:33).

5. The Nature of the Commentary

THIS commentary is planned to be a Jewish reader's commentary. The term describes the intent and the method followed in this volume as well as, presumably, in the other commentaries in this series. The fact that it is a reader's commentary defines and limits its concern. Unlike the more technical commentaries, it does not deal with linguistic analyses aimed at establishing the original and correct text. Hence there are rarely any suggested emendations of the text.

A reader's commentary begins with the text as we have it now, and since this is an English commentary, it starts with the Jewish Publication Society translation (1966) of the Book of Jeremiah. Since a translation in itself is the result of scholarly endeavors, it is by its very nature a sort of a commentary. Of course, if in the opinion of this commentator the meaning of an obscure passage can be brought out by an emendation suggested by some commentator, the emendation will be mentioned. But such occasions will be rare. The commentary is based upon the assumption that the text as we have it in our translation can generally be made understandable to the average reader.

This commentary is defined also as a Jewish reader's commentary. There has been a vast amount of first-class Christian scholarship applied to the Hebrew Bible, especially in the modern critical study of Scripture. Whatever in these critical studies may prove to be helpful will, as far as it is accessible to the commentator, be cited to help in the understanding of the text. However, while selective use will be made of the results of the critical study of Scripture, the chief use will be made of another literature entirely. The Jewish study of Jeremiah goes back virtually to the time of the prophet himself, if we count the emendations inserted into the text as we have it as a sort of commentary. But aside from these ancient interpolations, one of the earliest commentaries is the Aramaic translation, the Targum. Also the Mishnah and the Talmud and the Midrash react in their respective ways to various texts in Scripture. In the medieval period there were Jewish commentators by the scores; in southern Italy, in Spain, in the Provence, in northern France, and elsewhere. Each of these commentators naturally commented upon Scripture in the light of his own personality and interests. Some commentaries were linguistic, some merely expository, some legal, some philosophical, some cabalistic. Then there are modern and scientific commentators in the universities and secondary schools of modern Israel. All these commentaries together, or a fair marshaling of them, constitute the kaleidoscope of the reaction of historic world Jewry to the Scripture. Perhaps such a presentation will be of some value to general scholarship, since the commentaries of Jewish scholars are not generally available to Christian students. In general, a Jewish reader's commentary provides an opportunity to make clear the ancient and ongoing dialogue between Scripture and the Jewish people.

1

INTRODUCTORY chapter to the book and Jeremiah's call to become a prophet. The opening three verses of the chapter cover the time span of almost the entire book, and therefore are very likely the heading for the first booklet of prophecies which Jeremiah dictated to his friend and secretary, Baruch ben Neriah (chapter 36). So this heading presumably covers chapters 1-24, which is the main collection of the sermons.

After the heading there follows a description of the moment of inspiration that was Jeremiah's induction into the career of prophecy. Many of the great prophets speak of such a moment when they received the Divine commission and entered upon the prophetic life. Perhaps the most elaborate of these is the one in Ezekiel, with its description of a grand phenomenon of rolling chariots and blazing seraphs (Ezekiel 1 ff.). Also the great scene of Isaiah's vision of God enthroned in the Temple and the Voice which called out to him: "Whom shall I send, and who shall go for Me?" To which he answered: "Here am I, send me" (Isaiah 6:8). Here in Jeremiah, the Divine commission is given as in private conversation, a direct dialogue between God and the young prophet-to-be.

1. The words of Jeremiah the son of Hilkiah, of the priests that were in Anathoth in the land of Benjamin, 2. to whom the word of the LORD came in the days of Josiah the son of Amon, king of Judah,

Jeremiah

1

1:1 *Jeremiah the son of Hilkiah, of the priests . . . .* Jeremiah and later Ezekiel, the last two of the great prophets, were mem-

Jeremiah

1

in the thirteenth year of his reign. 3. It came also in the days of Johoiakim the son of Josiah, king of Judah, unto the end of the eleventh year of Zedekiah the son of Josiah, king of Judah, unto the carrying away of Jerusalem captive in the fifth month.

4. And the word of the Lord came unto me, saying:

5. Before I formed thee in the belly I knew thee,
And before thou camest forth out of the womb
    I sanctified thee;
I have appointed thee a prophet unto the nations.

bers of the priestly clan. Jeremiah is described as the son of Hilkiah. In II Kings 22:8 we are told that the priest who found the book of the law in the Temple (presumably our present Book of Deuteronomy) was named Hilkiah. Both Kimchi (quoting his father) and Joseph Ibn Nachmias say that the Hilkiah mentioned here as the father of Jeremiah is the same priest who found the book. Most scholars, however, reject this identification (so, for example, Luzzato). Hilkiah, the father of Jeremiah, was a descendant of the priest Eli (the tutor of Samuel), a member of the priestly clan related to Abiathar, who was exiled by King Solomon to Anathoth of the tribe of Benjamin, a few miles from Jerusalem. This priest was exiled after he had conspired with Adonijah to supplant Solomon as king of Israel. See I Kings 2:26 ff. "And unto Abiathar the priest said the king [Solomon]: 'Get thee to Anathoth, unto thine own fields; for thou art deserving of death. But I will not at this time put thee to death because thou didst bear the ark of the Lord God . . .'" Anathoth is also mentioned in Joshua 21:18 as one of the cities set aside for priestly residence.

1 : 2-3 *The word of the Lord came in the days of Josiah . . . also in the days of the Jehoiakim . . . unto the end of the eleventh year of Zedekiah . . . unto the carrying away of Jerusalem captive in the fifth month.* In other words, Jeremiah prophesied in the closing period of the Judean state. Actually, he remained for a while amid the ruins of the state, then was carried away to Egypt. Chapter 44 is a sermon of his which he delivered in Egypt.

1 : 5 *Before thou camest forth from the womb I sanctified thee . . .*

6. Then said I: 'Ah, Lord GOD! behold, I cannot speak; for I am a child.' 7. But the LORD said unto me:

Say not: I am a child;

For to whomsoever I shall send thee thou shalt go,

a prophet unto the nations.   This rather difficult concept, which has overtones of predestination, is explained in various ways by the commentators. Rashi, based upon rabbinic sources, says (Sanhedrin 38b) that God showed Adam all the leaders of the future, and thus at the very beginning of history Jeremiah's career was foreseen. Kimchi takes the concept more philosophically, basing his explanation upon Maimonides. He says that for a man to become a prophet certain potential characteristics must be in him at the beginning, and then, by intelligence, etc., they must be brought from potentiality into actuality.

A prophet unto the nations.   This Divine mandate created difficulties for the commentators. Jeremiah was a prophet to Israel, not to the nations. Rashi says, on the basis of a Midrash, that the phrase means that Jeremiah was a "prophet to Israel who, having forgotten their covenant with God, are acting like Gentiles and idolaters." Luzzato offers a simpler explanation. He says that the sentence does not mean that Jeremiah is to travel and preach among the nations, but he is to preach to Israel with regard to the nations of the world. Malbim: Your task is for *all* mankind. You are prophet for My purposes.

1 : 6   *Then said I . . . I cannot speak; for I am a child.*   Rashi says, not that Jeremiah meant that he was a child, but that he was immature or unprepared: How can I preach; I have not the experience or the status of Moses who preached to them close to his death and had previously performed many miracles to win their trust. Kimchi says that we must not wonder that prophecy came to Jeremiah when he was young, for behold it also came to Samuel when he was still younger.

1 : 7   *Say not: I am a child . . . to whomsoever I shall send thee thou shalt go.*   Rashi says this means "to the nations." Kimchi says the word of God came to Jeremiah in Anathoth, and God told him not to be afraid to go to Jerusalem and preach in the presence of the king, etc.

And whatsoever I shall command thee thou shalt
speak.

Jeremiah
1

8. Be not afraid of them;
For I am with thee to deliver thee,
Saith the LORD.

9. Then the LORD put forth His hand, and touched
my mouth; and the LORD said unto me:
Behold, I have put My words in thy mouth;

10. See, I have this day set thee over the nations and
over the kingdoms,
To root out and to pull down,
And to destroy and to overthrow;
To build, and to plant.

11. Moreover the word of the LORD came unto me,
saying: 'Jeremiah, what seest thou?' And I said:
'I see a rod of an ᵃalmond-tree,' 12. Then said the

1:9   *The Lord . . . touched my mouth . . . Behold, I have put My
words in thy mouth.*   The Targum, which always avoids too
human a description of God, rephrases as follows: "And the Lord
sent forth the word of His prophecy and arranged it in my
mouth." Kimchi, with the same motivation as the Targum, says
as follows: "The angel who appeared to him and spoke to him
in the Name of God did this. And it seemed to him in the vision
of prophecy that the angel actually did it." Kimchi adds that
the same metaphor is used by Isaiah at his consecration when he
says that the angel touched the coal to his lips.

1:10   *I have . . . set thee over . . . nations and . . . kingdoms . . .
to root out . . . and . . . to build.*   Then follow two visions
which, according to some modern commentators, constitute a
later addition to the consecration vision. This opinion is strength-
ened by the phrase used in verse 13. "The word of the Lord came
unto me the *second time* . . ." But even if so, the arranger of this
chapter, who might have been Jeremiah himself as he dictated to
Baruch, includes these two visions as appropriate to the initiation
narrative.

1:11-12   *A rod of an almond-tree. . . . I watch over My word to
perform it.*   This sentence is virtually untranslatable because
it is based upon a play on two Hebrew words. The Hebrew

ᵃ Heb. *shaked.*

18

LORD unto me: 'Thou hast well seen; for I ᵇwatch over My word to perform it.'

13. And the word of the LORD came unto me the second time, saying: 'What seest thou?' And I said: 'I see a seething pot; and the face thereof is from the north.' 14. Then the LORD said unto me: 'Out of the north the evil shall break forth upon all the inhabitants of the land. 15. For, lo, I will call all the families of the kingdoms of the north, saith the LORD; and they shall come, and they shall set every one his throne at the entrance of the gates of Jerusalem, and against all the walls thereof round about, and against all the cities of Judah. 16. And I will utter My judgments against them touching all their wickedness; in that they have forsaken Me, and have offered unto other gods, and worshipped the work of their own hands. 17. Thou therefore gird up thy loins, and arise, and speak unto them all that I command thee; be not dismayed at them, lest I dismay thee before them. 18. For, behold, I have made thee this day a fortified city, and an iron pillar, and brazen walls, against the whole land, against the kings of Judah, against the princes thereof, against the priests thereof, and against the people of the land. 19. And they shall fight against

Jeremiah

1

word *shaked*, "almond," can also sound like *shoked*, meaning "to watch." There is no pair of similar words in English to make the Hebrew play on words meaningful. Rashi makes the appropriateness of the phrase even more complex or striking than the similarity of the word *shaked*. He calls attention to the Midrash (Koheleth R, chapter 12) that from the seventeenth of Tammuz, when the Babylonians breached the walls of Jerusalem, to the ninth of Av, when the Temple was finally destroyed, is twenty-one days, which is precisely the time that passes from the blossoming of the almond to the ripening of its fruit.

1 : 13 *I see a seething pot; and the face . . . from the north.* Troubles are boiling up in the north, i.e., Babylon, and will blow their scalding heat over the land.

ᵇ Heb. *shoked.*

Jeremiah
1

thee; but they shall not prevail against thee; For I am with thee, saith the LORD, to deliver thee.'

1 : 15 *I will call all the families of the . . . north . . . they shall set . . . his throne at the . . . gates of Jerusalem.* This means that the various nations will set up courts of judgment at the gates of Jerusalem to judge between God and His people (Luzzato).

1 : 17 *Be not dismayed at them, lest I dismay thee before them.* Kimchi says: If you show courage before them, i.e., the kings, the priests, against whom I am sending you to preach, then I will be the Source of your strength and deliver you. Clearly it means: You be brave and your own courage will strengthen you. If you allow yourself to be afraid, your fear will destroy you. Be brave and I will make you as strong as "a fortified city and an iron pillar" (verse 18); "they shall fight against thee but shall not prevail against thee" (verse 19).

2

BRIGHT, IN THE Anchor Bible, considers this chapter to be a collection of various prophetic fragments. Nevertheless they now form a fairly consistent totality, so it may well be that the prophet himself put them together.

The general theme of the chapter seems to be that the prophet calls upon the people to explain the reason for their apostasy from God. Had not God been a loving Father to them since ancient times? Besides, no nation forsakes its gods even if they are only idols. In your idolatry you have been shameless, like a prostitute, wandering about.

1. And the word of the LORD came to me, saying:
2. Go, and cry in the ears of Jerusalem, saying: Thus saith the LORD:

   I remember for thee the affection of thy youth,

   The love of thine espousals;

   How thou wentest after Me in the wilderness,

   In a land that was not sown.

Jeremiah

2

2 : 2 *I remember . . . the affection of thy youth.* Rashi: God says, I will gladly take you back because I have not forgotten the lovable youthful years when you faithfully followed My messengers, Moses and Aaron, through the wilderness. Kimchi says: Even though I must now punish you, I will not destroy you

Jeremiah
2

3. Israel is the LORD's hallowed portion,
   His first-fruits of the increase;
   All that devour him shall be held guilty,
   Evil shall come upon them,
   Saith the LORD.

4. Hear ye the word of the LORD, O house of Jacob,
   And all the families of the house of Israel;

5. Thus saith the LORD:
   What unrighteousness have your fathers found
     in Me,
   That they are gone far from Me,
   And have walked after things of nought, and are
     become nought?

6. Neither said they:
   'Where is the LORD that brought us up
   Out of the land of Egypt;
   That led us through the wilderness,
   Through a land of deserts and of pits,
   Through a land of drought and of the shadow
     of death,
   Through a land that no man passed through,
   And where no man dwelt?'

7. And I brought you into a land of fruitful fields,
   To eat the fruit thereof and the good thereof;

utterly because I remember your loving youthfulness. Joseph Kara emphasizes the words "I remember" and explains the verse as follows: Even if *you* have quite forgotten, I have not forgotten those loving days, and I remind you now of My loving care in the past.

2 : 3 *Israel is the Lord's hallowed portion, His first-fruits.* Rashi explains that the phrase "first-fruit" refers to the first portions taken from the new crop, such as heave-offering, etc., which must be brought to the Temple as sacred and not eaten by the farmer. So Israel is compared to these parts of the crop to express the idea that he is God's sacred portion, and whoever destroys him will incur sin.

2 : 5 *What unrighteousness have your fathers found in Me?* Kimchi explains: For what reason did your ancestors who entered into the land of Canaan forget My loving care in the desert, abandon Me, and turn immediately to the idols of the Canaanites?

But when ye entered, ye defiled My land,
And made My heritage an abomination.

8. The priests said not: 'Where is the LORD?'
And they that handle the law knew Me not,
And the rulers transgressed against Me;
The prophets also prophesied by Baal,
And walked after things that do not profit.

9. Wherefore I will yet plead with you, said the LORD,
And with your children's children will I plead.

10. For pass over to the isles of the Kittites, and see,
And send unto Kedar, and consider diligently,
And see if there hath been such a thing.

11. Hath a nation changed its gods,
Which yet are no gods?
But My people hath changed its glory
For that which doth not profit.

12. Be astonished, O ye heavens, at this,
And be horribly afraid, be ye exceeding amazed,
Saith the LORD.

13. For My people have committed two evils:
They have forsaken Me, the fountain of living
waters,

Jeremiah

2

---

2 : 8 *The priests . . . they that handle the law . . . the rulers.* The prophet indicates that it was not only the untutored masses who turned at once to Canaanitish idolatry on entering the Holy Land, but all the leaders of the people were responsible. Thus Rashi says: "The handlers of the Torah" are the Sanhedrin, "the shepherds" are the kings. See, too, Kimchi. Cf. also 5:4.

2 : 10 *Kittites . . . Kedar.* Kittites refers to the sea-people from whom the Philistines came. Kedar refers to the wandering Bedouins of the desert, "tents of Kedar" (Psalm 120:5). Rashi elaborates the thought and says that the Bedouins move from place to place and must carry their gods from place to place. Nevertheless, though their gods cannot even travel alone, the Kedarites are still loyal to them.

2 : 11 *Hath a nation changed its gods which yet are no gods?* These idolatrous nations are loyal to their worthless gods, yet Israel has abandoned Me who has always led them and helped them.

2 : 13 *Broken cisterns.* Israel has committed a double sin or a

23

And hewed them out cisterns, broken cisterns,
That can hold no water.

Jeremiah

2

14. Is Israel a servant?
    Is he a home-born slave?
    Why is he become a prey?

15. The young lions have roared upon him,
    And let their voice resound;
    And they have made his land desolate,
    His cities are laid waste,
    Without inhabitant.

16. The children also of Noph and Tahpanhes
    Feed upon the crown of thy head.

17. Is it not this that doth cause it unto thee,
    That thou hast forsaken the LORD thy God,
    When He led thee by the way?

18. And now what hast thou to do in the way to Egypt,
    To drink the waters of Shihor?
    Or what hast thou to do in the way to Assyria,
    To drink the waters of the River?

19. Thine own wickess shall correct thee,
    And thy backslidings shall reprove thee:
    Know therefore and see that it is an evil and a
        bitter thing,
    That thou hast forsaken the LORD thy God,
    Neither is My fear in thee,
    Saith the Lord GOD of hosts.

double folly. First they abandoned Me. Second they supplanted Me with useless idols. The metaphor is: "They forsook the Fountain of living water and made leaky cisterns which do not hold the water."

2 : 14 ff.   Here the metaphor changes, and Israel is described as if he were a child of a slave whom nobody cares about, wandering around to Egypt or to Assyria, looking hopelessly for help.

2 : 19 *Thy backslidings shall reprove thee.*   Their own misfortunes should prove to them that their apostasy is a bitter error.

2 : 20 *Upon every high hill . . . playing the harlot.*   The hilltops were the places where the idolatrous shrines were set up, and certain trees were especially sacred. Hence apostasy is frequently described by the prophets as "playing the harlot on every high hill and under every leafy tree."

normal20. For of old time I have broken thy yoke,
And burst thy bands,
And thou saidst: 'I will not transgress';
Upon every high hill
And under every leafy tree
Thou didst recline, playing the harlot.

21. Yet I had planted thee a noble vine,
Wholly a right seed;
How then art thou turned into the degenerate plant
Of a strange vine unto Me?

22. For though thou wash thee with nitre,
And take thee much soap,
Yet thine iniquity is marked before Me,
Saith the Lord GOD.

23. How canst thou say: 'I am not defiled,
I have not gone after the Baalim';
See thy way in the Valley,
Know what thou hast done;
Thou art a swift young camel traversing her ways;

24. A wild ass used to the wilderness,
That snuffeth up the wind in her desire;
Her lust, who can hinder it?

2 : 21 *I . . . planted thee a noble vine.*   The same theme was used by Isaiah in his parable of the vineyard (Isaiah 5). God planted Israel as a noble vine, but it has now produced worthless grapes.

2 : 22 *Wash thee with . . . much soap.*   This idea is used elsewhere by Jeremiah (4:14) and means that the stain of sin is now so deep that it cannot be eradicated by soap or lye. The same theme was borrowed by Shakespeare in *Macbeth*, when Lady Macbeth tries in vain to wash the bloodstain from her hand: "Out, damned spot!" (*Macbeth*, v, 1, 39) The prophet will later use other metaphors to describe the deep stain of the sin and the difficulty of eradicating it. "Can the leopard change his spots or the Ethiopian his skin?" (Jer. 13:23)

2 : 23, 24   Here the metaphor of Israel running around wild in her idolatry changes to a description of animals in the wilderness, untamable, unrestrainable, "the young camel" and "the wild ass."

In her month they shall find her.   The wild animal, although untamable, can be reached and captured during the month of her lust (so Luzzato and Tur-Sinai).

All they that seek her will not weary themselves;
In her month they shall find her.

Jeremiah
2

25. Withhold thy foot from being unshod,
And thy throat from thirst;
But thou saidst: 'There is no hope;
No, for I have loved strangers, and after them
will I go.'

26. As the thief is ashamed when he is found,
So is the house of Israel ashamed;
They, their kings, their princes,
And their priests, and their prophets;

27. Who say to a stock: 'Thou art my father,'
And to a stone: 'Thou hast brought us forth,'
For they have turned their back unto Me, and not
their face;
But in the time of their trouble they will say:
'Arise, and save us.'

28. But where are thy gods that thou hast made thee?
Let them arise, if they can save thee in the time
of thy trouble;
For according to the number of thy cities
Are thy gods, O Judah.

29. Wherefore will ye contend with Me?
Ye all have transgressed against Me,
Saith the LORD.

30. In vain have I smitten your children—
They received no correction;
Your sword hath devoured your prophets,
Like a destroying lion.

2 : 27 *Who say to a stock* [i.e., to a stick]: *'Thou art my father.'*
They pretend that the wooden or stone idol is their Divine
father.

2 : 30 *I have smitten your children . . . your sword . . . devoured
your prophets.* Rashi: This refers to Zechariah and Isaiah, who
were slain. Zechariah is the priest mentioned in II Chronicles
24:21 ff., and Isaiah refers to the legend that Hezekiah's wicked
son Manasseh slew the prophet (Jebamot 49b). However, Kimchi doubts this explanation because of the phrase "*your*
prophets." He cites and accepts his father's explanation that the

31. O generation, see ye the word of the LORD:
    Have I been a wilderness unto Israel?
    Or a land of thick darkness?
    Wherefore say My people: 'We roam at large;
    We will come no more unto Thee'?

32. Can a maid forget her ornaments,
    Or a bride her attire?
    Yet My people have forgotten Me
    Days without number.

33. How trimmest thou thy way
    To seek love!
    Therefore—even the wicked women
    Hast thou taught thy ways;

34. Also in thy skirts is found the blood
    Of the souls of the innocent poor;
    Thou didst not find them breaking in;
    Yet for all these things

35. Thou saidst: 'I am innocent;
    Surely His anger is turned away from me'—
    Behold, I will enter into judgment with thee,
    Because thou sayest: 'I have not sinned.'

36. How greatly dost thou cheapen thyself
    To change thy way?
    Thou shalt be ashamed of Egypt also,
    As thou wast ashamed of Asshur.

verse means the false prophets whom you yourself in your fury destroyed when you heard the true phophecy proclaiming your doom. However, Tur-Sinai calls attention to the fact that the verse is not clear. The subject of the first part of the verse is "God": "I have smitten," and the subject of the second part of the verse is "the people": "your sword." He therefore emends the latter half of the verse to read as follows: In vain have I smitten your sons, and in vain have I slain your false prophets.

2 : 31 *We roam at large.*   The Hebrew word *radnu* has been given many explanations. Its plain meaning is "we will wander about." Rashi suggests it means: "We will separate ourselves from God." Kimchi takes it to mean: "We have our own authority, not God's."

2 : 32 ff.   Continues the metaphor of the faithless, evil woman.

Jeremiah

2

37. From him also shalt thou go forth,
    With thy hands upon thy head;
    For the LORD hath rejected them in whom thou
        didst trust,
    And thou shalt not prosper in them.

2 : 37   *With thy hands upon thy head.*   In modern terms this would mean a captive, a person who surrenders and puts his hands upon his head so as to be unable to make any threatening gesture. But Luzzato says that it is a sign of mourning, as Tamar after her tragedy left the house of her brother Amnon and put on symbols of mourning, and Scripture says, "She walked with her hands on her head" (II Kings 13:19).

3

MANY MODERN scholars regard verses 6-18, which compare the sinfulness of the northern kingdom and the southern kingdom, as an insertion into this chapter, and maintain that properly speaking the chapter begins with verse 1, goes to verse 5, continues with verse 19, and actually ends with verse 4 of the next chapter. Luzzato denies that verses 6-18 are an insertion. In fact the chapter makes fair sense if read as it is, since it has total relevance, as it must have had for the editor who placed this possible insertion here. The whole unit from chapter 3 to 4:4 speaks of the sinfulness of Israel and its apostasy, generally using the favorite prophetic metaphor of apostasy as adultery.

1.   . . . saying:
 If a man put away his wife,
 And she go from him,
 And become another man's,   **Jeremiah**
 May he return unto her again?   3
 Will not that land be greatly polluted?
 But thou hast played the harlot with many lovers;
 And wouldest thou yet return to Me?
 Saith the LORD.

3 : 1 . . . *Saying:* Ibn Caspi says that this is the only such beginning in Scripture. Clearly some words are missing, and most of the commentators supply the missing words, such as "Thus said the Lord unto me, speak to them, saying." Kimchi solves

Jeremiah

3

2. Lift up thine eyes unto the high hills, and see:
   Where hast thou not been lain with?
   By the ways hast thou sat for them,
   As an Arabian in the wilderness;
   And thou hast polluted the land
   With thy harlotries and with thy wickedness.
3. Therefore the showers have been withheld,
   And there hath been no latter rain;
   Yet thou hadst a harlot's forehead,
   Thou refusedst to be ashamed.

the problem simply by connecting this verse with the closing verse of the preceding chapter as follows: "The Lord hath rejected them whom thou didst trust, saying."

If a man put away his wife. Jeremiah here quotes the divorce law as it is given in Deuteronomy, namely, if a man divorces his wife, and then she marries another and the second man then divorces her, the first husband may never take her back again. Therefore the usual translation of this verse's closing words is: "Wouldst thou then return to Me? saith the Lord." In other words, having first been divorced from Me and now rejected by your idols, canst thou now return to Me? Certainly not. Kimchi therefore says: You can no longer be reconciled to Me. First your land must be destroyed and you must go into exile. Then and only then can I forgive you.

However, the Talmud (Yoma 86b) cites this verse as evidence of the great power of repentance. Repentance is so great, says the Talmud, that it can actually nullify a law of Scripture. The verse therefore (as the Talmud takes it) is as follows: By law you should never be permitted to return to Me (having been twice rejected), but if you repent, I will yet receive you, so great is the power of repentance. So Rashi, too, says: "*Nevertheless* return unto Me." Luzzato, however, takes the phrase to mean: After all these sins, wouldst thou then (thou hypocrite) imagine that thou canst return unto Me and say: "Will God keep His anger forever?" (verse 5).

3 : 3 *Therefore . . . showers have been withheld . . . yet thou hadst a harlot's forehead.* As a mark of God's punishment, rain is withheld from the fields. This theme is expressed a number of times in Scripture—for example, in Deuteronomy 11:16-17:

30

4. Didst thou not just now cry unto Me: 'My father,
Thou art the friend of my youth.

5. Will He bear grudge for ever?
Will He keep it to the end?'
Behold, thou hast spoken, but hast done evil things,
And hast had thy way.

6. And the LORD said unto me in the days of Josiah
the king: 'Hast thou seen that which backsliding
Israel did? she went up upon every high mountain
and under every leafy tree, and there played the
harlot. 7. And I said: After she hath done all these
things, she will return unto Me; but she returned
not. And her treacherous sister Judah saw it. 8. And
I saw, when, forasmuch as backsliding Israel had
committed adultery, I had put her away and given
her a bill of divorcement, that yet treacherous
Judah her sister feared not; but she also went and
played the harlot; 9. and it came to pass through
the lightness of her harlotry, that the land was

"Take heed lest ye serve other gods . . . and the anger of the
Lord shall be kindled and He shut up the heavens so that there be
no rain." See also Amos 4:7 and Isaiah 5:6.

Harlot's forehead. Modest women keep their faces
veiled, but thou dost show thyself shamelessly. The Talmud
further says that one reason for God withholding the rain from
the earth is that this is the special punishment for impudence
and immodesty. See Joseph and Nachmias and *Taanit* 7b.

3 : 6 *And the Lord said unto me in the days of Josiah the king.*
As has been mentioned, this passage (verses 6-18), comparing
the state of Judah with the destroyed state of Israel in the north,
is considered by many to be an addition or an interlude. This
opinion is supported by the fact that verse 6, "The Lord said
unto me," seems to be a new heading. Here the prophet says in
verse 8 that the northern kingdom was defeated, destroyed because of her adultery (i.e., her apostasy to idolatry), and the
southern kingdom in failing to learn the lesson of the fate of her
northern sister, is doubly sinful. But verse 14 says that God will
yet restore them and give them worthy leaders, "shepherds according to My heart" (verse 15).

polluted, and she committed adultery with stones and with stocks; 10. and yet for all this her treacherous sister Judah hath not returned unto Me with her whole heart, but feignedly, saith the LORD— 11. even the LORD said unto me—backsliding Israel hath proved herself more righteous than treacherous Judah. 12. Go, and proclaim these words toward the north, and say:

Return, thou backsliding Israel,
Saith the LORD.
I will not frown upon you;
For I am merciful, saith the LORD
I will not bear grudge for ever.

13. Only acknowledge thine iniquity,
That thou hast transgressed against the LORD thy God,
And hast scattered thy ways to the strangers
Under every leafy tree,
And ye have not hearkened to My voice,
Saith the LORD.

14. Return, O backsliding children, saith the LORD; for I am a lord unto you, and I will take you one of a city, and two of a family, and I will bring you to Zion; 15. and I will give you shepherds according to My heart, who shall feed you with knowledge and understanding. 16. And it shall come to pass, when ye are multiplied and increased in the land, in those days, saith the LORD, they shall say no

3 : 16 *They shall say no more: 'The ark of the covenant.'* All the commentators feel it necessary to explain why they will no longer speak of the ark of the covenant in the days of God's restoration. Rashi says this means: They will then be so holy that I will dwell in every assembly of theirs (not only in the ark). In addition, the following explanation is given: The ark of the covenant was always taken out as a palladium in wartime. Now it will no longer be necessary because the hostility of the surrounding people will have ceased in that blessed time. See Kimchi. Caspi says: When they were in exile, they had the arks of the law in their synagogues. But now that they are restored, they will swear by the very presence and throne of God.

more: The ark of the covenant of the LORD; neither shall it come to mind; neither shall they make mention of it; neither shall they miss it; neither shall it be made any more. 17. At that time they shall call Jerusalem The throne of the LORD; and all the nations shall be gathered unto it, to the name of the LORD, to Jerusalem; neither shall they walk any more after the stubbornness of their evil heart. 18. In those days the house of Judah shall walk with the house of Israel, and they shall come together out of the land of the north to the land that I have given for an inheritance unto your fathers.'

19. But I said: 'How would I put thee among the sons,
And give thee a pleasant land,
The goodliest heritage of the nations!'
And I said: 'Thou shalt call Me, My father;
And shalt not turn away from following Me.'

20. Surely as a wife treacherously departeth from her
    husband,
So have ye dealt treacherously with Me, O house
    of Israel,
Saith the LORD.

21. Hark! upon the high hills is heard
The suppliant weeping of the children of Israel;
For that they have perverted their way,
They have forgotten the LORD their God.

22. Return, ye backsliding children,
I will heal your backslidings.—
'Here we are, we are come unto Thee;
For Thou art the LORD our God.

23. Truly vain have proved the hills,
The uproar on the mountains;
Truly in the LORD our God
Is the salvation of Israel.

24. But the shameful thing hath devoured

3 : 23   *Truly vain have proved the hills.*   In their repentance they will realize that their apostasy on the hilltops, their idolatry there, was all in vain. So the next verse, "shame devoured our labor"; the word for "shame" here also means "idol," very likely specifically the idol Baal. See Tur-Sinai.

Jeremiah

3

The labour of our fathers from our youth;
Their flocks and their herds,
Their sons and their daughters.
25. Let us lie down in our shame,
And let our confusion cover us;
For we have sinned against the LORD our God,
We and our fathers,
From our youth even unto this day;
And we have not harkened
To the voice of the LORD our God.'

4

A DESCRIPTION chiefly of the threat of destruction which will be brought to the land by the invader from the north: "For I will bring evil from the north and a great destruction" (verse 6). This chapter also contains the first of the so-called confessions of Jeremiah, the self-expression of his inner sorrow at the harsh necessities that must be expressed in his message to his people— verses 19-21 ("My bowels, my bowels"). Other such confessions are 11:18-12:6; 15:10 f., 15-21; 17:14-18; 18:18-23; 20:7-13, 14-18 (for a discussion and listing, cf. Bright, pp. lxv ff.).

1. If thou wilt return, O Israel,
   Saith the LORD.
   Yea, return unto Me;
   And if thou wilt put away thy detestable things out
      of My sight,
   And wilt not waver;

Jeremiah
4

4 : 1 *If thou wilt return . . . return unto Me.* Most modern critics feel that verses 1-4 of this chapter are really to be considered the conclusion of the preceding thoughts or sermons of chapter 3.

The traditional commentators explain the apparent repetitiousness of the word "return" as follows: If you return to Me, saith the Lord, you will return to your former greatness (so Rashi). The Targum says it means: If you return to My worship, your repentance will be acceptable and the decree against you will not be sealed. So, too, Kimchi: If you return, you will not be exiled.

35

Jeremiah

4

2. And wilt swear: 'As the LORD liveth'
   In truth, in justice, and in righteousness;
   Then shall the nations bless themselves by Him,
   And in Him shall they glory.
3. For thus saith the LORD to the men of Judah and
   to Jerusalem:
   Break up for you a fallow ground,
   And sow not among thorns.
4. Circumcise yourselves to the LORD,
   And take away the foreskins of your heart,
   Ye men of Judah and inhabitants of Jerusalem;
   Lest My fury go forth like fire,
   And burn that none can quench it,
   Because of the evil of your doings.
5. Declare ye in Judah, and publish in Jerusalem,
   And say: 'Blow ye the horn in the land';
   Cry aloud and say:
   'Assemble yourselves, and let us go into the fortified
   cities.'
6. Set up a standard toward Zion;

4 : 2 *Swear . . . in truth.* Rashi calls attention to the fact that this is in contrast to their usual practice, as recorded in 5:2: "Though they say, 'As the Lord liveth,' surely they swear falsely." (So, too, Kimchi.)

4 : 4 *Circumcise . . . take away the foreskins of your heart.* This metaphor, describing the purifying of the heart by the removal of its uncleanliness as a spiritual circumcision, is frequently used in Scripture. Thus Deuteronomy 10:16: "Circumcise therefore the foreskin of your heart." So also Ezekiel 44:7: "Uncircumcised in heart." Jeremiah himself uses the metaphor again in 9:25: "For all the nations are uncircumcised, but all the house of Israel are uncircumcised in the heart." The Targum, which always avoids too physical a reference to God, is troubled by the fact that the metaphor here says "circumcise yourself to the Lord"; therefore it carefully paraphrases as follows: "Return to the worship of the Lord and remove the wickedness of your heart."

4 : 5 *Declare . . . publish in Jerusalem.* Kimchi paraphrases: Let it spread from ear to ear, through the streets of Jerusalem, that God will send you punishment for your sins.

36

Put yourselves under covert, stay not;
For I will bring evil from the north
And a great destruction.

7. A lion is gone up from his thicket,
And a destroyer of nations
Is set out, gone forth from his place;
To make thy land desolate,
That thy cities be laid waste, without inhabitant.

8. For this gird you with sackcloth,
Lament and wail;
For the fierce anger of the LORD
Is not turned back from us.

9. And it shall come to pass at that day,
Saith the LORD,
That the heart of the king shall fail,
And the heart of the princes;
And the priests shall be astonished,
And the prophets shall wonder.

10. Then said I: 'Ah, Lord GOD! surely Thou hast greatly deceived this people and Jerusalem, saying: Ye shall have peace; whereas the sword reacheth unto the soul.'

4 : 7 *A lion is gone up from his thicket.* The Targum paraphrases: "The king has left his fortress," etc. Kimchi makes the paraphrase more specific: Nebuchadnezzar, the king of Babylon, has begun his march, and he is compared to a lion because none can resist him.

4 : 8 *Gird you with sackcloth.* According to Rashi, this verse interrupts the above references to Babylon and goes back to the earlier tragedy of King Josiah, who was slain when he marched against Pharaoh-necoh (II Kings 23:29-30). Thus this verse and the next refer to the dismay and mourning on the death of the good King Josiah. But Kimchi says that the king mentioned in verse 9 is Zedekiah (the last king of Judea) and that the whole passage refers to the coming invasion by the lion from the north, Nebuchadnezzar.

4 : 10 *Lord God . . . Thou hast . . . deceived this people . . . saying: Ye shall have peace.* How did God deceive them? Rashi implies, and Kimchi is specific as to the answer, that God,

37

11. At that time shall it be said of this people and of
    Jerusalem.
    A hot wind of the high hills in the wilderness
    Toward the daughter of My people,
    Not to fan, nor to cleanse;

12. A wind too strong for this shall come for Me;
    Nor will I also utter judgments against them.

13. Behold, he cometh up as clouds,
    And his chariots are as the whirlwind;
    His horses are swifter than eagles.—
    'Woe unto us! for we are undone.'—

14. O Jerusalem, wash thy heart from wickedness,
    That thou mayest be saved.
    How long shall thy baleful thoughts
    Lodge within thee?

by being patient and tolerant of the false prophets who kept on
crying "Peace, peace, when there is no peace" (6:14; 8:11), has
thus, by His patience and tolerance, allowed the people to deceive itself with false hopes.

4 : 11 *A hot wind . . . in the wilderness . . . not to fan, nor to
cleanse.* Again a symbol of the coming destruction; it is like a
blazing desert wind—not like the useful winds that blow away
the chaff, but a wind so hot and strong that it will be totally
destructive.

4 : 12 *A wind . . . shall come for Me.* Our translation, capital-
izing the word "Me," takes the verse to mean that God speaks
and says: I will cause this hot destructive wind to blow. But
Kimchi says it is the prophet himself speaking here as a self-
personification of Israel, meaning therefore: A hot desert wind
is coming that will be too strong for me to resist. Kara says
that the word "Me" means the prophet who says: It is revealed
to me that the evil ones are like that powerful desert wind, good
only for destruction and not for any useful purpose. Luzzato
takes the verse differently; the "hot clear wind" is not a destructive wind at all, and the prophet is saying: A "hot clear
wind" of true prophecy will come to me from God. In other
words, the words "to me" mean Jeremiah.

Verses 13-18 carry out the thought that the blazing wind
of destruction is coming because of the wickedness of the
people.

15. For hark! one declareth from Dan,
    And announceth calamity from the hills of Ephraim:
16. Make ye mention to the nations:
    Behold—publish concerning Jerusalem—
    Watchers come from a far country,
    And give out their voice against the cities of Judah.'
17. As keepers of a field
    Are they against her round about;
    Because she hath been rebellious against Me,
    Saith the LORD.
18. Thy way and thy doings have procured
    These things unto thee;
    This is thy wickedness; yea, it is bitter,
    Yea, it reacheth unto thy heart.
19. My bowels, my bowels! I writhe in pain!
    The chambers of my heart!
    My heart moaneth within me!
    I cannot hold my peace!
    Because thou hast heard, O my soul, the sound
        of the horn,
    The alarm of war.
20. Destruction followeth upon destruction,
    For the whole land is spoiled;
    Suddenly are my tents spoiled,
    My curtains in a moment.

4 : 18 *Thy wickedness . . . reacheth unto thy heart.* Ibn Caspi
says: Their wickedness has corrupted them so thoroughly that it
has reached their very heart; that is, they are corrupt through
and through. He calls attention to King Solomon's phrase in
Proverbs 4:23: "Above all that thou guardest keep thy heart; for
out of it are the issues of life."

4 : 19-22 *My bowels . . . . My heart moaneth . . . .* In this series
of verses, 19-22, the prophet expresses his inner anguish. This is
the first of the prophet's so-called confessions, or self-expressions.
Jeremiah speaks of his physical misery and spiritual suffering at
the vision of the sudden evils that are coming because of the
folly of the people, who will not repent in time because they are
"Wise to do evil, but to do good they have no knowledge"
(verse 22). Kimchi says: I shudder in pain at the news of the
events that are coming.

39

21. How long shall I see the standard,
    Shall I hear the sound of the horn?

Jeremiah

4

22. For My people is foolish,
    They know Me not;
    They are sottish children,
    And they have no understanding;
    They are wise to do evil,
    But to do good they have no knowledge.

23. I beheld the earth,
    And, lo, it was waste and void;
    And the heavens, and they had no light.

24. I beheld the mountains, and, lo, they trembled,
    And all the hills moved to and fro.

25. I beheld, and, lo, there was no man,
    And all the birds of the heavens were fled.

26. I beheld, and, lo, the fruitful field was a wilderness,
    And all the cities thereof were broken down
    At the presence of the LORD,
    And before His fierce anger.

27. For thus saith the LORD:
    The whole land shall be desolate;
    Yet will I not make a full end.

28. For this shall the earth mourn,
    And the heavens above be black;
    Because I have spoken it, I have purposed it,
    And I have not repented, neither will I turn back
        from it.

29. For the noise of the horsemen and bowmen

The whole city fleeth;
They go into the thickets,
And climb up upon the rocks;
Every city is forsaken,
And not a man dwelleth therein.

30. And thou, that art spoiled, what doest thou,
That thou clothest thyself with scarlet,
That thou deckest thee with ornaments of gold,
That thou enlargest thine eyes with paint?
In vain dost thou make thyself fair;
Thy lovers despise thee, they seek thy life.
31. For I have heard a voice as of a woman in travail,
The anguish as of her that bringeth forth her
first child,
The voice of the daughter of Zion, that gaspeth
for breath,
That spreadeth her hands:
'Woe is me, now! for my soul fainteth
Before the murderers.'

4 : 30 *And thou, that art spoiled.* The translation here is misleading. It does not mean that the daughter of Zion is spoiled by
luxury. The Hebrew word here means "about to be despoiled,"
about to be robbed. The whole verse means: There is no use
decorating yourself up in your fine garments; you will not
attract any allies to save you from the invader.

5

THE PROPHET tells his hearers that God bids them to walk through the streets of Jerusalem and see whether there are any righteous people left. When they note how corruption, adultery, and social oppression have infected every social class, they will realize that destruction is inevitable, in spite of the false prophets and the priestly and secular leaders who assure them that all is well.

Jeremiah

5

1. Run ye to and fro through the streets of Jerusalem
And see now, and know,
And seek in the broad places thereof,
If ye can find a man,
If there be any that doeth justly, that seeketh truth;
And I will pardon her.

5 : 1 *And see now . . . if ye can find a man . . . that doeth justly . . . And I will pardon her.* This is similar to the discussion between Abraham and God when God announced that the wicked city of Sodom would be destroyed. Abraham pleaded with God and won His consent that the wicked city would be spared if there were a certain number of righteous men in it (Genesis 18:23-33). Kimchi says that his father, in his commentary, emphasized the words "the streets of Jerusalem," and

42

2. And though they say: 'As the LORD liveth,'
   Surely they swear falsely.
3. O LORD, are not Thine eyes upon truth?
   Thou hast stricken them, but they were not
      affected;
   Thou hast consumed them, but they have refused
      to receive correction;
   They have made their faces harder than a rock;
   They have refused to return.
4. And I said: 'Surely these are poor,
   They are foolish, for they know not the way of
      the LORD
   Nor the ordinance of their God;
5. I will get me unto the great men,
   And will speak unto them;

said that there were certainly some righteous people in Jerusalem; but they were hiding in fear of their lives. What the prophet meant, then, is: Go and see whether there is enough decency in the city of Jerusalem that righteous people are not afraid to appear on the streets.

5 : 2 *Surely they swear falsely.* Kimchi says that their usual oaths were in the names of their idols; on the rare occasions when they *did* swear in the Name of God, it was a false oath.

5 : 3 *O Lord . . . Thine eyes upon truth? Thou has stricken them . . . they have refused to return.* The sequence of these verses is not clear. Luzzato connects sentences 2 and 3 and explains them as follows: Thou, O Lord, seekest the truth (verse 3), but they swear falsely (verse 2). The proof of their falsehood is that they refuse to return to Thee even though Thou hast smitten them (verse 3). Other commentators take the word "truth" to mean "the true" or "the faithful worshipers of God." So Isaiah of Trani says: Thine eyes (i.e., Thy favor) are for the men of faith, but these wicked ones Thou dost punish.

5 : 4, 5 *These are poor . . . I will get me unto the great men and will speak unto them.* Kimchi says that the upper classes of the community are not worn out from having to earn a living and therefore should have time to meditate and to study the words of God. But, alas, they are just as evil, or just as sunk in iniquity, as the lower classes. The same thought is expressed in

43

For they know the way of the LORD
And the ordinance of their God.'
But these had altogether broken the yoke,
And burst the bands.

6. Wherefore a lion out of the forest doth slay them,
A wolf of the deserts doth spoil them,
A leopard watcheth over their cities,
Every one that goeth out thence is torn in pieces;
Because their transgressions are many,
Their backslidings are increased.

7. Wherefore should I pardon thee?
Thy children have forsaken Me,
And sworn by no-gods;
And when I had fed them to the full, they committed adultery,
And assembled themselves in troops at the harlots' houses.

8. They are become as well-fed horses, lusty stallions;
Every one neigheth after his neighbour's wife.

9. Shall I not punish for these things?
Saith the LORD;
And shall not My soul be avenged
On such a nation as this?

10. Go ye up into her rows, and destroy,
But make not a full end;
Take away her shoots;
For they are not the LORD'S.

2:8: "The priests . . . they that handle the law . . . the rulers have transgressed against Me."

5 : 10 *Go ye up into her rows.*   Rashi, who of course knew about vineyards and viticulture, says that God describes Israel as a vineyard and bids the enemy go into the vineyard and destroy the various shoots. Kimchi, however, following the Targum, says it is a command to the enemy to climb up the *walls* of Jerusalem (not the rows of the vineyard) and destroy its battlements.

However, Rashi's explanation of the metaphor seems more acceptable, especially because of the closing words of the sentence, "For they are not the Lord's." This is part of the

11. For the house of Israel and the house of Judah
    Have dealt very treacherously against Me,
    Saith the LORD.
12. They have belied the LORD,
    And said: 'It is not He,
    Neither shall evil come upon us;
    Neither shall we see sword nor famine;
13. And the prophets shall become wind,
    And the word is not in them;
    Thus be it done unto them.'
14. Wherefore thus saith the LORD, the God of hosts:
    Because ye speak this word,
    Behold, I will make My words in thy mouth fire,

Jeremiah

5

frequently used metaphor of Israel as God's vineyard; God complains that He had planted a good vine, but only wild and alien grapes have grown up, like weeds, instead. Thus Jeremiah 2:21: "Yet I had planted thee [as] a noble vine, wholly a right seed; how then art thou turned into the degenerate plant of a strange vine unto Me?"

5 : 12 *They have belied the Lord . . . it is not He.* Rashi and Kimchi both follow the Targum, which explains the words of the people as follows: It is not God Who is the source of our happiness, and He will not be the source of our misfortune. So, too, Isaiah of Trani: It is not God Who brings us blessings.

5 : 13 *And the prophets shall become wind.* The words themselves are clear enough, but it is uncertain who is saying them and to which prophets they apply. The Targum, Rashi, and Kimchi say that the people are saying the words, but that seems strange because they also say that the people are speaking of false prophets. The meaning seems to be as Luzzato, Malbim, and Isaiah of Trani all understand it (and perhaps, also, the earlier commentators), namely, the evil people are saying it, and they are saying it of the true prophet, whom they here scorn as a false prophet. Therefore, the people are saying that Jeremiah and his like are false prophets, and the evil which they threaten will not come to us. This explanation harmonizes with the close of the preceding verse in which the people confidently say: "Neither shall we see sword nor famine."

Thus be it done unto them. This closing phrase, then,

45

Jeremiah

5

And this people wood, and it shall devour them.

15. Lo, I will bring a nation upon you from far,
O house of Israel, saith the LORD;
It is an enduring nation,
It is an ancient nation,
A nation whose language thou knowest not,
Neither understandest what they say.

16. Their quiver is an open sepulchre,
They are all mighty men.

17. And they shall eat up thy harvest, and thy bread,
They shall eat up thy sons and thy daughters,
They shall eat up thy flocks and thy herds,
They shall eat up thy vines and thy fig-trees;
They shall batter thy fortified cities,
Wherein thou trustest, with the sword.

18. But even in those days, saith the LORD,
I will not make a full end with you.

19. And it shall come to pass, when ye shall say:
'Wherefore hath the LORD our God done all these
things unto us?' then shalt Thou say unto them:
'Like as ye have forsaken Me, and served strange
gods in your land, so shall ye serve strangers in
a land that is not yours.'

20. Declare ye this in the house of Jacob,
And announce it in Judah, saying.

21. Hear now this, O foolish people, and without
understanding,

is uttered by Jeremiah. The people call us false prophets and
deny that evil will come to them. But the evil thus described by
us will surely come, just as we have said. So it will be "done to
them."

5 : 15   *A nation whose language thou knowest not.*   Kimchi says
it is a special curse to be unable to converse or plead with their
conquerors. He calls attention to the fact that the same curse
is given in Deuteronomy 28:49: "The Lord will bring a nation
against thee from afar . . . a nation whose tongue thou shalt not
understand."

5 : 18-19   God will not destroy them utterly. These two verses
are understood by modern scholars to be a consolatory addition
written during the Exile.

46

That have eyes, and see not,
That have ears, and hear not:

22. Fear ye not Me? saith the LORD;
Will ye not tremble at My presence?
Who have placed the sand for the bound of the sea,
An everlasting ordinance, which it cannot pass;
And though the waves thereof toss themselves, yet
   can they not prevail;
Though they roar, yet can they not pass over it.

23. But this people hath a revolting and a rebellious
   heart;
They are revolted, and gone.

24. Neither say they in their heart:
'Let us now fear the LORD our God,
That giveth the former rain, and the latter in due
   season;
That keepeth for us
The appointed weeks of the harvest.'

25. Your iniquities have turned away these things,
And your sins have withholden good from you.

26. For among My people are found wicked men;
They pry, as fowlers lie in wait;
They set a trap, they catch men.

27. As a cage is full of birds,
So are their houses full of deceit;
Therefore they are become great, and waxen rich;

28. They are waxen fat, they are become sleek;
Yea, they overpass in deeds of wickedness;
They plead not the cause, the cause of the
   fatherless,
That they might make it to prosper;
And the right of the needy do they not judge.

5 : 24 *Appointed weeks of the harvest.* God, Who is Master of
the seasons and brings the rains and the harvest at the proper
time, should have won their loyalty by the very trustworthiness
of these regular seasonal blessings.

5 : 28 *They overpass in deeds of wickedness.* Kimchi says that
for these oppressors it is not enough to acquire wealth. They
will continue with their evil even after they are enriched. Luz-

Jeremiah
5

29. Shall I not punish for these things?
    Saith the LORD;
    Shall not My soul be avenged
    On such a nation as this?
30. An appalling and horrible thing
    Is come to pass in the land:
31. The prophets prophesy in the service of falsehood,
    And the priests bear rule at their beck;
    And My people love to have it so;
    What then will ye do in the end thereof?

zato says that "they overpass" means "they pass by." When they see unfortunates needing help, they pass by and ignore them.

5 : 31 *The priests bear rule at their beck.*   The priests exercise their authority, which is bolstered by the reassuring predictions of the false prophets.

6

CONTINUING THE denunciation of the people's sinfulness, which makes their sacrificial worship unacceptable to God and the doom of the nation inevitable.

1. Put yourselves under covert, ye children of Benjamin,
   Away from the midst of Jerusalem,
   And blow the horn in Tekoa,
   And set up a signal on Bethcherem;
   For evil looketh forth from the north,
   And a great destruction.
2. The comely and delicate one,
   The daughter of Zion, will I cut off.
3. Shepherds with their flocks come unto her;

Jeremiah

6

6 : 1   *Blow the horn . . . set up a signal.*   When war threatens, various signals (horns, bonfires) are used to warn the countryfolk to come into the walled city for safety.

From the midst of Jerusalem.   But now that the walled city of Jerusalem itself is doomed to fall, the countryfolk are advised to *leave* the city (where they may be dwelling temporarily) and flee and scatter for safety's sake. Kimchi suggests that Jeremiah here addresses his kinfolk (whose home village is Anathoth in Benjamin), warning them to flee now for safety *out* of Jerusalem.

6 : 3   *Shepherds with their flocks.*   Rashi and Kimchi follow

49

They pitch their tents against her round about;
They feed bare every one what is nigh at hand.

Jeremiah
6

4. 'Prepare ye war against her;
   Arise, and let us go up at noon!'
   'Woe unto us! for the day declineth,
   For the shadows of the evening are stretched out!'
5. 'Arise, and let us go up by night,
   And let us destroy her palaces.'
6. For thus hath the LORD of hosts said;
   Hew ye down her trees,
   And cast up a mound against Jerusalem;
   This is the city to be punished;
   Everywhere there is oppression in the midst of her.
7. As a cistern welleth with her waters,
   So she welleth with her wickedness;
   Violence and spoil is heard in her;
   Before Me continually is sickness and wounds.
8. Be thou corrected, O Jerusalem,
   Lest My soul be alienated from thee,
   Lest I make thee desolate,
   A land not inhabited.

the Targum here to the effect that this means the invading kings and their armies will encamp in the conquered city.

6 : 4-5   *Prepare ye war . . . at noon . . . the day declineth . . . go up by night.*   Most of the commentators take this to mean that the prophet identifies himself with the invading enemy, as if the enemy is saying: Let us start early in the morning against this city; but alas, they say, we are losing time; it is already the afternoon. And the prophet adds (verse 5): Then attack at night (Kimchi and Luzzato).

6 : 6   *The city to be punished.*   Rashi here follows the Targum to the effect that the time of retribution has finally come for Jerusalem.

6 : 7   *As a cistern welleth with her waters.*   Most of the commentators understand this to mean that just as a living fountain keeps bubbling up freshly with its waters, so does Jerusalem keep on creating and re-creating its sins.

6 : 8   *A land not inhabited.*   The Targum says: Like the wicked city of Sodom, which could never be inhabited again (so, also, Kimchi).

50

9. Thus saith the Lord of hosts:
   They shall thoroughly glean as a vine
   The remnant of Israel;
   Turn again thy hand
   As a grape-gatherer upon the shoots.
10. To whom shall I speak and give warning,
    That they may hear?
    Behold, their ear is dull,
    And they cannot attend;
    Behold, the word of the Lord to become unto
      them a reproach,
    They have no delight in it.
11. Therefore I am full of the fury of the Lord,
    I am weary with holding in:
    Pour it out upon the babes in the street,
    And upon the assembly of young men together;
    For even the husband with the wife shall be taken,
    The aged with him that is full of days.
12. And their houses shall be turned unto others,
    Their fields and their wives together;
    For I will stretch out My hand upon the in-
      habitants of the land,
    Saith the Lord.
13. For from the least of them even unto the greatest
      of them
    Every one is greedy for gain;
    And from the prophet even unto the priest
    Every one dealeth falsely.
14. They have healed also the hurt of My people lightly,
    Saying: 'Peace, peace,' when there is no peace.

6 : 9 *Turn again thy hand as a grape-gatherer.* Rashi says that
  this refers to the constantly returning attacks of the enemy, first
  to destroy King Jehoiakim, then Jehoiachin, and finally Zedekiah,
  just as the gleaner of grapes keeps on returning to the vineyard
  until the very last grapes are gathered.
6 : 13 *Prophet . . . priest . . . dealeth falsely.* Jeremiah frequently mentions prophets and priests together as those who
  should be the responsible leaders of the people. So in the preceding chapter, verse 31.
6 : 14 *Lightly . . . peace, peace.* The word "lightly" here is

Jeremiah

6

15. They shall be put to shame because they have
    committed abomination;
    Yea, they are not at all ashamed,
    Neither know they how to blush;
    Therefore they shall fall among them that fall,
    At the time that I punish them they shall stumble,
    Saith the LORD.
16. Thus saith the LORD:
    Stand ye in the ways and see,
    And ask for the old paths,
    Where is the good way, and walk therein,
    And ye shall find rest for your souls.
    But they said: 'We will not walk therein.'
17. And I set watchmen over you:
    'Attend to the sound of the horn';
    But they said: 'We will not attend.'
18. Therefore hear, ye nations,
    And know, O congregation, what is against them.
19. Hear, O earth:

interpreted in a number of ways, though they all mean virtually the same thing. The Targum says: They utter these false words. Rashi says it means that it is a light task, an easy task, to reassure the people and say "Peace." Kimchi says it means it is a light word with no reality behind it. Luzzato says "lightly" means they act as if the sickness of the people is only a trivial ailment that can be easily cured.

6 : 15 *Put to shame . . . not at all ashamed.*   They all should be deeply ashamed because of their evil deeds; but since they refuse to be ashamed, God will put them to shame.

6 : 16 *Stand ye in the ways . . . ask for the old paths.*   Kimchi calls attention to the parallel with the words which the Prophet Elijah spoke to the prophets of Baal on Mount Carmel, namely, "How long will ye halt between two opinions; if the Lord be God, follow Him, but if Baal, follow him" (I Kings 18:21). In other words, Jeremiah says to the people: Make up your mind, pick the proper path, the old established path.

6 : 18 *And know, O congregation, what is against them.*   The Targum explains: "Know, O congregation of Israel, what are your sins" (that are counted against you).

52

Behold, I will bring evil upon this people,
Even the fruit of their thoughts,
Because they have not attended unto My words,
And as for My teaching, they have rejected it.

20. To what purpose is to Me the frankincense that
cometh from Sheba,
And the sweet cane, from a far country?
Your burnt-offerings are not acceptable,
Nor your sacrifices pleasing unto Me.

21. Therefore thus saith the LORD:
Behold, I will lay stumblingblocks before this
people,
And the fathers and the sons together shall
stumble against them,
The neighbour and his friend, and they shall
perish.

22. Thus saith the LORD:
Behold, a people cometh from the north country,
And a great nation shall be roused from the utter-
most parts of the earth.

23. They lay hold on bow and spear,
They are cruel, and have no compassion;
Their voice is like the roaring sea,
And they ride upon horses;
Set in array, as a man for war,
Against thee, O daughter of Zion.

24. 'We have heard the fame thereof,
Our hands wax feeble,
Anguish hath taken hold of us,
And pain, as of a woman in travail.'

25. Go not forth into the field,
Nor walk by the way;

6 : 20   *To what purpose . . . the frankincense . . . your burnt-
offerings are not acceptable.*   Kimchi: If because of your sins
your burnt-offerings, the sacrifices themselves, are not acceptable
to Me, then what good are the incidentals, the expensive frankincense and other spices which accompany them?

6 : 22-26   Again a description of the terrible invasion brought by
the invading enemy.

53

For there is the sword of the enemy,
And terror on every side.

Jeremiah

6

26. O daughter of my people, gird thee with sackcloth,
And wallow thyself in ashes;
Make thee mourning, as for an only son,
Most bitter lamentation;
For the spoiler shall suddenly come upon us.
27. I have made thee a tower and a fortress among
My people;
That thou mayest know and try their way.
28. They are all grievous revolters,
Going about with slanders;
They are brass and iron;
They all of them deal corruptly.
29. The bellows blow fiercely,
The lead is consumed of the fire;
In vain doth the founder refine,
For the wicked are not separated.
30. Refuse silver shall men call them,
Because the LORD hath rejected them.

6 : 27 *I have made thee a tower.* As the watchman in a high tower can see all the traffic in the city below, so thou as a watchman "mayest know and try their way."

6 : 28 *They are brass and iron.* The precise meaning of this metaphor is not clear. Rashi takes it to mean that they are stubborn and strong in their evildoings, like brass and iron. Kimchi, following the Targum, speaks of brass and iron being melted together to form a strong alloy.

54

6 : 29-30   *The bellows blow . . . the lead is consumed . . . in vain doth the founder refine . . . refuse silver.*   The difficulty in this sentence is the meaning of the phrase "the lead is consumed." Clearly the verse uses a metaphor drawn from the refining of silver. If so, what has the lead to do with it? Therefore Tur-Sinai believes that the word "lead" was mistakenly moved from the preceding sentence, where the description of the people should be "they are brass and iron and lead."

However, most of the classic commentators, including Kimchi, Isaiah of Trani, and Abarbanel, say that lead is an essential part of the process of refining silver—the refiner puts lead into the crucible with the silver to help in some way with the purification; presumably, when the lead is melted away, it will have combined itself with the dregs of the silver and thus the silver will be purified.

These medieval commentators are correct. They were describing a process with which they were actually acquainted. R. J. Forbes, in his *Metallurgy in Antiquity*, p. 209, says: "In antiquity it was customary to smelt silver with lead to insure complete extraction of all the silver" (cf. also p. 213; information provided by David J. Kusler, U.S. Bureau of Mines).

The verse now becomes quite clear. The bellows are heated, the fire waxes hot, so hot indeed that all the lead is melted away; but in spite of that fact, the silver is not purified. In other words, the people are so sinful that in spite of the flame of suffering, they still remain impure. Hence they are called "refuse" or "low-grade" (verse 30).

7

THE TEMPLE sermon. Jeremiah is directed to preach to the people in the Temple and tell them that they are mistaken in their belief that no matter what they do, God will never allow His sacred Temple to be destroyed, and that for the sake of the Temple, the city of Jerusalem will be safe and the people secure. Jeremiah tells them that just as God did not hesitate to remove His presence from the sanctuary in Shiloh, where Eli and his evil sons officiated, so the sinful people today cannot rely upon being protected by the Temple buildings.

Jeremiah   1. The word that came to Jeremiah from the LORD,
7   saying: 2. Stand in the gate of the LORD's house, and proclaim there this word, and say: Hear the

7 : 2 *The gate of the Lord's house . . . enter in at these gates.* The commentators call attention to the singular "gate" and then later in the sentence the plural "gates." Thus Kimchi: Jeremiah was to stand at the eastern gate, which was the main entrance of the Temple precincts. There were two other gates giving access from the south, and two other gates still giving access from the north. (There was, of course, no gate in the west, where the Holy of Holies came up against the outside wall, which still stands today as a remnant of Herod's Temple and is called "the western wall.")

56

word of the LORD, all ye of Judah, that enter in at these gates to worship the LORD. 3. Thus saith the LORD of hosts, the God of Israel:

Amend your ways and your doings, and I will cause you to dwell in this place. 4. Trust ye not in lying words, saying: 'The temple of the LORD, the temple of the LORD, the temple of the LORD, are these.' 5. Nay, but if ye thoroughly amend your ways and your doings; if ye thoroughly execute justice between a man and his neighbour; 6. if ye oppress not the stranger, the fatherless, and the widow, and shed not innocent blood in this place, neither walk after other gods to your hurt; 7. then will I cause you to dwell in this place, in the land that I gave to your fathers, for ever and ever. 8. Be-

7 : 3 *Amend your ways . . . and I will cause you to dwell in this place.* Kimchi says this means that if you amend your ways you will not be exiled from "this place," i.e., from Jerusalem. However "in this place" could mean the Temple itself. Therefore Ehrlich emends the text to read that God says: "and *I* shall continue to dwell in this place."

7 : 4 *Trust ye not in lying words. . . . the temple . . . the temple . . . the temple.* Ibn Caspi interprets the people's words as follows: Jerusalem will always be safe because God will never allow His Temple to be destroyed. Isaiah of Trani, commenting on the fact that the word "Temple" is used three times, says: Do not imagine that you will be safe because you come three times a year to this Temple on the pilgrimage. Kimchi, quoting his father, says that the word "Temple" is used three times because there the Temple had three main halls. Malbim gives the sentence a spiritual interpretation: The "lying words" are the claim that the buildings themselves are God's sanctuary. So Jeremiah says: Do not imagine that the building is God's sanctuary; your deeds and the way of your life can be His sanctuary; and they determine God's presence or absence.

7 :5, 6, 7 *Amend your ways . . . shed not innocent blood . . . neither walk after other gods . . . I will cause you to dwell.* This is the basis for Malbim's homily that not the building but their actions are God's true sanctuary.

Jeremiah
7

hold, ye trust in lying words, that cannot profit. 9. Will ye steal, murder, and commit adultery, and swear falsely, and offer unto Baal, and walk after other gods whom ye have not known, 10. and come and stand before Me in this house, whereupon My name is called, and say: 'We are delivered,' that ye may do all these abominations? 11. Is this house, whereupon My name is called, become a den of robbers in your eyes? Behold, I, even I, have seen it, saith the LORD. 12. For go ye now unto My place which was in Shiloh, where I caused My name to dwell at the first, and see what I did to it for the wickedness of My people Israel. 13. And now, because ye have done all these works, saith the LORD, and I spoke unto you, speaking betimes and often, but ye heard not, and I called you, but ye answered not; 14. therefore will I do unto the house, whereupon My name is called, wherein ye trust, and unto the place which I gave to you and to your fathers, as I have done to Shiloh. 15. And I will cast you out of My sight, as I have cast out all your brethren, even the whole seed of Ephraim.

16. Therefore pray not thou for this people, neither lift up cry nor prayer for them, neither make intercession to Me; for I will not hear thee. 17. Seest thou not what they do in the cities of

7 : 9-11 *Steal, murder . . . is this house . . . a den of robbers?* After all your evil actions, you come and worship here as if this house will justify you. Is it a den of robbers that it should approve your actions?

7 : 12-15 *Go . . . unto My place which was in Shiloh . . . will I do unto the house . . . as I have done to Shiloh . . . as I have cast out all your brethren.* Shiloh was the most sacred shrine. My ark was there. Yet I allowed the ark to be captured by the Philistines, and I removed My presence from Shiloh, and the whole northern kingdom (the house of Ephraim) was exiled. Therefore do not imagine that this building will keep you safe.

7 : 17 *What they do in the . . . streets.* The idolatrous actions

Judah and in the streets of Jerusalem? 18. The children gather wood, and the fathers kindle the fire, and the women knead the dough, to make cakes to the queen of heaven, and to pour out drink-offerings unto other gods, that they may provoke Me. 19. Do they provoke Me? saith the LORD; do they not provoke themselves, to the confusion of their own faces? 20. Therefore thus saith the Lord GOD: Behold, Mine anger and My fury shall be poured out upon this place, upon man, and upon beast, and upon the trees of the field, and upon the fruit of the land; and it shall burn, and shall not be quenched.

21. Thus saith the LORD of hosts, the God of Israel: Add your burnt-offerings unto your sacrifices, and eat ye flesh. 22. For I spoke not unto your fathers, nor commanded them in the day that I brought them out of the land of Egypt, concern-

Jeremiah
7

described in the next verses are carried on shamelessly in the very streets of the city (Kimchi).

7 : 18   *Cakes to the queen of heaven.*   According to the Targum, they worshiped the "star of heaven," called "the queen of heaven," which was very likely the bright star Venus, although Luzzato says it means the moon. At all events, the queen of heaven was worshiped by the baking and offering of special cakes. The same worship continued among the people even after the destruction of the state. When they fled to Egypt and abducted Jeremiah, they still continued offering cakes to the queen of heaven. See Jeremiah 44:17-19.

7 : 21   *Add your burnt-offerings unto your sacrifices, and eat ye flesh.*   The peace-offerings (*shelamim*) were sacrificed at the Temple and eaten festively by the people. Certain other sacrifices were eaten only by the priests. But the burnt-offering was the most sacred of all. No one could eat of it. It had to be burned up entirely on the altar. What the prophet says to them here is: Even the most sacred are not sacred at all. You might as well add them to your other offerings and eat them as you eat the peace offerings, etc.

7 : 22   *I spoke not unto your fathers . . . in the day that I brought*

59

them out of . . . Egypt, concerning burnt-offerings or sacrifices.
This verse has been the subject of great discussion. On the face
of it, the prophet seems to say that at the beginning of Jewish
history, when God brought the descendants of the Patriarchs out
of Egypt and they became a nation, He gave them no commandments to offer sacrifices. Amos (5:21-25) makes a somewhat
analogous statement that during the years in the wilderness the
Children of Israel did not offer any sacrifices. This is a startling
statement because the Pentateuch, particularly the Book of
Leviticus, is full of the minutest ordinances as to the various
types of sacrifices to be offered in the Tabernacle in the wilderness.

To the radical critics of the last generation, this contradiction
between Jeremiah and Leviticus involved no difficulty at all.
They accepted the words of Jeremiah as literally true, maintain-
ing that the whole account of the sacrificial cult in Leviticus,
pertaining to the Tabernacle in the wilderness, was written later,
and that Jeremiah and the people knew there had been no sacrificial cult in the wilderness (see Duhm, pp. 81 ff.). However,
later critical scholars of Scripture have a more balanced opinion.
Thus Bright (p. 57) says: "It is unlikely, however, that it is to
be taken either as a categorical rejection of the sacrificial system
as such or as a statement that there was no sacrifice in the wilderness. The point lies in the balance. . . . God's essential demands
(e.g., as found in the Decalogue) did not concern ritual matters,
but the keeping of the covenant stipulations."

Bright's opinion was anticipated by the Jewish commentators,
who generally take the point of view that God's commandments
to Israel when they came out of Egypt did not concern sacrifices.
Maimonides says that the paschal lamb ordained to be offered in
Egypt was an exception for a special occasion. The commands
that the children of Israel received in Marah, their first stopping-
place (Exodus 15:23), had to do with the Sabbath and with the
laws of justice (Sanhedrin 56b). Then, when they came to
Mount Sinai, what was given to them was the Ten Commandments, which were all ethical mandates.

See especially the long discussion of the passage in Don Isaac
Abarbanel. Abarbanel bases his discussion upon the rather bold
opinion of Maimonides in the *Guide to the Perplexed*, book 3,
chapter 33. Maimonides says that God's concern and commandments all had to do with the ethical requirements which ennoble

ing burnt-offerings or sacrifices; 23. but this thing I commanded them, saying: 'Hearken unto My voice, and I will be your God, and ye shall be My people; and walk ye in all the way that I command you, that it may be well with you.' 24. But they hearkened not, nor inclined their ear, but walked in their own counsels, even in the stubbornness of their evil heart, and went backward and not forward, 25. even since the day that your fathers came forth out of the land of Egypt unto this day; and though I have sent unto you all My servants the prophets, sending them daily betimes and often, 26. yet they hearkened not unto Me, nor inclined their ear, but made their neck stiff; they did worse than their fathers.

27. And thou shalt speak all these words unto them, but they will not hearken to thee; thou shalt also call unto them, but they will not answer thee. 28. Therefore thou shalt say unto them:
This is the nation that hath not hearkened
To the voice of the LORD their God,

human character. It was only after the people sinned with the golden calf that God permitted sacrifices. This was a concession to the universal type of worship of the period, so that the people would not be led to sacrifice to idols but at least would sacrifice to God Himself. Abarbanel does not accept Maimonides's opinion that the sacrifices were given as an inferior alternative. But he says that what Jeremiah means is: At Mount Sinai My commandments did not concern sacrifices but the ethical ideals of the Ten Commandments.

This is the line of thought followed by all the Jewish commentators from the beginning, and, in fact, it is the implication of Jeremiah himself in verse 23: "But this thing I commanded them, hearken unto My Voice and I shall be your God and ye shall be My people." So Rashi says: the first condition of the covenant was that "ye shall hearken to My Voice," etc. So, too, Kimchi. Malbim puts it as follows, reading verses 22 and 23 together: When I commanded the sacrifices, My purpose was mainly, primarily, that you should hearken unto My Voice.

Nor received correction;
Faithfulness is perished,
And is cut off from their mouth.

29. Cut off thy hair, and cast it away,
And take up a lamentation on the high hills;
For the LORD hath rejected and forsaken the gen-
eration of His wrath.

30. For the children of Judah have done that which

7 : 30 *Their detestable things in the house.* As Kimchi says,
the evil kings Ahaz and Manasseh set up idols in the very Temple.

7 : 31 *Topheth ... in the valley of ... Hinnom, to burn their sons
and their daughters.* This refers to the sacrificing of children
to the god Moloch by throwing them into the fire. The name
of the place, Topheth, is connected by the commentators to the
word *toph*, which means "a timbrel." The priests of Moloch,
they say, would sound loud the timbrels to drown out the cries
of the burning children.

Which I commanded not, neither came it into My mind.
Abarbanel wonders at this phrase. Why is it necessary? How
could one imagine that the prophet needs to deny that God ever
commanded such a cruel action? But, he says, it is an answer to
some who said: "Did not God command Abraham to sacrifice

is evil in My sight, saith the LORD; they have set their detestable things in the house whereon My name is called, to defile it. 31. And they have built the high places of Topheth, which is in the valley of the son of Hinnom, to burn their sons and their daughters in the fire; which I commanded not, neither came it into My mind. 32. Therefore, behold, the days come, saith the LORD, that it shall no more be called Topheth, nor The valley of the son of Hinnom, but The valley of slaughter; for they shall bury in Topheth, for lack of room. 33. And the carcasses of this people shall be food for the fowls of the heaven, and for the beasts of the earth; and none shall frighten them away. 34. Then will I cause to cease from the cities of Judah, and from the streets of Jerusalem, the voice of mirth and the voice of gladness, the voice of the bridegroom and the voice of the bride; for the land shall be desolate.

Jeremiah
7

his son Isaac as a burnt-offering," and therefore this is a precedent for the Moloch-sacrificers. To which God answers: I never intended that Isaac should be burnt as a burnt-offering.

8

THE FIRST three verses continue the theme with which chapter 7 closed—that the bodies of the leaders of the people will be taken from their graves and thrown to the fowl of the heavens and the beasts of the earth.

The new theme begins with verse 4. The prophet denounces the people for their complacent certainty that they are not violating God's law. He speaks of their leaders, who reassure them that there will be peace, and ends with a dirge on his vision of the coming doom of his people.

Jeremiah

8

1. At the time, saith the LORD, they shall bring out the bones of the kings of Judah, and the bones of his princes, and the bones of the priests, and the bones of the prophets, and the bones of the inhabitants of Jerusalem, out of their graves; 2. and they shall spread them before the sun, and the moon, and all the host of heaven, whom they have loved, and whom they have served, and after whom they have walked, and whom they have sought, and whom they have worshipped; they shall not be gathered, nor be buried, they shall be for dung upon the face of the earth. 3. And death

8 : 3   *And death shall be chosen rather than life.*   Rashi comments: The survivors, even though they shall see the dishonored

64

shall be chosen rather than life by all the residue
that remain of this evil family, that remain in all
the places whither I have driven them, saith the
LORD of hosts.

4. Moreover thou shalt say unto them:
Thus saith the LORD:
Do men fall, and not rise up again?
Doth one turn away, and not return?

5. Why then is this people of Jerusalem slidden back
By a perpetual backsliding?
They hold fast deceit,
They refuse to return.

6. I attended and listened,
But they spoke not aright;
No man repenteth him of his wickedness,
Saying: 'What have I done?'
Every one turneth away in his course,
As a horse that rusheth headlong in the battle.

7. Yea, the stork in the heaven
Knoweth her appointed times;
And the turtle and the swallow and the crane
Observe the time of their coming;
But My people know not
The ordinance of the LORD.

death of the leaders, nevertheless will find life so bitter that they
will prefer a dishonored death to their unhappy life. Isaiah of
Trani says that the verse refers to the captives, who will prefer
death to their miserable life.

8 : 4   *Doth one turn away, and not return?*   Rashi, following the
Targum, says in effect that even if they do repent, they will
regret their repentance and return again to their sin.

8 : 6   *Every one turneth away . . . headlong.*   Nothing can stop
them in their evil course. As Kimchi puts it: They are like a war-
horse charging onward in battle whom no one can stop any more
than one could stop a rushing torrent.

8 : 7   *The stork . . . the turtle . . . the swallow . . . the crane. .*   The
turtle, of course, means here the turtledove, as in *Song of Songs*
2:12: "The time of singing is come, and the voice of the turtle is
heard in our land." The prophet here describes the birds, always

65

8. How do ye say: 'We are wise,
   And the Law of the LORD is with us'?
   Lo, certainly in vain hath wrought
   The vain pen of the scribes.

9. The wise men are ashamed,
   They are dismayed and taken;
   Lo, they have rejected the word of the LORD;
   And what wisdom is in them?

10. Therefore will I give their wives unto others,
    And their fields to them that shall possess them;
    For from the least even unto the greatest

returning in due season. But you do not return to God. You rush on headlong in your sin.

8 : 8   *How do ye say: 'We are wise . . . the Law of the Lord is with us'? . . . vain pen of the scribes.*   The earlier biblical critics use this as proof-text for their opinion that Jeremiah was opposed to the Deuteronomic reformation. According to them, the prophet is saying here that the Book of Deuteronomy, which you boast is the Law of God, is only the vain work of lying scribes (see Duhm, p. 88). However, later critical writers are not so positive. See Bright, p. 64: "It is most unlikely that Jeremiah is saying that Deuteronomy is a fraud . . . nor can we derive from these words evidence regarding Jeremiah's original attitude toward Josiah's reform. . . . indeed the delusion or falsehood which the scribes have created seems to be not so much the law itself as the result and conceit that possession of the law gives all necessary wisdom."

In this opinion Bright comes very close to the opinion of the classical Jewish commentators. According to Kimchi, Jeremiah is saying to the people: What is the good of the scribes writing the Torah if you do not obey it? So, too, Nachmias. So, too, Luzzato. The general understanding of this verse by the Jewish commentators is that the mere possession of a written scroll without the people obeying it is utterly useless. This interpretation fits well with the next verse, which says that their wise men have rejected the word of the Lord.

8 : 9   *They have rejected the word of the Lord . . . what wisdom is in them?*   Kimchi, reflecting the controversies of his day as to what place secular studies should have in the curriculum of Jewish learning, says (on verses 8 and 9) that if they neglect the study of the Torah, external studies will be of no use.

Every one is greedy for gain,
From the prophet even unto the priest
Every one dealeth falsely.

11. And they have healed the hurt of the daughter of My people lightly,
Saying: 'Peace, peace,' when there is no peace.
12. They shall be put to shame because they have committed abomination;
Yea, they are not at all ashamed,
Neither know they how to blush;
Therefore shall they fall among them that fall,
In the time of their visitation they shall stumble,
Saith the LORD.
13. I will utterly consume them, saith the LORD;
There are no grapes on the vine,
Nor figs on the fig-tree,
And the leaf is faded;
And I gave them that which they transgress.
14. 'Why do we sit still?
Assemble yourselves, and let us enter into the fortified cities,
And let us be cut off there;
For the LORD our God hath cut us off,
And given us water of gall to drink
Because we have sinned against the LORD.
15. We looked for peace, but no good came;
And for a time of healing, and behold terror!'
16. The snorting of his horses is heard from Dan;
At the sound of the neighing of his strong ones
The whole land trembleth;
For they are come, and have devoured the land and all that is in it,
The city and those that dwell therein.

Jeremiah
8

8:11 *Peace, peace.* A restatement of the words cited from the false prophets in 6:14.
8:13 *I will utterly consume them.* Rashi calls attention to the words of the Prophet Zephaniah (Zephaniah 1:2): "I will utterly consume all things . . ."
I gave them that which they transgress. Rashi: I am punishing them because I gave them a Law which they transgress.

67

Jeremiah

8

17. For, behold, I will send serpents, basilisks, among
    you,
    Which will not be charmed;
    And they shall bite you, saith the LORD
18. Though I would take comfort against sorrow,
    My heart is faint within me.
19. Behold the voice of the cry of the daughter of
    my people
    From a land far off:
    'Is not the LORD in Zion?
    Is not her King in her?'—
    'Why have they provoked Me with their graven
    images,
    And with strange vanities?'

8 : 17 *Serpents . . . which will not be charmed.* Rashi says that the adder becomes deaf after a while and therefore can no longer be controlled by the music of the snake charmer and remains dangerous. The same thought is expressed in Psalm 58:5-6: "They are like the deaf asp . . . which hearkeneth not to the voice of charmers." In other words, as Kimchi expands the meaning, they will face murderous enemies who cannot be appeased.

Verse 18 to the end of the chapter is another outburst of the prophet's emotions and an expression of his grief at the doom of his people.

8 : 19 *A land far off.* Rashi explains that Jeremiah in his imagination visualizes the people as already in exile and hears "the voice of the daughter of Zion" crying in anguish from "a land far away."

20. 'The harvest is past, the summer is ended.
    And we are not saved.'
21. For the hurt of the daughter of my people am I
    seized with anguish;
    I am black, appalment hath taken hold on me.
22. Is there no balm in Gilead?
    Is there no physician there?
    Why then is not the health
    Of the daughter of my people recovered?
23. Oh that my head were waters,
    And mine eyes a fountain of tears,
    That I might weep day and night
    For the slain of the daughter of my people!

8 : 20   *The harvest is past . . . we are not saved.*   Rashi says that
this refers specifically to Egypt. We counted on the Egyptians
coming to our rescue after they had reaped their annual harvest.
But the Egyptian harvest is now past and yet they have not come
to help us. Kimchi says the verse simply means that the harvest,
which should be a time for joy is past now and we are not saved.
Luzzato says: As a man counts on the harvest to repay him for
all his toil, we counted on deliverance and we are disappointed.

8 : 22   *Is there no balm in Gilead?*   Gilead is the part of the land
where the balsam, a medicinal plant, is grown. The same phrase
is used in Jeremiah 46:11: "Go up into Gilead, and take balm,
O virgin daughter of Egypt." The prophet means that there is
no medicine and no healing available for the agony of his people.

8 : 23   *Oh that my head were waters.*   The Targum paraphrases:
Would that my head were like a river and my eyes like a fountain so that I could weep day and night over the death of the
congregation of my people.

9

AN EXPRESSION of despair at the seemingly incurable evil of the people. Their treachery to each other is one of their paramount sins. The prophet mourns the impeding tragedy.

Jeremiah

9

1. Oh that I were in the wilderness,
   In a lodging-place of wayfaring men,
   That I might leave my people,
   And go from them!
   For they are all adulterers,
   An assembly of treacherous men.
2. And they bend their tongue, their bow of falsehood;
   And they are grown mighty in the land, but not for truth;
   For they proceed from evil to evil,
   And Me they know not,
   Saith the LORD.
3. Take ye heed every one of his neighbour,

9 : 2 *They bend their tongue, their bow of falsehood.* The word for "bend" in Hebrew is from the same root as the word "to tread," as if the phrase were, "they tread their tongue." Rashi, having in mind the stiff crossbows in use in France in his day (he uses the word "arbalest"), says that the bow is bent with the help of the feet.

9 : 3 *Every brother acteth subtly.* The Hebrew (as Kimchi indicates) means "acteth deceitfully."

70

And trust ye not in any brother;
For every brother acteth subtly,
And every neighbour goeth about with slanders.

4. And they deceive every one his neighbour,
And truth they speak not;
They have taught their tongue to speak lies,
They weary themselves to commit iniquity.

5. Thy habitation is in the midst of deceit;
Through deceit they refuse to know Me,
Saith the LORD.

6. Therefore thus saith the LORD of hosts:
Behold, I will smelt them, and try them;
For how else should I do,
Because of the daughter of My people?

7. Their tongue is a sharpened arrow,
It speaketh deceit;
One speaketh peaceably to his neighbour with
his mouth,
But in his heart he layeth wait for him.

8. Shall I not punish them for these things?
Saith the LORD;
Shall not My soul be avenged
On such a nation as this?

9. For the mountains will I take up a weeping and
wailing,

9 : 5 *Thy habitation is in the midst of deceit.* God here speaks
to Jeremiah and says: You are dwelling amidst a deceitful people;
you cannot bring them back to Me (Kimchi).

9 : 6 *Behold, I will smelt them.* Rashi, following the Targum,
says this means: I will purify them in the crucible of suffering.
Because of the daughter of My people? Kimchi connects
both halves of the verse in the following explanation: I will purify
them in the crucible; what else can I do? After all, they are My
people. In a similar way Isaiah of Trani says: I will punish them
with exile, yet I shall not destroy them; they are, after all, My
people.

9 : 7 *Their tongue . . . speaketh deceit.* This verse should be
read as if it followed verse 4, thus: "Their tongues speak lies"
(verse 4), "their tongue is a sharpened arrow" (verse 7).

9 : 9 *I take up a weeping and wailing.* Luzzato explains that

71

And for the pastures of the wilderness a lamentation,

Because they are burned up, so that none passeth through,

And they hear not the voice of the cattle;

Both the fowl of the heavens and the beast

Are fled, and gone.

10. And I will make Jerusalem heaps,

A lair of jackals;

And I will make the cities of Judah a desolation,

Without an inhabitant.

11. Who is the wise man, that he may understand this?

And who is he to whom the mouth of the LORD hath spoken, that he may declare it?

Wherefore is the land perished

And laid waste like a wilderness, so that none passeth through?

12. And the LORD saith:

Because they have forsaken My law which I set before them.

And have not hearkened to My voice, neither walked therein;

13. But have walked after the stubbornness of their own heart

And after the Baalim, which their fathers taught them.

with this sentence Jeremiah interrupts what he was saying in the Name of God, in order now to express his own sorrow at what is bound to happen in the city of Jerusalem.

9 : 11   *Who is the wise man, that he may understand . . . ? And who is he to whom . . . the Lord hath spoken . . . ?*   According to both Rashi and Kimchi, this means: Who is able to understand the situation by his own good sense, and who will be the prophet who will tell them what must be the consequence of their sins?

9 : 12   *And the Lord saith: Because they have forsaken My law.* The reason for their punishment is clear, and they should all be able to understand it. Therefore Kimchi parallels this statement with that of Deuteronomy 30: 12-13. It is not overseas or in the heavens but in your hearts that ye may know it.

14. Therefore thus saith the LORD of hosts, the God
    of Israel:
    Behold, I will feed them, even this people, with
    wormwood,
    And give them water of gall to drink.
15. I will scatter them also among the nations,
    Whom neither they nor their fathers have known;
    And I will send the sword after them,
    Till I have consumed them.
16. Thus saith the LORD of hosts:
    Consider ye, and call for the mourning women,
    that they may come;
    And send for the wise women, that they may
    come;
17. And let them make haste, and take up a wailing
    for us,
    That our eyes may run down with tears,
    And our eyelids gush out with waters.
18. For a voice of wailing is heard out of Zion:
    'How are we undone!
    We are greatly confounded, because we have for-
    saken the land,
    Because our dwellings have cast us out.'
19. Yea, hear the word of the LORD, O ye women,
    And let your ear receive the word of His mouth,
    And teach your daughters wailing,
    And every one her neighbour lamentation:
20. 'For death is come up into our windows,
    It is entered into our palaces,

9 : 16-19 Describes the professional wailing women that were
    hired at times of bereavement. Wailing was evidently a practiced
    art, for the prophet also calls them "the wise women" (verse 16),
    and asks them to transmit their melancholy art to others: "Teach
    your daughters wailing" (verse 19).
9 : 20 *Death ... into our windows ... into our palaces.* Kimchi
    explains that high palaces are so secure, and their windows gen-
    erally so inaccessible to intruders, that they are always kept open
    and unbarred. But now the enemy has come so suddenly that the
    people had no time to close and bar the windows.

To cut off the children from the street,
And the young men from the broad places.—

Jeremiah 9

21. Speak: Thus saith the LORD—
And the carcasses of men fall
As dung upon the open field,
And as the handful after the harvestman,
Which none gathereth.'

22. Thus saith the LORD:
Let not the wise man glory in his wisdom,
Neither let the mighty man glory in his might,
Let not the rich man glory in his riches;

23. But let him that glorieth glory in this,
That he understandeth, and knoweth Me,
That I am the LORD who exercise mercy,
Justice, and righteousness, in the earth;
For in these things I delight,
Saith the LORD.

9 : 21 *The carcasses of men.* The same thought as in 8:1 ff.

9 : 22, 23 *Let not the wise man . . . but let him that glorieth glory in this.* These two verses have had a curious destiny. Modern critical scholars tend to brush them aside. Duhm (p. 97) considers them more or less meaningless, a "harmless and insignificant" addition written into the text of Jeremiah's prophecy by some reader without any taste. Bright, in his *Jeremiah*, counts these verses as a later edition, which they well might be.

Yet contrary to the cavalier manner in which modern commentators treat these verses, the traditional Jewish commentators of the Middle Ages wrote virtual essays in their enthusiastic commentation of them. To the Jewish commentators they represent a description of the growth of the human personality from the lowest level to the greatest height, the true knowledge of God.

Maimonides devotes the last chapter of his *Guide to the Perplexed* to these verses, which to him represent the ladder of en-

74

24. Behold, the days come, saith the Lord, that I will punish all them that are circumcised in their uncircumcision: 25. Egypt, and Judah, and Edom, and the children of Ammon, and Moab, and all that have the corners of their hair polled, that dwell in the wilderness;

For all the nations are uncircumcised,

But all the house of Israel are uncircumcised in the heart.

lightenment toward human perfection. With variations, the same is the opinion of Kimchi and, of course, of Don Isaac Abarbanel. Abarbanel makes of these three stages, "the wise man, the mighty man, and the rich man," a parallel to the three classes in society (equivalent of Plato's classes in the *Republic*). The wise man is the governing philosopher, the mighty man is the warrior, and the rich man is the worker and the merchant.

Nearly all of the Jewish commentators also comment on the phrase "righteousness in the earth" as an indication that God's providence rules not only in the changeless heavens, as some philosophers think, but also in the earth. At all events, the essence of traditional commentation is that of all human achievements, the knowledge of God's justice and essential purposes is the highest stage of human enlightenment.

9 : 24 *I will punish all them . . . circumcised in their uncircumcision.* This theme has been previously used by the prophet (Jeremiah 4:4), namely, that evil is a sort of uncircumcision of the heart which God will punish. The various nations mentioned include "all that have the corners of their hair polled." This refers to the wandering Arabs in the desert, who cut their hair short. After mentioning all the nations, he repeats that the people of Israel are "uncircumcised in heart" and for this (i.e., their obdurate sinfulness) they will be punished.

10

CHAPTERS 8 AND 9 dealt primarily with the obdurate sinfulness of the people and the prophet's grief at their doom, which he saw to be inevitable.

This general thought is interrupted in chapter 10. Here Jeremiah warns the people against the folly of idolatry. But in verse 17 of this chapter he returns to the general theme of chapters 8 and 9, a dirge for the tragedy which awaits the people.

Jeremiah   1. Hear ye the word which the LORD speaketh unto you, O house of Israel; 2. thus saith the LORD:
10   Learn not the way of the nations,

10 : 2 *Be not dismayed at the signs of heaven.*   Rashi: Be not terrified as the nations are at the eclipses of the sun, etc. Kimchi takes the verse to be a warning against worshiping the heavenly bodies out of fear, for example, that the crops may fail if the sun is not friendly. These heavenly bodies, says Kimchi, are God's servants. Do not worship them. Worship their Master. So, too, Isaiah of Trani.

It is quite likely that this is a somewhat later chapter and has reference to the Babylonians, who were deeply immersed in, and whose life was governed by, their astrology. See the denunciation of Babylon by Isaiah in which he says: "Let now the astrologers, the star-gazers . . . , stand up and save thee" (Isaiah 47:13).

And be not dismayed at the signs of heaven;
For the nations are dismayed at them.

3. For the customs of the peoples are vanity;
For it is but a tree which one cutteth out of the
forest,
The work of the hands of the workman with the
axe.

4. They deck it with silver and with gold,
They fasten it with nails and with hammers, that
it move not.

5. They are like a pillar in a garden of cucumbers,
and speak not;
They must needs be borne, because they can-
not go.
Be not afraid of them, for they cannot do evil,
Neither is it in them to do good.

6. There is none like unto Thee, O LORD;

Verses 3-5 and also verses 9 and 14 give a description of the
workingmen building the idol. This is almost identical with the
descriptions given in the Second Isaiah, 40:18-20, 41:6-7, 44:9-20,
46:5-7.

10 : 5 *A pillar in a garden of cucumbers.* The Hebrew of this
verse is not clear; the modern translations vary considerably and
are not quite understandable. What is a pillar doing in a garden
of cucumbers? Bright tries to make the verse meaningful by
imaginatively translating the word *tomer* as a "scarecrow" in a
garden of cucumbers. The word translated "cucumbers," *mik-
shah*, is amended by Tur-Sinai to read *shikmah*, meaning "sycamore," and he translates the verse, "like the trunk of a sycamore
tree," meaning that the idol has been hammered smooth and
straight. This explanation is close to the explanation of the classical commentators who say the verse means that the idol is like a
column beaten smooth and straight. In fact Kimchi calls attention to the word for column, *tomer*, which can be normally
translated here as "palm tree." The palm tree rises up straight a
long distance without branches. So the traditional translation of
the verse is not "a pillar in a cucumber field," but "a palmlike
column beaten smooth."

10 : 6 *None like unto Thee.* In the heavens above or on the
earth below, there is none like God (Kimchi).

Jeremiah
10

Thou are great, and Thy name is great in might.

7. Who would not fear Thee, O King of the nations?
For it befitteth Thee;
Forasmuch as among all the wise men of the
nations, and in all their royalty,
There is none like unto Thee.

8. But they are altogether brutish and foolish:
The vanities by which they are instructed are but
a stock;

9. Silver beaten into plates which is brought from
Tarshish,
And gold from Uphaz,
The work of the craftsman and of the hands of
the goldsmith;
Blue and purple is their clothing;
They are all the work of skilful men.

10. But the LORD God is the true God,
He is the living God, and the everlasting King;
At His wrath the earth trembleth,
And the nations are not able to abide His in-
dignation.

11. Thus shall ye say unto them: 'The gods that have
not made the heavens and the earth, these shall
perish from the earth, and from under the heavens.'

10 : 7 *Who would not fear thee . . . ?* Luzzato shows the
contrast here with verse 5. The prophet speaking of the idols in
verse 5, says: "Be not afraid of them." Here, speaking of God, he
says: "Who would not fear Thee?"

Verses 6 and 7, speaking of God, seem to be an interruption
in the description of the making of the idols, which now continues in verses 8 and 9. It would make easier reading if 6 and 7
were read after 9 or after verse 10.

10 : 8 *The vanities . . . are but a stock.* This verse means that
the vain and useless gods in whose names the priests give the
people their instructions are merely lumps of wood.

10 : 11 *Say unto them.* This verse is entirely in the Aramaic
language. In explaining why the prophet should suddenly change
from Hebrew to Aramaic, both Rashi and Kimchi accept the
paraphrase of the Targum, which reads as follows: "This is the

78

12. He that hath made the earth by His power,
    That hath established the world by His wisdom,
    And hath stretched out the heavens by His under-
        standing;
13. At the sound of His giving a multitude of waters
        in the heavens,
    When He causeth the vapours to ascend from the
        ends of the earth;
    When He maketh lightnings with the rain,
    And bringeth forth the wind out of His treasuries;
14. Every man is proved to be brutish, without knowl-
        edge,
    Every goldsmith is put to shame by the graven
        image,
    His molten image is falsehood, and there is no
        breath in them.
15. They are vanity, a work of delusion;
    In the time of their visitation they shall perish.
16. Not like these is the portion of Jacob;
    For He is the former of all things,
    And Israel is the tribe of His inheritance;
    The LORD of hosts is His name.

copy of the letter which the Prophet Jeremiah sent to the leaders of the exile in Babylon: 'If the Chaldeans say to you, worship our idols, then answer them as follows.' " When Jeremiah spoke these words, the exile of Jehoiachin and his followers were already in Babylon. This supposed letter is addressed to them and it is in Aramaic, which is the language of the Babylonians, or Chaldeans, so it is meant to be the actual answer to them in their new language. As a thought it fits well, except for the sudden change of language, in this chapter which denounces idolatry.

10 : 12-13   A description of the grandeur of God as expressed in the manifestations of nature. The words of verse 13 are almost exactly those found in Psalm 135:7.

Verses 14 and 15 return to the description of the worthlessness of the idols.

10 : 15   *Their visitation.*   When God gives them retribution, they shall all perish.

From verse 17 to the end, the chapter reverts to the general

17. Gather up thy wares from the ground,
    O thou that abidest in the siege.
18. For thus saith the LORD: Behold, I will sling out the inhabitants of the land at this time, and will distress them, that they may feel it.
19. Woe is me for my hurt!
    My wound is grievous;
    But I said: 'This is but a sickness,
    And I must bear it.'
20. My tent is spoiled,
    And all my cords are broken;
    My children are gone forth of me, and they are not;
    There is none to stretch forth my tent any more,
    And to set up my curtains.
21. For the shepherds are become brutish,
    And have not inquired of the LORD;
    Therefore they have not prospered,
    And all their flocks are scattered.

theme of chapters 8 and 9, the dirge on the coming doom of the nation.

10 : 17 *Gather up thy wares from the ground.* Perhaps a description of a poor merchant with his few pitiful wares displayed on the ground around him. Or perhaps, in general a call on the people to gather their possessions for the march into exile when "I will sling out the inhabitants of the land" (verse 18).

Verse 19 to the end of the chapter is a dirge of Jeremiah.

10 : 19 *I said: 'This is but a sickness'.* At first I thought that the troubles which had come to us might be transient, like a passing sickness which I simply must bear until it goes away. But now "my cords are broken" (verse 20), the land is entirely destroyed. This is no transient sickness, but an enduring tragedy.

10 : 21 *The shepherds are become brutish.* The leaders of the people have lost all good sense, the flock is now scattered, and the destruction comes down "out of the north country" (verse 22).

22. Hark! a report, behold, it cometh,
    And a great commotion out of the north country,
    To make the cities of Judah desolate.
    A dwelling-place of jackals.
23. O Lord, I know that man's way is not his own;
    It is not in man to direct his steps as he walketh.
24. O Lord, correct me, but in measure;
    Not in Thine anger, lest Thou diminish me.
25. Pour out Thy wrath upon the nations that know
        Thee not,
    And upon the families that call not on Thy name;
    For they have devoured Jacob,
    Yea, they have devoured him and consumed him,
    And have laid waste his habitation.

Jeremiah

10

10 : 23, 24 *Man's way is not his own . . . correct me, but in measure.* The prophet argues here with God. He says that, after all, a human being is not entirely responsible for his actions and therefore does not deserve utter destruction. "Correct us, O God," indeed, but do not destroy us utterly. The classic commentators all give virtually the same explanation of these verses, though they offer different reasons for the fact that we are not entirely responsible for what we do and therefore should be dealt with mercifully. Rashi says that the evil inclination, which God Himself has implanted in us, often leads us astray. Kimchi recalls the legend that Nebuchadnezzar had almost decided to march against the Ammonites instead of against Jerusalem. At the cross-roads he cast lots, and the lots decided him to march against Jerusalem (Ezekiel 21:23-27). Can we, the children of Israel, therefore say that our fate is entirely our fault? Does not chance, which God directs, play a part in it?

10 : 25 *Pour out Thy wrath.* If Thou must destroy, O Lord, then destroy those who have destroyed us unjustly. The whole verse is also found in Psalm 79:6 ff.

11

THE CHAPTER speaks of the covenant between God and the people, which the people have now violated. The probabilities, of course, are that the covenant here referred to is the one spoken of in II Kings 23:1-3 in connection with the book found in the Temple, which is the basis of the present Book of Deuteronomy. This covenant was to create a religious revolution, abolishing all the minor sanctuaries in the land and concentrating the worship in the Temple in Jerusalem. That the Deuteronomic reformation, as this event is referred to, is the one meant here, is supported, first, by the fact that we know of no other great national religious covenant in the lifetime of Jeremiah other than this one in the reign of King Josiah; second, because the language used here is strongly reminiscent of the language in Deuteronomy. For example, verse 3 of this chapter, "Cursed be the man that heareth not the words of this covenant," is exactly the wording used in the ceremony of the adoption of the Deuteronomic covenant. See Deuteronomy 27, especially verse 26. At each sentence of curse in Deuteronomy, the listeners agree by saying "Amen," and here the prophet in verse 5: "Then answered I, and said: 'Amen, O Lord.'" In Deuternomy 4:21 the slavery in Egypt is described as the "iron furnace." So here too in verse 4. It is therefore evident that the covenant here refers to the Deuteronomic covenant.

Since the earlier biblical critics believed that the Prophet Jeremiah was bitterly opposed to the Deuteronomic reformation, they are compelled to explain this chapter away. Thus Duhm maintains that the chapter is poor in thought and superficial, claiming it was inserted here by some late Deuteronomic author who perhaps lived as late as the post-exilic period. However, later critical authors are not so certain that Jeremiah was completely opposed to the Deuteronomic reformation. Bright (p. 89) says: "There is no reason to doubt that it [i.e., this chapter] reflects Jeremiah's actual sentiments and activity. It represents him first as urging obedience to 'his covenant,' then as bitterly censuring the people for their breach of it. . . . . In all probability it is Josiah's covenant that is referred to here."

Jeremiah
11

1. The word that came to Jeremiah from the LORD, saying: 2. 'Hear ye the words of this covenant, and speak unto the men of Judah, and to the inhabitants of Jerusalem; 3. and say thou unto them: Thus saith the LORD, the God of Israel: Cursed be the man that heareth not the words of this covenant, 4. which I commanded your fathers in the day that I brought them forth out of the land of Egypt, out of the iron furnace, saying: Hearken to My voice, and do them, according to all which I command you; so shall ye be My people, and I will be your God; 5. that I may establish the oath which I swore unto your fathers, to give them a land flowing with milk and honey, as at this day.' Then answered I, and said: 'Amen, O LORD.'

6. And the LORD said unto me: 'Proclaim all these words in the cities of Judah, and in the streets of Jerusalem, saying: Hear ye the words of this covenant, and do them. 7. For I earnestly forewarned your fathers in the day that I brought them up out of the land of Egypt, even unto this day, forewarning betimes and often, saying: Hearken to My voice. 8. Yet they hearkened not, nor inclined their ear, but walked every one in the stubbornness of their evil heart; therefore I brought upon them all the words of this covenant, which I commanded them to do, but they did them not.'

9. And the LORD said unto me: 'A conspiracy is

11 : 9   *A conspiracy.*   Kimchi explains the word by saying that after they had made the covenant with Josiah they all rebelled

Jeremiah
11

found among the men of Judah, and among the inhabitants of Jerusalem. 10. They are turned back to the iniquities of their forefathers, who refused to hear My words; and they are gone after other gods to serve them; the house of Israel and the house of Judah have broken My covenant which I made with their fathers. 11. Therefore thus saith the LORD: Behold, I will bring evil upon them, which they shall not be able to escape; and though they shall cry unto Me, I will not hearken unto them. 12. Then shall the cities of Judah and the inhabitants of Jerusalem go and cry unto the gods unto whom they offer; but they shall not save them at all in the time of their trouble. 13. For according to the number of thy cities are thy gods, O Judah; and according to the number of the streets of Jerusalem have ye set up altars to the shameful thing, even altars to offer unto Baal. 14. Therefore pray not thou for this people, neither lift up cry nor prayer for them; for I will not hear them in the time that they cry unto Me for their trouble.'

15. What hath My beloved to do in My house,
Seeing she hath wrought lewdness with many,
And the hallowed flesh is passed from thee?
When thou doest evil, then thou rejoicest.

against it. Luzzato says that the word "conspiracy" is used to indicate that they all sinned together as if they had made a conspiracy to do so.

11 : 13 *Altars to the shameful thing.* The Hebrew word for "shameful thing" is *boshet*, an uglification of "Baal," the name of the idol. Thus, for example, Saul's son Eshbaal is called in uglified form "Ishbosheth" (I Chronicles 8:33 and II Samuel 3:8).

11 : 15 *What hath My beloved to do in My house.* Tur-Sinai quite properly says that this verse is so difficult that none of the versions helps us to understand it. The proof of the verses's difficulty is revealed by the variety of explanations offered by the various commentators. There are at least three different explanations of who is meant by "My beloved." The Targum (and following the Targum, Rashi and Isaiah of Trani) says that "My

16. The Lord called thy name
A leafy olive-tree, fair with goodly fruit;
With the noise of a great tumult
He hath kindled fire upon it,
And the branches of it are broken.

17. For the Lord of hosts, that planted thee, hath pronounced evil against thee, because of the evil of the house of Israel and of the house of Judah, which they have wrought for themselves in provoking Me by offering unto Baal.

beloved" means "My beloved people Israel." God says to them: Why do you My (once) beloved people still come to My Temple since you have become so evil? Kimchi says that Jeremiah is here speaking to God, Who is the "beloved": Why do You, our beloved God, continue to let Your presence rest on this house which has become so corrupt? Luzzato says that "beloved" means the Prophet Jeremiah and God addresses him as such: Why do you, My beloved prophet, continue to come to this Temple to pray for this people? And the Talmud (Menachot 53b) says that the sentence is the epitome of a dialogue between God and Abraham, the beloved of God.

The hallowed flesh is passed from thee. The sacrifices are no longer hallowed since you do evil. Another interpretation is: You have masked the evidence of the sacred covenant of circumcision.

11:16 *A leafy olive-tree.* The olive-tree and the grapevine are two metaphors used frequently in Scripture for the people of Israel. Thus Psalm 52:10: "But as for me, I am like a leafy olive-tree in the house of the Lord." So too Hosea 14:7: "His branches shall spread and his beauty shall be as the olive-tree."

From verse 18 to the end of the chapter is an account of a conspiracy by the townsmen of Anathoth to take Jeremiah's life. It is not clear why his townsmen (possibly those men of Anathoth who lived in Jerusalem) wanted to kill Jeremiah. In verse 21 the reason they give is: "Thou shalt not prophesy in the Name of the Lord, that thou die not by our hand." Why should the men of Anathoth, more than the other inhabitants of Jerusalem, be so aroused by Jeremiah's doleful preaching as to make a threat of murder? Perhaps they felt that since he was their townsman,

18. And the Lord gave me knowledge of it, and I
    knew it;
    Then Thou showedst me their doings.
19. But I was like a docile lamb that is led to the
    slaughter;
    And I knew not that they had devised devices
    against me:
    'Let us destroy the tree with the fruit thereof,
    And let us cut him off from the land of the living.
    That his name may be no more remembered.'
20. But, O Lord of hosts, that judgest righteously,
    That triest the reins and the heart,
    Let me see Thy vengeance on them;
    For unto Thee have I revealed my cause.
21. Therefore thus saith the Lord concerning the men
    of Anathoth, that seek thy life, saying: 'Thou shalt
    not prophesy in the name of the Lord, that thou
    die not by our hand'; 22. therefore thus saith the
    Lord of hosts:
    Behold, I will punish them;
    The young men shall die by the sword,
    Their sons and their daughters shall die by famine;
23. And there shall be no remnant unto them;
    For I will bring evil upon the men of Anathoth,
    Even the year of their visitation.

the hatred his preaching was bound to arouse would endanger
them. At all events, Jeremiah describes himself as not realizing
their murderous intent. He speaks of himself as being "like a
docile lamb that is led to the slaughter" (verse 19).

Then, after becoming aware of their intent and escaping
from their hands, he utters a curse in the Name of God against
them: "I will punish them. The young men shall die by the
sword . . . ."

12

A DEBATE with God as to the justice of His ways, the same theme that is basic to the Book of Job. There are other resemblances to Job in the Book of Jeremiah. For example, in chapter 3 Job curses the fact that he was born and says: "Why died I not from the womb?" (Job 3:11). So, too, Jeremiah says: "Woe is me, my mother, that thou hast borne me" (Jeremiah 15:10), "Cursed be the day wherein I was born; the day wherein my mother bore me . . ." (Jeremiah 20:14 ff.).

1. Right wouldest Thou be, O LORD,
   Were I to contend with Thee,
   Yet will I reason with Thee:
   Wherefore doth the way of the wicked prosper?
   Wherefore are all they secure that deal very treacherously?

Jeremiah

12

12 : 1   *Right wouldest Thou be, O Lord . . . Yet will I reason with Thee.*   If Jeremiah knows beforehand that God is just ("Right wouldest Thou be"), what is the use of all the argument? Rashi explains as follows: I do indeed know beforehand that Thou art right; I am only arguing with You in order to learn the meaning of Thy ways. Kimchi says: I am arguing simply because I am in a state of confusion.

The way of the wicked prosper.   Isaiah of Trani says that Jeremiah here refers to the wicked conspirators of Anathoth who sought his life. In this way Isaiah of Trani connects this chapter with the end of the preceding one. They may be connected. In the preceding chapter (verse 19) Jeremiah describes himself as

Jeremiah

12

2. Thou hast planted them, yea, they have taken root;
They grow, yea, they bring forth fruit;
Thou art near in their mouth,
And far from their reins.

3. But Thou, O Lord, knowest me,
Thou seest me, and triest my heart toward Thee;
Pull them out like sheep for the slaughter,
And prepare them for the day of slaughter.

4. How long shall the land mourn,
And the herbs of the whole field wither?
For the wickedness of them that dwell therein, the
beasts are consumed, and the birds;
Because they said: 'He seeth not our end.'

5. 'If thou hast run with the footmen, and they have
wearied thee,
Then how canst thou contend with horses?
And though in a land of peace thou art secure,
Yet how wilt thou do in the thickets of the Jordan?

"a lamb led to the slaughter." And here he asks for God's retribution against them, saying: "Pull them out like sheep for the slaughter."

12 : 2   *Near in their mouth, and far from their reins.*   The verse means that they are hypocritical. God is on their lips but far from their hearts, except that here, instead of using the heart as the seat of the conscience or the emotions, Jeremiah uses the "reins," that is, the kidneys. The ancients believed that the kidneys were the seat of the emotions, or of certain emotions. Thus Jeremiah 11:20: "Lord of hosts, that judgest righteously, that triest the reins and the heart." So in 17:10: "I the Lord search the heart, I try the reins." So, too, in Psalm 7:10: "For the righteous God trieth the hearts and reins."

12 : 4   *The land mourn . . . the herbs . . . wither.*   It is because of the wickedness of the people that nature and the whole land mourn.

12 : 5   *If thou hast run with the footmen.*   God says to Jeremiah: If you cannot outrun footmen in a footrace, how can you expect to outrun horses? Then the idea is repeated in another form: If you feel safe in a peaceful land, how can you expect to feel safe in the thickets of the Jordan (a jungle inhabited by lions and other wild beasts)?

88

The primary meaning of this double comparison is clear enough, but its application to the thought of the chapter is not clear, and as a result there have been many different interpretations. The Targum, instead of a translation, gives a long paraphrase of the verse which is worth citing first, to indicate how the Targum brings in midrashic material, and also because, in one way or another, the paraphrase is used by the classical commentators. "This is the answer," says the Targum, "to Jeremiah the prophet: You are like a man who has gotten weary in a foot-race. How do you expect to race with horses? If you feel secure in a peaceful valley, how do you expect to cope with the wild beasts in the Jordan valley? If you wonder at the kindness that I am doing to Nebuchadnezzar, who walked on foot, what will you say when I show you the kindness that I will do to our righteous fathers, who rushed like horses to do good deeds?"

The Targum's reference to Nebuchadnezzar's footsteps is given in the Talmud in Sanhedrin 96a. Nebuchadnezzar, when he was secretary to the king of Babylon, followed a messenger on foot to recall a letter to the king of Israel which was not respectfully addressed (cf. Ginzberg's *Legends*, vol. 4, p. 300). The Targum's paraphrase is meant to serve as an answer to Jeremiah's questioning of God's justice. In other words, God answers: You cannot understand the kindnesses that I do to a certain wicked king because of some small merit that he has. Can you, then, understand the great kindness which I will do to the righteous people? The explanation offered by the Targum, midrashic as it is, is in effect the basis of all the traditional explanations of the metaphor in this verse. The answer to his question about God's justice amounts to this: You cannot understand simple things; how can you understand great and profound things? Rashi has an additional explanation of the metaphor about footmen and horses: God says to Jeremiah, if you could hardly cope with your own townsmen who threatened your life, what will you do when I send you against princes and kings? Kimchi, quoting his father, virtually follows the Targum as to what God says to Jeremiah, but he puts it in somewhat more sophisticated terms: Your townsmen had conspired against you and yet you knew nothing of it. Now if you could not read the minds of your fellow townsmen, how do you expect to understand My purposes?

6. For even thy brethren, and the house of thy father,
   Even they have dealt treacherously with thee,
   Even they have cried aloud after thee;
   Believe them not, though they speak fair words
       unto thee.'
7. I have forsaken My house,
   I have cast off My heritage;
   I have given the dearly beloved of My soul
   Into the hand of her enemies.
8. My heritage is become unto Me
   As a lion in the forest;
   She hath uttered her voice against Me;
   Therefore have I hated her.
9. Is My heritage unto Me as a speckled bird of prey?
   Are the birds of prey against her round about?
   Come ye, assemble all the beasts of the field,
   Bring them to devour.

12 : 7 *I have forsaken My house.*   Since they are so wicked, I have forsaken the Temple (Luzzato).

12 : 8 *As a lion . . . she hath uttered her voice against Me.*   As a threatening roar of a lion is heard afar, so the cry of the violence of Jerusalem has come before Me; as in Genesis 18:20: "The cry of the city of Sodom is great . . . ."

12 : 9 *Is My heritage . . . a speckled bird of prey?*   The verse is difficult. Who is the vulture here, "the bird of prey," and who is the prey that is being devoured? Beginning with the second line of the sentence, it is clear that the city of Jerusalem, surrounded by enemies, is being attacked as by vultures, and is the prey. The succeeding four verses confirm this explanation since they describe the nation being devoured. The difficulty is in the first line, "Is My heritage unto Me as a speckled bird of prey?" This would indicate that God's heritage, the people of Israel, is not the victim, as the sense of the entire section requires, but is itself a vulture. Therefore Rashi treats the words "speckled bird" as if they mean "a victim," and thus harmonizes them with the rest of the sentence. He says that a "speckled bird" means a special sort of bird which, because it is different, other birds attack. Tur-Sinai solves the difficulty by omitting the first word, *ayyit,* "a vulture." Joseph Nachmias gives an explanation which does not

10. Many shepherds have destroyed My vineyard,
    They have trodden My portion under foot,
    They have made My pleasant portion
    A desolate wilderness.
11. They have made it a desolation,
    It mourneth unto Me, being desolate;
    The whole land is made desolate,
    Because no man layeth it to heart.
12. Upon all the high hills in the wilderness spoilers
      are come;
    For the sword of the LORD devoureth
    From the one end of the land even to the other end
      of the land,
    No flesh hath peace.
13. They have sown wheat, and have reaped thorns;
    They have put themselves to pain, they profit not:
    Be ye then ashamed of your increase,
    Because of the fierce anger of the LORD.
14. Thus saith the LORD: As for all Mine evil neigh-
    bours, that touch the inheritance which I have

require any omission or emendation: Vultures, with their keen vision, see the fallen prey first, and then all the other animals gather after the vulture swoops down upon the prey. He takes, therefore, the passage to mean this: Is My heritage (i.e., Israel) a bloodstained vulture, that it has attracted all the other animals which now surround it?

12 : 10   *Many shepherds.*   This means many powerful kings, as the phrase is used in Jeremiah 6:3.

12 : 12   *The sword of the Lord.*   This refers to the Babylonian army, just as in an earlier era Isaiah said: "O Assyria, rod of Mine anger" (Isaiah 10:5).

12 : 13   *Sown wheat . . . reaped thorns.*   Rashi calls attention to the verse in Jeremiah 4:3, in which the prophet tells the peo-ple: Plough up fallow land to destroy the thorns first before you sow. So Rashi says that they did not destroy the thorns; they continued to sin.

   Ashamed of your increase.   Rashi: Ashamed of your crop of evil deeds. 14 to the end is a denunciation of the various neigh-boring nations who are attacking Israel.

Jeremiah
12

caused My people Israel to inherit, behold, I will pluck them up from off their land, and will pluck up the house of Judah from among them. 15. And it shall come to pass, after that I have plucked them up, I will again have compassion on them; and I will bring them back, every man to his heritage, and every man to his land. 16. And it shall come to pass, if they will diligently learn the ways of My people to swear by My name: 'As the LORD liveth,' even as they taught My people to swear by Baal; then shall they be built up in the midst of My people. 17. But if they will not hearken, then will I pluck up that nation, plucking up and destroying it, saith the LORD.

12 : 15   *I will again have compassion on them.*   After God has punished the nations that attack Israel and sent them away into exile, just as Israel has gone into exile, then God will have compassion on them, as He will have compassion on Israel, and He will restore them. Jeremiah repeats this thought in 48:47: "I will turn the captivity of Moab," and 49:6: "I will bring back the captivity of the children of Ammon"; Isaiah 19:24 ff. also expresses the thought that God will bless both Egypt and Assyria.

12 : 16   *If they will diligently learn the ways of My people.*   The redemption of the various nations is dependent upon their abandoning their idol-worship and turning to the worship of God.

13

THIS CHAPTER is a sermon based upon two symbols which are used as object lessons. One is a girdle which will be allowed to rot away, and the other is an earthen wine-bottle which will be smashed. The prophets often build their sermons around some familiar object as a symbol and object lesson, or they dress in some special way and base the sermon on the unusual mode of dress. Thus, for example, in Isaiah 8 the prophet is asked to take a tablet and write on it in large letters that all may read it. So also in Isaiah 20, the prophet is told to walk "naked" and barefoot. Also in Jeremiah 18, Jeremiah goes down to the potter's working-place and builds his object lesson around a marred and broken piece of pottery. In chapter 27 Jeremiah puts a yoke on his shoulders as a symbol upon which his sermon will be based.

1. Thus said the LORD unto me: 'Go, and get thee a linen girdle, and put it upon thy loins, and put it not in water.' 2. So I got a girdle according to the word of the LORD, and put it upon my loins.
3. And the word of the LORD came unto me the second time, saying: 4. 'Take the girdle that thou hast

Jeremiah

13

13 : 1-4 *The girdle.* It is to be worn for a while and remain unwashed, then to be put in a cleft by the riverbank; after it has decayed there, the prophet is to take it and build his sermon upon it.

13 : 4 *Take the girdle . . . go to Perath.* Our translation here

gotten, which is upon thy loins, and arise, go to Perath, and hide it there in a cleft of the rock.' 5. So I went, and hid it in Perath, as the LORD commanded me. 6. And it came to pass after many days, that the LORD said unto me: 'Arise, go to Perath, and take the girdle from thence, which I commanded thee to hide there.' 7. Then I went to Perath, and digged, and took the girdle from the place where I had hid it; and, behold, the girdle was marred, it was profitable for nothing.

8. Then the word of the LORD came unto me, saying:

9. Thus saith the LORD: After this manner will I mar the pride of Judah, and the great pride of Jerusalem, 10. even this evil people, that refuse to hear My words, that walk in the stubbornness of their heart, and are gone after other gods to serve them, and to worship them, that it be as this girdle, which is profitable for nothing. 11. For as the girdle cleaveth to the loins of a man, so have I caused to cleave unto Me the whole house of Israel and the whole house of Judah, saith the LORD, that they might be unto Me for a people, and for a name, and for a praise, and for a glory; but they would not hearken.

carefully avoids the usual translation, which is found, for example, in the King James version. The word *Perath* is usually translated "Euphrates." But the usual translation raises a problem. How could the prophet be sent all the way to the Euphrates River on the border of Mesopotamia, and then come back after a while to pick up the girdle which is to be his object lesson? Luzzato gives various opinions of different commentators attempting to solve the problem of the word *Perath*, or "Euphrates," mentioning one which suggests that *Perath* is also the name of a village near Jerusalem. However, Maimonides (who is cited by Kimchi) cuts across the entire difficulty with an interpretation which is characteristic of his philosophic approach to prophecy. He says that the whole series of events is merely a vision that came to Jeremiah. Kimchi's reference is to the end of chapter 46 in book 2 of Maimonides' *Guide to the Perplexed*. Maimonides says: "In

12. Moreover thou shalt speak unto them this word: Thus saith the LORD, the God of Israel: 'Every bottle is filled with wine'; and when they shall say unto thee: 'Do we not know that every bottle is filled with wine?' 13. Then shalt thou say unto them: Thus saith the LORD: Behold, I will fill all the inhabitants of this land, even the kings that sit upon David's throne, and the priests, and the prophets, and all the inhabitants of Jerusalem, with drunkenness. 14. And I will dash them one against another, even the fathers and the sons together, saith the Lord; I will not pity, nor spare, nor have compassion, that I should not destroy them.

15. Hear ye, and give ear, be not proud;
    For the LORD hath spoken.
16. Give glory to the LORD your God.
    Before it grow dark,
    And before your feet stumble
    Upon the mountains of twilight,

Jeremiah

13

reference to this command given to Jeremiah to conceal the girdle on the banks of the Euphrates . . . all this is allegorical, shown in a vision. Jeremiah did not go forth from Palestine to Babylon and did not see the Euphrates."

13 : 12-14 Jeremiah changes the metaphor from the rotted girdle to earthenware wine-bottles which will smash against each other.

13 : 12 *Every bottle.* Rashi explains that this means an earthenware bottle (i.e., not a wineskin) since in verse 14 the bottles will be smashed against each other and shattered.

13 : 14 *Dash them one against another.* The same verb is used here as in Psalm 2:9. "Thou shalt dash them in pieces like a potter's vessel." Our translation would be clearer here if after "dash them" it also had the words "in pieces," or perhaps translated simply, "smash them against each other." Kimchi develops the metaphor of the jugs smashing against each other by explaining it as follows: When their punishment comes, their sorrows will be so great that "fathers and sons together" will be desperate and confused enough to forget all natural pity toward each other and do each other harm.

13 : 16 *Your feet stumble upon the mountains of twilight.*

Jeremiah

13

And, while ye look for light,
He turn it into the shadow of death,
And make it gross darkness.

17. But if ye will not hear it,
My soul shall weep in secret for your pride;
And mine eye shall weep sore, and run down with
    tears
Because the LORD's flock is carried away captive.

18. Say thou unto the king and to the queen-mother:
'Sit ye down low;
For your headtires are come down,
Even your beautiful crown.'

19. The cities of the South are shut up,
And there is none to open them;
Judah is carried away captive all of it;
It is wholly carried away captive.

Rashi explains: Your going into exile will be like going into darkness. Kimchi adds: You will hit your feet against stone, as happens when one walks in the darkness.

The rocky roads of the land gave rise to the natural metaphor of hitting one's foot against a stone and stumbling. Therefore, speaking of sin, Hosea (14:2) says: "Thou hast stumbled in thine iniquity," and the same symbol is used in Psalm 91:11 ff. to describe God's protection: "He will give His angels charge over thee . . . lest thou dash thy foot against a stone."

13 : 17 *My soul shall weep . . . for your pride.* Rashi says this means: For your pride, which will now be brought down to dust. But Tur-Sinai emends the word which means "pride" (*gevah*) to *navehu*, which means "His dwelling-place." The verse, then, would simply mean that Jeremiah weeps because of the Temple, God's dwelling-place, which will be destroyed.

13 : 18-19 Here Jeremiah addresses himself to the king and queen, telling them how they will be humbled. This verse fits better with the traditional reading of the preceding verse, "because of pride" (which will now be humbled).

13 : 18 *Headtires.* That is, the attire of the head, possibly the tiara or crown.

13 : 19 *The cities of the South.* The invader is coming down from the north; therefore, when the cities of the south are conquered, it will mean that the whole land has been overrun.

96

20. Lift up your eyes, and behold
    Them that come from the north;
    Where is the flock that was given thee,
    Thy beautiful flock?
21. What wilt thou say, when He shall set the friends
        over thee as head,
    Whom thou thyself hast trained against thee?
    Shall not pangs take hold of thee,
    As of a woman in travail?
22. And if thou say in thy heart:
    'Wherefore are these things befallen me?'—
    For the greatness of thine iniquity are thy skirts
        uncovered,
    And thy heels suffer violence.
23. Can the Ethiopian change his skin,
    Or the leopard his spots?
    Then may ye also do good,
    That are accustomed to do evil.
24. Therefore will I scatter them, as the stubble that
        passeth away
    By the wind of the wilderness.
25. This is thy lot, the portion measured unto thee
        from Me,
    Saith the LORD;

13 : 21 *Friends over thee as head, whom thou thyself hast trained.*
Rashi explains the phrases "the friends whom thou thyself hast
trained" who will now be "over thee as head." He says it means:
You yourself sent messengers time and again to Babylon asking
their friendship and their help; that is to say, you yourself
have taught them to be master over you. Kimchi gives perhaps a
clearer example. King Ahaz sent to the king of Assyria saying
"I am thy servant and thy son" (II Kings 16:7).

13 : 22 *Thy heels suffer violence.* Kimchi says the captive woman is allowed no privacy. (So too Isaiah of Trani). In other
words the whole body, from head to heels, is open to the gaze
of the oppressor.

13 : 23 *Can the Ethiopian change his skin . . . ?* Evil has become
so habitual that it seems to be an inherent part of your nature.

13 : 25 *Thy . . . portion measured unto thee.* According to the
rabbinic idea, God punishes for our sins, like for like, "measure
for measure" (B. Sabbath 105b).

Because thou hast forgotten Me,
And trusted in falsehood.

Jeremiah 13

26. Therefore will I also uncover thy skirts upon thy face,
    And thy shame shall appear.
27. Thine adulteries, and thy neighings, the lewdness of thy harlotry,
    On the hills in the field have I seen thy detestable acts.
    Woe unto thee, O Jerusalem! thou wilt not be made clean!
    When shall it ever be?

13 : 27   *When shall it ever be?*   Trani says that the prophet implies the answer, namely, only after the exile "will it ever be" that you will be purified.

14

THIS CHAPTER is based upon a drought that overtook the land. The country was always subject to drought, and there was a long and elaborate tradition for a sequence of fasts as a drought continued. The Talmud treatise *Taanit* deals entirely with fasting, chiefly in time of drought. In this chapter the people pray; but God says that because of their sins, He will not listen to them. He directs Jeremiah not to plead for them. The chapter continues with a dirge by the prophet and ends up with a renewed prayer by the people.

1. The word of the LORD that came to Jeremiah concerning the droughts.
2. Judah mourneth, and the gates thereof languish,
   They bow down in black unto the ground;
   And the cry of Jerusalem is gone up.
3. And their nobles send their lads for water:
   They come to the pits, and find no water;
   Their vessels return empty;

Jeremiah

14

14 : 2 *The gates thereof languish.* Rashi says that "the gates" simply means the cities of Judea (not only the countryside). "The gate" is an appropriate symbol for a city. Aside from the obvious fact that it was a busy center of activity, deserted only when all traffic between city and country had ceased, the gate was the place where, in earlier times, the city's elders sat to take

99

They are ashamed and confounded, and cover their
heads.

Jeremiah
14

4. Because of the ground which is cracked,
For there hath been no rain in the land,
The plowmen are ashamed, they cover their heads.

5. Yea, the hind also in the field calveth, and for-
saketh her young,
Because there is no grass.

6. And the wild asses stand on the high hills,
They gasp for air like jackals;
Their eyes fail, because there is no herbage.

7. Though our iniquities testify against us,
O Lord, work Thou for Thy name's sake;
For our backslidings are many,
We have sinned against Thee.

8. O Thou hope of Israel,
The Saviour thereof in time of trouble,
Why shouldest Thou be as a stranger in the land,
And as a wayfaring man that turneth aside to tarry
for a night?

9. Why shouldest Thou be as a man overcome,

counsel with each other and to execute justice. Therefore the
sentence in Deuteronomy 16:18: "Judges and officers shalt thou
make thee in all thy gates."

Bow down in black. As a sign of mourning (Luzzato).
The same word is used in 8:21: "I am seized with anguish; I am
black."

14 : 3-6 A description of the drought. There is no water in the
wells. The ground is so dry and crumbly that it cannot be
ploughed, and even the wild animals languish.

14 : 7-9 The prayer of the people during the drought, asking that
God forgive their sins, be near to them, and not keep a distance
between them as if He were "a stranger in the land . . . a wayfaring man."

14 : 8 *Thou hope of Israel.* Kimchi explains: Although we
know we have sinned, Thou still remainest the sole hope of our
deliverance.

14 : 9 *As a man overcome.* Rashi: As a man overcome with
fear who flees from the battle.

As a mighty man that cannot save?
Yet Thou, O Lord, art in the midst of us,
And Thy name is called upon us;
Leave us not.

10. Thus saith the Lord unto this people:
Even so have they loved to wander,
They have not refrained their feet;
Therefore the Lord doth not accept them,
Now will He remember their iniquity,
And punish their sins.

11. And the Lord said unto me: 'Pray not for this people for their good. 12. When they fast, I will not hear their cry; and when they offer burnt-offering and meal-offering, I will not accept them; but I will consume them by the sword, and by the famine, and by the pestilence.' 13. Then said I: 'Ah, Lord God! behold, the prophets say unto them: Ye shall not see the sword, neither shall ye have famine; but I will give you assured peace in this place.' 14. Then the Lord said unto me: 'The prophets prophesy lies in My name; I sent them not, neither have I commanded them, neither spoke I unto them; they prophesy unto you a lying vision, and divination, and a thing of nought, and the deceit of their own heart. 15. Therefore thus saith the Lord: As for the prophets that prophesy in My name, and I sent them not, yet they say: Sword and famine shall not be in this land, by sword and famine shall those prophets be consumed. 16. and the people to whom they prophesy shall be cast out in the streets of Jerusalem because of the famine and the sword; and they shall have none to bury them, them, their wives, nor their sons, nor their daughters; for I will pour their evil upon them.'

Jeremiah

14

14 : 10 *Loved to wander.* Kimchi: God says to the people, you have loved to wander down to Egypt and Assyria for help; all this against My warnings. Now I will make you wander in exile.
14 : 11-18 A dialogue between Jeremiah and God. God tells the

17. And thou shalt say this word unto them:
    Let mine eyes run down with tears night and day,
    And let them not cease;
    For the virgin daughter of my people is broken
        with a great breach,
    With a very grievous blow.

18. If I go forth into the field,
    Then behold the slain with the sword!
    And if I enter into the city,
    Then behold them that are sick with famine!
    For both the prophet and the priest are gone about
    to a land, and knew it not.

19. Hast Thou utterly rejected Judah?
    Hath Thy soul loathed Zion?
    Why hast Thou smitten us, and there is no healing
        for us?

prophet not to pray for the people. Jeremiah says: Their prophets are reassuring them that they will have food and peace (therefore how can they be expected to repent?) God responds: These are false prophets: "As for the prophets that prophesy in My name, I sent them not" (verse 15). These prophets will be punished, and you, Jeremiah, weep for them. When they ask you why you are weeping, explain it is because of the sorrows that await them (verses 17 and 18).

We looked for peace, but no good came;
And for a time of healing, and behold terror!

20. We acknowledge, O LORD, our wickedness,
Even the iniquity of our fathers;
For we have sinned against Thee.

21. Do not contemn us, for Thy name's sake,
Do not dishonour the throne of Thy glory;
Remember, break not Thy covenant with us.

22. Are there any among the vanities of the nations
that can cause rain?
Or can the heavens give showers?
Art not Thou He, O LORD our God, and do we not
wait for Thee?
For thou hast made all these things.

14 : 19 *Hast Thou utterly rejected Judah?*　Kimchi: In spite of God's command: "Pray not for this people" (verse 11), nevertheless Jeremiah here *does* pray for them. The meaning of his prayer, according to Rashi, is: If You have not *completely* rejected them, then do not punish them so much that they cannot be cured.

14 : 22 *Can the heavens give showers?*　The rains do not come of their own accord but by Thy will. Therefore if we are suffering it is because we have sinned against Thee.

15

THIS CHAPTER continues the theme of chapter 14, where God told Jeremiah not to pray for the people. God now says: Even if Moses and Samuel came and pleaded for them, I would not listen. There follows another passage of Jeremiah's self-expression (a "confession"), and a repetition of the promise that God gave at the beginning of Jeremiah's career. See chapter 1, especially verse 18, that God will give Jeremiah the strength of an iron and brazen wall; the people will not be able to overcome him.

Jeremiah
15

1. Then said the LORD unto me: 'Though Moses and Samuel stood before Me, yet My mind could not be toward this people; cast them out of My sight, and let them go forth. 2. And it shall come to pass,

15 : 1 *Moses and Samuel.* Moses and Samuel were held to be the noblest among the prophets. Kimchi recalls the verse in Psalm 99:6: "Moses and Aaron among His priests, and Samuel among them that call upon His Name, did call upon the Lord and He answered them." Rashi explains why Moses and Samuel were able to win God's assent when they pleaded for the people. It was because Moses and Samuel first persuaded the people to repent and *then* pleaded for God's pardon. But thou, Jeremiah, hast not won them to repentance; therefore, even pleas by Moses and Samuel would be of no avail.

15 : 2-3 *Death . . . sword . . . famine . . . captivity . . . four kinds.* The four types of national and social destruction. It is very likely

when they say unto thee: Whither shall we go forth? then thou shalt tell them: Thus saith the LORD: Such as are for death, to death; and such as are for the sword, to the sword; and such as are for the famine, to the famine; and such as are for captivity, to captivity. 3. And I will appoint over them four kinds, saith the LORD: the sword to slay, and the dogs to drag, and the fowls of the heaven, and the beasts of the earth, to devour and to destroy. 4. And I will cause them to be a horror among all the kingdoms of the earth, because of Manasseh the son of Hezekiah king of Judah, for that which he did in Jerusalem.

5. For who shall have pity upon thee, O Jerusalem?
Or who shall bemoan thee?
Or who shall turn aside to ask of thy welfare?

6. Thou hast cast Me off, saith the LORD,
Thou art gone backward;
Therefore do I stretch out My hand against thee,
   and destroy thee;
I am weary with repenting.

7. And I fan them with a fan in the gates of the land;
I bereave them of children, I destroy My people,
Since they return not from their ways.

8. Their widows are increased to Me above the sand
   of the seas;
I bring upon them, against the mother, a chosen
one,

upon this passage that the author of the New Testament Book of Revelation (the Apocalypse) based his picture of the four horsemen of destruction: "The Four Horsemen of the Apocalypse."

15 : 4 *Because of Manasseh.*   The evil King Manasseh was the son of the righteous Hezekiah, the friend of Isaiah. Manasseh reintroduced idolatry and even child-sacrifices. See II Kings 21:1-8.

15 : 5-9 A dirge visualizing the impending doom.

15 : 8 *Against the mother, a chosen one.*   Rashi and Trani: "The mother" means Jerusalem, which is the mother-city, a phrase used elsewhere in the Bible for a great city. II Samuel 20:19: "Seekest thou to destroy a city and a mother in Israel?" (the same use as in the Greek *metro-polis*, i.e., mother-city).

Even a spoiler at noonday;
I cause anguish and terrors to fall upon her suddenly.

Jeremiah

15

9. She that hath borne seven languisheth;
Her spirit droopeth;
Her sun is gone down while it was yet day,
She is ashamed and confounded;
And the residue of them will I deliver to the sword
before their enemies,
Saith the LORD.'

10. Woe is me, my mother, that thou hast borne me
A man of strife and a man of contention to the
whole earth!
I have not lent, neither have men lent to me;
Yet every one of them doth curse me.

11. The LORD said: 'Verily I will release thee for good;

A chosen one. The enemy whom I have chosen as My instrument. But Kimchi takes "the chosen one" to mean the chosen
heroes will not be able to resist the enemy.

15 : 9 *She that hath borne seven languisheth.* Rashi says that
this refers to the northern kingdom, which had been destroyed.
The northern kingdom had produced seven dynasties, the families of Jeroboam, Omri, etc. However, Trani says that "seven"
is just a round number, and he calls attention to the verse in
Proverbs 24:16: "For a righteous man falleth seven times and
riseth again."

15 : 10 Here Jeremiah utters a dirge on his own life, regretting
that he ever was born, having to face unremitting hatred from
the people around him. The relevance of the dirge in this place
may be the reference to a bereaved mother in verse 9, which
brought the thought of his own mother to his mind (Malbim sees
this connection).

I have not lent. Kimchi explains that sometimes the borrower is enraged at the lender (for dunning him), and sometimes
the lender is enraged at the borrower (for not repaying). But I,
says Jeremiah, am in no such relations to them ("Neither a borrower nor a lender be," *Hamlet*, i, 3, 75), and yet they curse me.

15 : 11 *I will release thee for good.* There are many interpretations of this rather difficult passage. The Targum translates it:

verily I will cause the enemy to make supplication unto thee in the time of evil and in the time of affliction. 12. Can iron break iron from the north and brass? 13. Thy substance and thy treasures will I give for a spoil without price, and that for all thy sins, even in all thy borders. 14. And I will make thee to pass with thine enemies into a land which thou knowest not; for a fire is kindled in My nostril, which shall burn upon you.'

Thy future will be happy. Kimchi follows the Targum: The rest of your life will be happy. Neither of these explanations renders "release" as the meaning of the word *sheritich* used here. They take the Hebrew word to mean *she'erit*, "the rest" or "the remainder," i.e., of your life. Luzzato also takes the word to mean "remnant," but gives this interpretation (God saying to Israel): I will not destroy you to such an extent that you will just be a broken remnant; I will punish you for your own good. However Rashi (as also Abarbanel) takes the word as our translation here takes it, to mean "release," and sees it as a sort of preview of what occurred after the Babylonians captured the city. The Babylonian officer released Jeremiah from the shackles in which he was found and offered to give him a new home in Babylon "for his own good." Jeremiah 40:2-4: "The captain of the guard took Jeremiah, and said . . . 'now behold, I loose thee this day from the chains . . . .'"

The enemy to make supplication. Rashi, continuing his explanation of what will happen when the Babylonians free him from his chains, takes these words to mean: At that time the Judeans (hitherto hostile to you) will plead with you to intercede for them.

15 : 12 *Can iron break iron from the north?* Rashi: Can your weapons defeat the weapons of Nebuchadnezzar (who comes down from the north)? So Kimchi indicates: It means that the iron of the north, namely Nebuchadnezzar's weaponry, is stronger than yours. To describe that strong northern iron, Kimchi uses the French word *acier* (steel).

15 : 13 *Spoil without price.* There will be so much booty that the market will be glutted; it will not be possible to sell it even at the cheapest price.

Jeremiah

15

15. Thou, O LORD, knowest;
    Remember me, and think of me, and avenge me
        of my persecutors;
    Take me not away because of Thy long-suffering;
    Know that for Thy sake I have suffered taunts.
16. Thy words were found, and I did eat them;
    And Thy words were unto me a joy and the re-
        joicing of my heart;
    Because Thy name was called on me, O LORD God
        of hosts.
17. I sat not in the assembly of them that make merry,
        nor rejoiced;
    I sat alone because of Thy hand;
    For Thou hast filled me with indignation.
18. Why is my pain perpetual,
    And my wound incurable, so that it refuseth to be
        healed?
    Wilt Thou indeed be unto me as a deceitful brook.
    As waters that fail?

15 to the end. Again an outburst of self-expression by Jeremiah, telling how much he has suffered for speaking the words
which God directed him to speak.

15 : 15 *Take me not away because of Thy long-suffering.* Because Thou art merciful ("long-suffering") let me live. It is "for
Thy sake I have suffered taunts."

15 : 16 *Thy words were found, and I did eat them.* There are
a number of examples of the metaphor, likening God's words to
the prophet to welcome food. So Ezekiel 2:8 (God says to the
prophet): "Open thy mouth and eat what I give thee." Abarbanel: Thy words were as sweet to me as if they were the finest
dainties in the world.

15 : 18 *Why is my pain perpetual . . . ? Wilt Thou indeed be unto
me as a deceitful brook?* The rivers in the south often dry up.
The traveler, trudging through the desert, expecting to find
water, finds only a sandy riverbed. Jeremiah complains that God
has become to him like a dried-up stream, granting him no re-
freshment or help, and he wants to know why he must suffer so

108

19. Therefore thus saith the LORD:
    If thou return, and I bring thee back,
    Thou shalt stand before Me;
    And if thou bring forth the precious out of the vile,
    Thou shalt be as My mouth;
    Let them return unto thee,
    But thou shalt not return unto them.
20. And I will make thee unto this people a fortified
    brazen wall;
    And they shall fight against thee,
    But they shall not prevail against thee;
    For I am with thee to save thee and to deliver thee,
    Saith the LORD.
21. And I will deliver thee out of the hand of the
    wicked,
    And I will redeem thee out of the hand of the
    terrible.

endlessly and be constantly hated. Similarly Job, speaking of his
untrustworthy friends, says: "My brothers have dealt deceitfully
as a brook" (Job 6:15). The Targum, seeking to avoid this harsh
reference to God as if He were a disappointing brook in the
south, paraphrases: Let not Your words be like a fountain whose
water has ceased.

15 : 19 *If thou return, and I bring thee back.* Kimchi says that
God addresses these words to the prophet and says: If you repent
of the bitter words you have just spoken, I will restore you. Trani
says: If you succeed in bringing Israel back to Me, I will restore
you. Luzzato, however, says it means: If you return to your task
(i.e., and not despair), I will give you strength again.

The precious out of the vile. Rashi: If you bring forth the
goodness which is in the evil man; i.e., if you lead him to repentance.

15 : 20 *I will make thee . . . a fortified brazen wall.* This renews
God's promise to Jeremiah at the beginning of his ministry
(Jeremiah 1:18): "For, behold, I have made thee this day . . .
an iron pillar, and brazen walls, against the whole land, against
the kings . . . the princes . . . the priests . . . the people."

16

JEREMIAH IS told never to marry and have children because the fate of children will be tragic when the country is overrun.

Jeremiah

16

1. The word of the LORD came also unto me, saying:
2. Thou shalt not take thee a wife,
   Neither shalt thou have sons or daughters in this place.
3. For thus saith the LORD concerning the sons and concerning the daughters that are born in this place, and concerning their mothers that bore them, and concerning their fathers that begot them in this land:
4. They shall die of grievous deaths;
   They shall not be lamented, neither shall they be buried,
   They shall be as dung upon the face of the ground;
   And they shall be consumed by the sword, and by famine;
   And their carcasses shall be meat for the fowls of heaven,
   And for the beasts of the earth.

16 : 4 *Neither shall they be buried.* This is the same dire prediction which the prophet had made (in 8:1) concerning the bodies of the kings, priests, and false prophets.

5. For thus saith the LORD: Enter not into the house of mourning, neither go to lament, neither bemoan them for I have taken away My peace from this people, saith the LORD, even mercy and compassion. 6. Both the great and the small shall die in this land; they shall not be buried; neither shall men lament for them, nor cut themselves, nor make themselves bald for them; 7. neither shall men break bread for them in mourning, to comfort them for the dead; neither shall men give them the cup of consolation to drink for their father or for their mother. 8. And thou shalt not go into the house

16 : 5 *Enter not into the house of mourning.* The prophet's demeanor is often meant to be a prevision of the destiny of the people. The time is coming when the defeated people, dragged off into captivity, will not have time to bury their dead and certainly not to lament for them. Therefore now, as a prevision of the dire future before the calamity has come, the prophet is told not to participate in mourning. Kimchi says it means: Since I, the Lord, have now removed My mercy from them, do not you, Jeremiah, try to console them.

16 : 6 *Neither shall men . . . cut themselves . . . nor make . . . bald for them.* It was the custom of the peoples roundabout, in times of mourning, to display their grief by cutting their flesh and making a bald spot on their foreheads. This is expressly forbidden to the children of Israel in Deuteronomy 14:1: "Ye are children of the Lord your God: ye shall not cut yourselves nor make any baldness between your eyes for the dead." But the prohibition creates some difficulty with this text. If such marks of mourning are forbidden, why should their absence be described as part of the tragedy that will take place when the nation is invaded? Kimchi and Trani say: Of course these things were forbidden, but the people nevertheless followed the customs of the nations around them. So too Luzzato.

16 : 7 *Break bread . . . cup of consolation.* Of these two customs, the providing of food for the mourners by their friends still remains a traditional practice.

16 : 8 *Thou shalt not go into the house of feasting.* This completes the thought of verse 5. Jeremiah was not to participate

of feasting to sit with them, to eat and to drink.
9. For thus saith the LORD of hosts, the God of Israel:

Behold, I will cause to cease out of this place,
Before your eyes and in your days,
The voice of mirth and the voice of gladness,
The voice of the bridegroom and the voice of the bride.

10. And it shall come to pass, when thou shalt tell this people all these words, and they shall say unto thee: 'Wherefore hath the LORD pronounced all this great evil against us? or what is our iniquity? or what is our sin that we have committed against the LORD our God?' 11. then shalt thou say unto them: 'Because your fathers have forsaken Me, saith the LORD, and have walked after other gods, and have served them, and have worshipped them, and have forsaken Me, and have not kept My law; 12. and ye have done worse than your fathers; for behold, ye walk every one after the stubbornness of his evil heart, so that ye hearken not unto Me; 13. therefore will I cast you out of this land into a land that ye have not known, neither ye nor your fathers; and there shall ye serve other gods day and night; forasmuch as I will show you no favour.'

14. Therefore, behold, the days come, saith the

either in their mourning or in their feasting as a prevision of the fact that God will abolish both. There will be no time for mourning, and there will be no reason for rejoicing.

16 : 9   *The voice of mirth . . . bridegroom . . . bride.*   Follows the preceding verse; just as following verse 5 God said there would be no mourning for the dead, so here He says there will be no rejoicing at weddings. This sequence of "mirth," "gladness," "bridegroom," "bride," occurs three other times in the Book of Jeremiah, in 7:34, 25:10, and 33:11.

16 : 10-13 is a dialogue between the people and Jeremiah, the people asking: Why has God punished us so much? and the prophet answering: It is because of your idolatry.

16 : 14-15   These verses, speaking of the coming deliverance, inter-

LORD, that it shall no more be said: 'As the
LORD liveth, that brought up the children of Israel
out of the land of Egypt,' but: 15. 'As the LORD
liveth, that brought up the children of Israel
from the land of the north, and from all the countries whither He had driven them'; and I will bring
them back into their land that I gave unto their
fathers.

16. Behold, I will send for many fishers, saith the
LORD, and they shall fish them; and afterward I
will send for many hunters, and they shall hunt
them from every mountain, and from every hill,
and out of the clefts of the rocks.

17. For Mine eyes are upon all their ways,
They are not hid from My face;
Neither is their iniquity concealed from Mine eyes.

18. And first I will recompense their iniquity and their
sin double;
Because they have profaned My land;
They have filled Mine inheritance

rupt the sequence, which speaks only of the coming doom. As a
matter of fact, these verses are found also in Jeremiah 23:7-8,
where they do fit into the sequence. Perhaps some later writer
inserted them here to mitigate the gloom of the prophecy.

16 : 14   *It shall no more be said.*   The deliverance from Babylon
will be so blessedly welcome that people will swear by that event
as they used to swear by the deliverance from Egypt. This explanation, given by the various commentators, is based upon the
Talmud (B. Beracoth 12b).

16 : 16   *Fishers . . . hunters.*   After the interruption of verses 14
and 15, this verse resumes the description of the coming calamity.
Luzzato makes an interesting explanation of why the prophet
first speaks of fishermen and then of hunters. Fishermen, using
nets, capture large numbers of fish all at once. Hunters pursue
one stag at a time. When the enemy comes, they will first capture the city and get vast numbers of captives at one time (like
a fisherman with his net). Then those who have fled into the
hills will be hunted down, one by one.

16 : 18   *I will recompense their . . . sin double.*   Kimchi: Since
they adopted and repeated the iniquities of their fathers and even

With the carcasses of their detestable things and
their abominations.

Jeremiah

16

19. O LORD, my strength, and my stronghold,
And my refuge, in the day of affliction,
Unto Thee shall the nations come
From the ends of the earth, and shall say:
'Our fathers have inherited nought but lies,
Vanity and things wherein there is no profit.'

20. Shall a man make unto himself gods,
And they are no gods?

21. Therefore, behold, I will cause them to know,
This once will I cause them to know
My hand and My might;
And they shall know that My name is the LORD.

added to them, I will punish them double, as it is said: Visiting
the iniquities of the fathers upon the children (Exodus 20:5).
Deutero-Isaiah, speaking during the captivity, says: "Bid Jerusalem take heart, she hath received of the Lord's hand double for
all her sins." However, Luzzato says it does not really mean double punishment, but parallel punishment, one for one.

16 : 19   *O Lord, my strength . . . unto Thee shall the nations come.*

The prophet, declaring that God is his strength, is certain that someday the nations will discover that their idolatry is all foolishness and cannot help them, and that God is the only source of strength.

16 : 21 *This once will I cause them to know.* This sentence is rather difficult. God will cause whom to know His might once more? What has this prediction to do with the prophecy that the nations will someday abandon their idols and return to God? Kimchi suggests it means: I will cause Israel to know My might, and thus the nations will learn of God's power in the world. Trani has a similar explanation. He reads the preceding verse, which speaks of the unreality of the idols, as the words spoken by the Gentiles to God. The two verses therefore come together in this meaning. The Gentiles say: Since we have now discovered that the idols are worthless, why do the people Israel remain idolatrous? To which God says: Therefore I will punish them (Israel) once more that they may be rid of their idols. Luzzato gives a similar explanation. Malbim gives an entirely different meaning to the phrase "this time," etc. He says that at some *future* date the nations will learn that the idols are worthless. But God wishes Israel to know that truth immediately. Therefore He will send Israel punishment now, so that they may know God's reality *now*, at *this time.*

17

MOST MODERN scholars agree that this chapter is a miscellany of various unconnected pieces of prose and poetry. The chapter begins with a statement of the nation's sin of idolatry; then follows a denunciation of those who put their trust in man rather than in God; then the prophet asks God to heal him from the hurt caused by the hostility of the people to whom he is preaching. The chapter ends with a plea to observe the Sabbath.

Jeremiah

17

1. The sin of Judah is written
   With a pen of iron, and with the point of a diamond;
   It is graven upon the tablet of their heart,
   And upon the horns of your altars.
2. Like the symbols of their sons are their altars,

17 : 1 *Pen of iron . . . point of a diamond . . . graven upon the tablet of their heart.* Rashi: The metal instrument incises the words so that they are ineradicable. Their sin is so deeply engraved that it cannot be removed. It is now part of their nature. This is just what Jeremiah meant in 13:23: "Can the Ethiopian change his skin, or the leopard his spots?" The sin has become inherent and permanent.

Just as evil impulses can be looked upon as engraved upon the heart, so also Scripture speaks of virtues as thus engraved. So Proverbs 3:3: "Let not kindness and truth forsake thee . . . Write them upon the table of thy heart." See also Proverbs 7:3.

17 : 2 *Like the symbols of their sons.* The Hebrew word *zecher*

116

And their Asherim are by the leafy trees,
Upon the high hills.

3. O thou that sittest upon the mountain in the field,
And thy high places, because of sin, throughout
all thy borders.

4. And thou, even of thyself, shalt discontinue from
thy heritage
That I gave thee;
And I will cause thee to serve thine enemies
In the land which thou knowest not;
For ye have kindled a fire in My nostril,
Which shall burn forever.

5. Thus saith the LORD:
Cursed is the man that trusteth in man,

literally means, not "symbols," as here translated, but "memory" or "recollection." So all the classic commentators take this verse to mean: As it is a joy for a man to think of a beloved son, so does the thought of their idolatries make them happy (Rashi, Kimchi, Luzzato, Trani). This explanation is found in the Talmud, B. Sanhedrin 63b.

17 : 3 *Sittest upon the mountain.* The city of Jerusalem (Rashi).

17 : 4 *Thou, even of thyself, shalt discontinue.* The verse is difficult. It seems to mean: Thou shalt give up thine inheritance by thine own doings, i.e., thy sins will cause thee to be disinherited. Trani rearranges the text (saying that it is not in proper order) and then gives it this meaning: You yourself will surrender the inheritance which I have given thee. Malbim refers the verse to the time after the capture of Jerusalem. The Babylonians left the land relatively unspoiled, but the people, of their own accord (i.e., "even of thyself"), abandoned the land and emigrated to Egypt.

17 : 5-8 These verses say that a man who trusts in man rather than God is like a tree growing in the desert, which is always on the verge of drying up. The one who trusts in God is like a tree growing in a well-watered land.

17 : 5-13 These verses seem to express a unified theme, that of trusting in God rather than in man.

17 : 5 *Trusteth in man.* Kimchi says this refers to the fact that they trusted in help from Egypt instead of relying upon God for their safety.

And maketh flesh his arm,
And whose heart departeth from the LORD.

Jeremiah
17

6. For he shall be like a tamarisk in the desert,
And shall not see when good cometh;
But shall inhabit the parched places in the wilderness,
A salt land and not inhabited.

7. Blessed is the man that trusteth in the LORD,
And whose trust the LORD is.

8. For he shall be as a tree planted by the waters,
And that spreadeth out its roots by the river,
And shall not see when heat cometh,
But its foliage shall be luxuriant;
And shall not be anxious in the year of drought,
Neither shall cease from yielding fruit.

9. The heart is deceitful above all things,
And it is exceeding weak—who can know it?

10. I the LORD search the heart,
I try the reins,
Even to give every man according to his ways,
According to the fruit of his doings.

11. As the partridge that broodeth over young which she hath not brought forth,

17 : 8 *Not be anxious in the year of drought.* The tree growing in the well-watered land has roots going deep to the underground water and so can outlast a season of drought. Similarly, the man who "trusteth in God" (verse 7) has roots and can outlive misfortunes.

17 : 9 *The heart is deceitful ... who can know it?* Kimchi connects this verse with the preceding verses, which speak of trusting God. Trust in God depends upon the deep impulses of the heart. Thus verse 5 describes those who do not trust in God as those "whose heart departeth from the Lord." But the heart (the emotions) is so unpredictable, who can understand it? Thereupon verse 10 answers the question of verse 9: "I the Lord search the heart."

17 : 10 *I try the reins.* The kidneys as the seat of the emotions. See the comment to 12:2.

17 : 11 *As the partridge ... broodeth.* According to some of

So is he that getteth riches, and not by right;
In the midst of his days he shall leave them,
And at his end he shall be a fool.

12. Thou throne of glory, on high from the beginning,
Thou place of our sanctuary,

13. Thou hope of Israel, the LORD!
All that forsake Thee shall be ashamed;
They that depart from Thee shall be written in the
earth,
Because they have forsaken the LORD,
The fountain of living waters.

14. Heal me, O LORD, and I shall be healed;
Save me, and I shall be saved;
For Thou art my praise.

Jeremiah
17

the commentators, the partridge gathers the eggs of other birds
and hatches them. Others give virtually the same explanation but
say that the partridge gathers young chicks and raises them.
But all her efforts are in vain. The chicks are never the partridge's
offspring. They leave her as soon as they can fly. So (the verse
continues) the man who gains his wealth dishonestly will lose it
soon, just as the partridge loses the alien chicks.

17 : 12 *Thou throne of glory.* The Targum connects this with
the preceding verse as follows: The wicked will be punished from
the throne of glory.

17 : 13 *They . . . shall be written in the earth.* The commentators find this verse difficult, so there are many different interpretations. Trani says it means that the wicked are written down
(not for life, but) for death, to be buried in the earth. Luzzato
cites a number of commentators who say the verse means that
the wicked will be written in the dust. In other words, the memory of them will be blown away. But he himself prefers to
interpret it as follows. The wicked will be recorded on earth (en-
duringly) to be remembered for their wickedness. Duhm quotes
a number of modern critics who emend the word used here,
yikotevu, to *yikolemu*, and translate: "the wicked will be put to
shame." Tur-Sinai emends the word to *yikoretu*, meaning: "they
will be cut off from the earth."

17 : 14-18 Another outburst ("confession") of Jeremiah, asking
God for healing and for protection from his persecutors.

119

15. Behold, they say unto me:
    'Where is the word of the LORD? let it come now.'

16. As for me, I have not hastened from being a
    shepherd after Thee;
    Neither have I desired the woeful day; Thou
    knowest it;
    That which came out of my lips was manifest be-
    fore Thee.

17. Be not a ruin unto me;
    Thou art my refuge in the day of evil.

18. Let them be ashamed that persecute me, but let not
    me be ashamed;
    Let them be dismayed, but let not me be dismayed;
    Bring upon them the day of evil,
    And destroy them with double destruction.

19. Thus said the LORD unto me: Go, and stand in the
    gate of the children of the people, whereby the
    kings of Judah come in, and by which they go out,
    and in all the gates of Jerusalem; 20. and say unto
    them:
    Hear ye the word of the LORD, ye kings of
    Judah, and all Judah, and all the inhabitants of

17 : 16 *I have not hastened from being a shepherd . . . neither have I desired the woeful day.*   I have not run away from the bitter task which you assigned me (to be a shepherd to a doomed flock) nor did I enjoy the bitter predictions which I had to make. Luzzato emends the text so as to read it as follows: As a shepherd I never urged you to carry out your threats; I never did desire that the evil day should come.

17 : 18 *With double destruction.*   This is the same thought as in 16:18: "I will recompense their iniquity and their sin double."

17 : 19-27 A sermon against the violation of the Sabbath by carrying burdens. The earlier critical scholars, who generally take the point of view that the prophets were against all ceremonial ("cult"), cannot believe that a sermon calling upon the people to observe the Sabbath could possibly come from Jeremiah the Prophet. So Duhm (p. 149), citing most critical scholarship, says that this passage was long recognized as not genuine; it represents the mood and concerns of a later day (Trito-Isaiah

Jerusalem, that enter in by these gates; 21. thus saith the LORD: Take heed for the sake of your souls, and bear no burden on the sabbath day, nor bring it in by the gates of Jerusalem; 22. neither carry forth a burden out of your houses on the sabbath day, neither do ye any work; but hallow ye the sabbath day, as I commanded your fathers; 23. but they hearkened not, neither inclined their ear, but made their neck stiff, that they might not hear, nor receive instruction. 24. And it shall come to pass, if ye diligently hearken unto Me, saith the LORD, to bring in no burden through the gates of this city on the sabbath day, but to hallow the sabbath day, to do no work therein; 25. then shall there enter in by the gates of this city kings and princes sitting upon the throne of David, riding in chariots and on horses, they, and their princes, the men of Judah, and the inhabitants of Jerusalem; and this city shall be inhabited for ever. 26. And they shall come from the cities of Judah, and from the places round about Jerusalem, and from the land of Benjamin, and from the Lowland, and from

Jeremiah

17

and Nehemiah). However the more recent critical scholar, Bright, says (p. 120): "There is every likelihood that it [this passage] does develop actual words of Jeremiah on the subject. Jeremiah must certainly have held the Sabbath in respect."

The text of this long passage is well preserved and presents no difficulty to the reader. Rashi, for example, has almost no commentary on the entire passage.

17 : 19   *In the gate of the children of the people.*   Luzzato says that each of the gates of Jerusalem had its own special name. Jeremiah was to preach this sermon in the gate called "Children of the People."

17 : 21, 24   *Gates of Jerusalem . . . gates of this city.*   Kimchi comments on the use of the word "gates" and says: The violation of the Sabbath was only in carrying goods in and out of the gates. Carrying on the Sabbath *within* the city of Jerusalem was no sin, since it was a walled city with its gates closed at night. (So too Abarbanel.)

Jeremiah
17

the mountains, and from the South, bringing burnt-offerings, and sacrifices, and meal-offerings, and frankincense, and bringing sacrifices of thanksgiving, unto the house of the LORD. 27. But if ye will not hearken unto Me to hallow the sabbath day, and not to bear a burden and enter in at the gates of Jerusalem on the sabbath day; then will I kindle a fire in the gates thereof, and it shall devour the palaces of Jerusalem, and it shall not be quenched.

18

JEREMIAH HERE uses the symbol of a potter working at his wheel. When a vessel seems misshapen, the potter remakes it into a perfect vessel. So God can restore Israel if the people would only repent. But they refuse to repent. Instead they plot against Jeremiah's life. He prays for the defeat of his enemies.

1. The word which came to Jeremiah from the LORD, saying: 2. 'Arise, and go down to the potter's house, and there I will cause thee to hear My words.' 3. Then I went down to the potter's house, and, behold, he was at his work on the wheels. 4. And whensoever the vessel that he made of the clay was marred in the hand of the potter, he made it again another vessel, as seemed good to the potter to make it.

5. Then the word of the LORD came to me, saying: 6. 'O house of Israel, cannot I do with you as this potter? saith the LORD. Behold, as the clay in the potter's hand, so are ye in My hand, O house

Jeremiah

18

18 : 1-4   The potter remakes a spoiled vessel, so God says to Israel: "As the clay in the potter's hand, so are ye in My hand, O house of Israel" (verse 6). If, then, the nation "turn from their evil" (verse 8), God will forgive them: "I frame evil against you . . . return ye now every one from his evil way" (verse 11).

of Israel. 7. At one instant I may speak concerning a nation, and concerning a kingdom, to pluck up and to break down and to destroy it; 8. but if that nation turn from their evil, because of which I have spoken against it, I repent of the evil that I thought to do unto it. 9. And at one instant I may speak concerning a nation, and concerning a kingdom, to build and to plant it; 10. but, if it do evil in My sight, that it hearken not to My voice, then I repent of the good, wherewith I said I would benefit it. 11. Now therefore do thou speak to the men of Judah, and to the inhabitants of Jerusalem, saying: Thus saith the LORD: Behold, I frame evil against you, and devise a device against you; return ye now every one from his evil way, and amend your ways and your doings. 12. But they say: There is no hope; but we will walk after our own devices, and we will do every one after the stubbornness of his evil heart.'

13. Therefore thus saith the LORD:
Ask ye now among the nations,

18 : 12 *But they say . . . we will do every one after the stubbornness of his evil heart.* Luzzato calls attention to the fact that this sentence is supposed to be spoken by the people themselves. If that is the case, it is impossible that they should refer to their own impulses as their "evil heart." Therefore these words are really Jeremiah's rewording of what the people are thinking and saying.

18 : 14 *Snow of Lebanon . . . rock of the field . . . strange cold flowing waters.* A difficult verse, and therefore there are many interpretations. The individual words cannot be adequately interpreted or fitted into place. Nevertheless, the general thought is clear enough. People do not give up the fine, clear, flowing water that comes from the melted snow of the Lebanon, and yet My people have abandoned Me. This metaphor of God as the clear sparkling water which the people have foolishly abandoned was used previously by Jeremiah. He says in 2:13: "They have forsaken Me, the Fountain of living waters."

Who hath heard such things;
The virgin of Israel hath done
A very horrible thing.

14. Doth the snow of Lebanon fail
From the rock of the field?
Or are the strange cold flowing waters
Plucked up?

15. For My people hath forgotten Me,
They offer unto vanity;
And they have been made to stumble in their ways,
In the ancient paths,
To walk in bypaths,
In a way not cast up;

16. To make their land an astonishment,
And a perpetual hissing;
Every one that passeth thereby shall be astonished,
And shake his head.

17. I will scatter them as with an east wind
Before the enemy;
I will look upon their back, and not their face,
In the day of their calamity.

18. Then said they:
'Come, and let us devise devices against Jeremiah;
For instruction shall not perish from the priest,
Nor counsel from the wise, nor the word from the
    prophet.
Come, and let us smite him with the tongue,

18 : 17 *Their back, and not their face.* The Hebrew here
merely has the words "back" and "face" without "their," so it is
not clear whose back and whose face are referred to. Rashi (followed by Luzzato) says the verse means (God speaking): I will
watch them when they are defeated and turn their back on the
enemy, and yet I will not help them. Kimchi says (again God
speaking): Since they have turned their face away from Me and
turned their back on Me, I will punish them "measure for measure" and turn My back on them.

18 : 18 *Against Jeremiah; For instruction shall not perish from
the priest.* Both Rashi and Kimchi say that these words are
spoken by the men of Anathoth plotting against Jeremiah; and

And let us not give heed to any of his words.'

Jeremiah

18

19. Give heed to me, O LORD,
    And hearken to the voice of them that contend
    with me.

20. Shall evil be recompensed for good?
    For they have digged a pit for my soul.
    Remember how I stood before Thee
    To speak good for them.
    To turn away Thy wrath from them.

21. Therefore deliver up their children to the famine,
    And hurl them to the power of the sword;
    And let their wives be bereaved of their children,
    and widows;
    And let their men be slain of death,
    And their young men smitten of the sword in battle.

22. Let a cry be heard from their houses,
    When thou shalt bring a troop suddenly upon them;
    For they have digged a pit to take me,
    And hit snares for my feet.

23. Yet, LORD, Thou knowest
    All their counsel against me to slay me;
    Forgive not their iniquity,
    Neither blot out their sin from Thy sight;
    But let them be made to stumble before Thee;
    Deal Thou with them in the time of Thine anger.

what they are saying, in effect, is this: We men of Anathoth are priests in our own right; what if we do slay Jeremiah? There will still be priestly wisdom, etc., i.e., coming from us.

In the rest of the chapter Jeremiah calls upon God to punish the enemies who plot against him.

19

JEREMIAH, AT God's command, visits the workingplace of the potters in the valley of Hinnom, at the place called Tophet, where the children were sacrificed to the idol Moloch. Jeremiah publicly smashes a vessel as a symbol of how God will break up the nation for this bloody type of idolatry. This sin, taking place in the same valley, had already been described by Jeremiah in 7:30-34.

1. Thus said the LORD: Go and get a potter's earthen bottle, and take of the elders of the people, and of the elders of the priests; 2. and go forth unto the valley of the son of Hinnom, which is by the entry of the gate Harsith, and proclaim there the words

Jeremiah

19

19 : 2   *Valley of the son of Hinnom.*   Generally called "the valley of Hinnom," named, as we see here, after the family Hinnom, which owned the land. In Hebrew the "valley of Hinnom" is *Gehinnom*, which, because it was the place of the fires lighted to the god Moloch, got to be the name of the fires of hell, Gehinnom, or, in Christian spelling, Gehenna.

The gate Harsith.   *Cheres*, which is the root of the name, means a "broken piece of pottery," a "potsherd." So the Targum translates the name of this gate as the Gate of the Spoiled Pieces. The gate got its name because it was near where the potters worked with the clay, and it was there, through the gate, that they threw the broken pieces of spoiled pottery.

that I shall tell thee; 3. and say: Hear ye the word of the LORD, O kings of Judah, and inhabitants of Jerusalem; thus saith the LORD of hosts, the God of Israel:

Behold, I will bring evil upon this place, which whosoever heareth, his ears shall tingle; 4. because they have forsaken Me, and have estranged this place, and have offered in it unto other gods, whom neither they nor their fathers have known, nor the kings of Judah; and have filled this place with the blood of innocents; 5. and have built the high places of Baal, to burn their sons in the fire for burnt-offerings unto Baal; which I commanded not, nor spoke it, neither came it into My mind. 6. Therefore, behold, the days come, saith the LORD, that this place shall no more be called Topheth, nor The valley of the son of Hinnom, but The valley of slaughter; 7. and I will make void the counsel of Judah and Jerusalem in this place; and I will cause them to fall by the sword before their enemies, and by the hand of them that seek their life; and their carcasses will I give to be food for the fowls of the heaven, and for the beasts of the earth; 8. and I will make this city an

19 : 3   *I will bring evil upon this place, which whosoever heareth, his ears shall tingle.*   The phrase is used frequently in Scripture. Thus when God reveals to the child Samuel the evil that will come to the wicked house of Eli, He says that the "ears of them that hear of it shall tingle" (I Samuel 3:11). Rashi says that the word for "tingle" has the same Hebrew root as the word for a "timbrel" or "tambourine," as used in Psalm 150. Trani says it means really a "reverberation." Evidently, then, just as a timbrel keeps on sounding for quite a while after it is struck, so the people hearing of the calamity will not forget what they have heard. It will continue to reverberate in their ears.

19 : 5-6   A description of the murderous worship of Moloch, using almost the same language as in Jeremiah 7:30-34.

19 : 8   *An astonishment and a hissing.*   Besides the phrase "tingle" of the ears used in verse 3, this phrase, "astonishment and

astonishment, and a hissing; every one that passeth thereby shall be astonished and hiss because of all the plagues thereof; 9. and I will cause them to eat the flesh of their sons and the flesh of their daughters, and they shall eat every one the flesh of his friend, in the siege and in the straitness, where-with their enemies, and they that seek their life, shall straiten them. 10. Then shalt thou break the bottle in the sight of the men that go with thee, 11. and shalt say unto them: Thus saith the LORD of hosts. Even so will I break this people and this city, as one breaketh a potter's vessel, that cannot be made whole again and they shall bury in To-pheth, for want of room to bury. 12. Thus will I do unto this place, saith the LORD, and to the in-habitants thereof, even making this city as Topheth; 13. and the houses of Jerusalem, and the houses of the kings of Judah, which are defiled, shall be as the place of Topheth, even all the houses upon whose roofs they have offered unto all the host of heaven, and have poured out drink-offerings unto other gods.

14. Then came Jeremiah from Topheth, whither the LORD had sent him to prophesy; and he stood

hissing," is also frequently used. Thus, for example, I Kings 9:8, Jeremiah 18:16, 25:9, 49:17. Evidently, just as a modern person might express astonishment by whistling, the ancients hissed in astonishment.

19:9   *Eat the flesh of their sons.*   So great will be the famine during the siege that cannibalism will break out. Almost the same language is used in Deuteronomy 28:53: "And thou shalt eat . . . the flesh of thy sons . . . in the siege."

In the straitness, wherewith their enemies . . . shall straiten them.   Almost the same phrase is used in the Deuteronomy verse cited above. The word means "narrowness," "squeezing." In time of trouble we feel hemmed in, but in happiness we feel free and expansive. The same thought is used in Psalm 118:5: "Out of my straits I called upon the Lord; He answered me with great enlargement."

Jeremiah
19

in the court of the LORD's house, and said to all the people: 15. 'Thus saith the LORD of hosts, the God of Israel: Behold, I will bring upon this city and upon all her towns all the evil that I have pronounced against it; because they have made their neck stiff, that they might not hear My words.'

20

THE CHIEF priest and superintendent of the Temple, Pashhur, hears the address given by Jeremiah in the potter's field, and he angrily strikes him and puts him in the stocks. In the morning he releases Jeremiah, who curses him. The chapter ends with an emotional outburst (a "confession") in which Jeremiah expresses the wish that he had never been born.

Jeremiah
20

1. Now Pashhur the son of Immer the priest, who was chief officer in the house of the LORD, heard Jeremiah prophesying these things. 2. Then Pashhur smote Jeremiah the prophet, and put him in the stocks that were in the upper gate of Benjamin, which was in the house of the LORD. 3. And it came to pass on the morrow, that Pashhur brought forth Jeremiah out of the stocks. Then said Jeremiah unto him: 'The LORD hath not called thy name Pashur, but ᵃMagormissabib. 4. For thus

20 : 2 *Put him in the stocks.* Some of the commentators believe that Pashhur put him in a prison; but Kimchi says, in the name of his father, that the word used here means two pieces of wood with a place for the prisoner's neck. If Joseph Kimchi is right, then the correct translation here should be "pillory," not "stocks." The stocks held a culprit's feet; the pillory held his head.

ᵃ That is, *Terror on every side.*

saith the LORD; Behold, I will make thee a terror to thyself, and to all thy friends; and they shall fall by the sword of their enemies, and thine eyes shall behold it, and I will give all Judah into the hand of the king of Babylon, and he shall carry them captive to Babylon, and shall slay them with the sword. 5. Moreover I will give all the store of this city, and all the gains thereof, and all the wealth thereof, yea, all the treasures of the kings of Judah will I give into the hand of their enemies, who shall spoil them, and take them, and carry them to Babylon. 6. And thou, Pashhur, and all that dwell in thy house shall go into captivity; and thou shalt come to Babylon, and there thou shalt die, and there shalt thou be buried, thou, and all thy friends, to whom thou hast prophesied falsely.'

7. O LORD, Thou hast enticed me, and I was enticed,
   Thou hast overcome me, and hast prevailed;
   I am become a laughing-stock all the day,
   Every one mocketh me.
8. For as often as I speak, I cry out,
   I cry: 'Violence and spoil';
   Because the word of the LORD is made
   A reproach unto me, and a derision, all the day.

20 : 6 *And thou, Pashhur . . . shalt come to Babylon.* Jeremiah predicts that Pashhur, for trying to prevent him from prophesying, will be completely despoiled when the invaders come and will be carried away to Babylon. The same type of imprecation was made by Amos when the priest Amaziah told him to stop preaching.

To whom thou hast prophesied falsely. Evidently this means that Pashhur, speaking to his friends, contradicted the dire prophecy of Jeremiah and said, as all the false prophets said, that there would be peace.

20 : 7-18 A "confession" of Jeremiah in two parts. The first part, 7-13, says that God had "enticed" Jeremiah to prophesy. He could not resist the persuasion of God; even though everyone laughs at him, he continues to prophesy. May God punish those who mock him.

9. And if I say: 'I will not make mention of Him,
   Nor speak any more in His name,'
   Then there is in my heart as it were a burning fire
   Shut up in my bones,
   And I weary myself to hold it in,
   But cannot.

10. For I have heard the whispering of many,
    Terror on every side:
    'Denounce, and we will denounce him';
    Even of all my familiar friends,
    Them that watch for my halting:
    'Peradventure he will be enticed, and we shall pre-
       vail against him,
    And we shall take our revenge on him.'

11. But the LORD is with me as a mighty warrior;
    Therefore my persecutors shall stumble, and they
       shall not prevail;
    They shall be greatly ashamed, because they have
       not prospered,
    Even with an everlasting confusion which shall
       never be forgotten.

12. But, O LORD of hosts, that triest the righteous,
    That seest the reins and the heart,
    Let me see Thy vengeance on them:
    For unto Thee have I revealed my cause.

13. Sing unto the LORD,
    Praise ye the LORD;

20 : 10 *Even of all my familiar friends.* Even those I thought of as my friends have proved to be false. Perhaps Jeremiah here refers to his fellow-townsmen, the men of Anathoth, who plotted against him.

The second half of the "confession" closely resembles the plaint in 15:10, expressing sorrow that his mother ever brought him into this world. Here this regret is much more fully expressed and closely resembles, even in its wording, the similar complaint in Job 3. Like Job, Jeremiah wishes the impossible wish that the day on which he was born had never come into existence. If he had not been born, he would not have to endure, as he does, "labor and sorrow" and "days . . . consumed in shame" (verse 18).

For He hath delivered the soul of the needy
From the hand of evil-doers.

Jeremiah
20

14. Cursed be the day
Wherein I was born;
The day wherein my mother bore me,
Let it not be blessed.

15. Cursed be the man who brought tidings
To my father, saying:
'A man-child is born unto thee';
Making him very glad.

16. And let that man be as the cities
Which the LORD overthrew, and repented not;
And let him hear a cry in the morning,
And an alarm at noontide;

17. Because He slew me not from the womb;
And so my mother would have been my grave,
And her womb always great.

18. Wherefore came I forth out of the womb
To see labour and sorrow,
That my days should be consumed in shame?

21

A NARRATIVE, and words of solemn prophecy at the time of the siege of Jerusalem by the Babylonian army. The king asks Jeremiah to pray for the city. Jeremiah answers that there is no hope now. The city will be captured. Only those who surrender to the Babylonians will survive.

Luzzato believes that this chapter properly belongs between chapters 37 and 38, which record the events of Zedekiah's reign and the last days of Jerusalem. Whoever placed the chapter here found it appropriate to do so because of its similarity to chapter 22, which speaks of justice and righteousness as the function of the king. The same thought is expressed here in verses 12 ff.

1. The word which came unto Jeremiah from the LORD, when king Zedekiah sent unto him Pashhur the son of Malchiah, and Zephaniah the son of Masseiah the priest, saying: 2. 'Inquire, I pray thee, of the LORD for us; for Nebuchadrezzar king of Babylon maketh war against us; peradventure the LORD will deal with us according to all His wondrous works, that he may go up from us.'

Jeremiah

21

3. Then said Jeremiah unto them: Thus shall ye say

21 : 2   *Inquire . . . of the Lord for us.*   The word for "inquire" also means "seek" or "plead." Therefore the Targum translates: "pray to the Lord for us."

Jeremiah
21

to Zedekiah: 4. Thus saith the LORD, the God of Israel:

Behold, I will turn back the weapons of war that are in your hands, wherewith ye fight against the king of Babylon, and against the Chaldeans, that besiege you without the walls, and I will gather them into the midst of this city. 5. And I myself will fight against you with an outstretched hand and with a strong arm, even in anger, and in fury, and in great wrath. 6. And I will smite the inhabitants of this city, both man and beast; they shall die of a great pestilence. 7. And afterward, saith the LORD, I will deliver Zedekiah king of Judah, and his servants, and the people, and such as are left in this city from the pestilence, from the sword, and from the famine, into the hand of Nebuchadrezzar king of Babylon, and into the hand of their enemies, and into the hand of those that seek their life; and he shall smite them with the edge of the sword; he shall not spare them, neither have pity, nor have compassion.

8. And unto this people thou shalt say: Thus saith the LORD: Behold, I set before you the way of life and the way of death. 9. He that abideth in this city shall die by the sword, and by the famine, and by

21 : 4 *I will turn back the weapons of war . . . in your hands.* Trani explains: The arrows you shoot against the Babylonians will turn back and fall into the city. In other words, all your weapons are worthless against the Babylonians.

21 : 3-7 Addressed to the royal court. Jeremiah predicts that the city will be captured and the court taken captive.

21 : 8-10 Here Jeremiah turns from the court and addresses the people, urging them to surrender to the Babylonians and thus save their lives.

21 : 10-14 He turns again to address the court, saying: All this

the pestilence; but he that goeth out, and falleth away to the Chaldeans that besiege you, he shall live, and his life shall be unto him for a prey. 10. For I have set My face against this city for evil, and not for good, saith the LORD; it shall be given into the hand of the king of Babylon, and he shall burn it with fire.

11. And unto the house of the king of Judah: Hear ye the word of the LORD; 12. O house of David, thus saith the LORD:

Execute justice in the morning,

And deliver the spoiled out of the hand of the oppressor,

Lest My fury go forth like fire,

And burn that none can quench it,

Because of the evil of your doings.

13. Behold, I am against thee, O inhabitant of the valley,

And rock of the plain, saith the LORD;

Ye that say: 'Who shall come down against us?

Or who shall enter into our habitations?'

14. And I will punish you according to the fruit of your doings,

Saith the LORD.

And I will kindle a fire in her forest

And it shall devour all that is round about her.

misfortune will come to you because you have perverted justice.

21 : 12 *Justice in the morning.* Kimchi: In the early morning, before you turn to your own affairs, go to the courts and deal out judgment to the people. Thus Moses did: "Moses sat to judge the people from the morning" (Exodus 18:13).

21 : 13 *O inhabitant of the valley.* This refers to Jerusalem. Although Jerusalem was on a hill, the hill was surrounded by a valley (Rashi and Kimchi).

22

IN THIS CHAPTER Jeremiah refers to or addresses four successive kings of Judah. The first is Josiah, the second is Jehoahaz (Shallum), Josiah's fourth son (I Chronicles 3:15). Jehoahaz succeeded to the throne when Josiah was killed during his campaign against the Egyptians. After a reign of only three months, however, he was captured by the Egyptians, imprisoned in Ribla, and then was taken to Egypt, where he died. He was succeeded by his brother Jehoiakim, who laid heavy taxes on the people to pay for his grandiose building program. The chapter finally refers to Jehoiakim's son, Jehoaichin (Coniah), who was captured by the Babylonians and spent the rest of his life as a captive in Babylon.

Jeremiah calls on the kings of Judah to do justice, describing the tragic fate each will experience because of his various injustices.

Jeremiah 22

1. Thus said the LORD: Go down to the house of the king of Judah, and speak there this word, 2. and say: Hear the word of the LORD, O king of Judah, that sittest upon the throne of David, thou, and thy servants, and thy people that enter in by these gates. 3. Thus saith the LORD:

Execute ye justice and righteousness, and deliver

22:3 *The stranger, the fatherless . . . the widow.* Virtually the same phraseology as in Deuteronomy 10:18.

the spoiled out of the hand of the oppressor; and do no wrong, do no violence, to the stranger, the fatherless, nor the widow, neither shed innocent blood in this place. 4. For if ye do this thing indeed, then shall there enter in by the gates of this house kings sitting upon the throne of David, riding in chariots and on horses, he, and his servants, and his people. 5. But if ye will not hear these words, I swear by Myself, saith the LORD, that this house shall become a desolation. 6. For thus saith the LORD concerning the house of the king of Judah:

Thou art Gilead unto Me,
The head of Lebanon;
Yet surely I will make thee a wilderness,
Cities which are not inhabited.
7. And I will prepare destroyers against thee,
Every one with his weapons;
And they shall cut down thy choice cedars,
And cast them into the fire.
8. And many nations shall pass by this city, and they shall say every man to his neighbour: 'Wherefore hath the LORD done thus unto this great city?' 9. Then they shall answer: 'Because they forsook

22 : 6 *Gilead unto Me, the head of Lebanon.* The verse seems to say to Jerusalem: You are as precious as Gilead was to Me, but I will make you into a wilderness as I did to Gilead. But why compare Jerusalem to Gilead in particular? Rashi explains that the Temple was like Gilead from which came the healing balm for all the world (Jeremiah 8:22: "Is there no balm in Gilead?"). But Trani says that Gilead was a preview of what would happen to Jerusalem. It was destroyed by Tiglath-pileser, and its people were carried away captive (II Kings 15:29).

22 : 8 *Nations . . . shall say . . . 'Wherefore hath the Lord done thus . . . ?'* The thought seems to be that for many years to come the people of nation after nation will pass by the ruins of Jerusalem and ask why God made this great destruction. The same idea is found almost word for word in Deuteronomy 29:23-24.

Jeremiah 22

the covenant of the LORD their God, and worshipped other gods, and served them.'

10. Weep ye not for the dead,
Neither bemoan him;
But weep sore for him that goeth away,
For he shall return no more,
Nor see his native country.

11. For thus saith the LORD touching Shallum the son of Josiah, king of Judah, who reigned instead of Josiah his father, and who went forth out of this place: He shall not return thither any more; 12. but in the place whither they have led him captive, there shall he die, and he shall see this land no more.

13. Woe unto him that buildeth his house by unrighteousness,
And his chambers by injustice;
That useth his neighbour's service without wages,
And giveth him not his hire;

14. That saith: 'I will build me a wide house
And spacious chambers,'
And cutteth him out windows,
And it is ceiled with cedar, and painted with vermilion.

22 : 10 *Weep ye not for the dead.* Those who die in battle are more fortunate than those who survive only to suffer the miseries of captivity. "But weep sore for him that goeth away."

22 : 11 *Shallum the son of Josiah . . . shall not return.* The preceding verse, which speaks of the bitter lot of the captives in an alien land, refers, of course, to all the captives but specifically also to Shallum (Jehoahaz), who died in captivity in Egypt.

22 : 13-19 Now Jeremiah speaks of Shallum's brother, Jehoiakim, who took the throne after him. Jehoiakim built large palaces, exacting the money from the poor. Hence Jeremiah denounces him, predicting that he will die unwept and will receive a shameful burial.

22 : 13 *Woe unto him that buildeth . . . by unrighteousness.* Rashi: This is directed at King Jehoiakim, as indicated in verse 18.

140

15. Shalt thou reign, because thou strivest to excel in
      cedar?
    Did not thy father eat and drink, and do justice and righteousness?
    Then it was well with him.

Jeremiah

22

15. Shalt thou reign, because thou strivest to excel in
      cedar?
    Did not thy father eat and drink, and do justice
      and righteousness?
    Then it was well with him.
16. He judged the cause of the poor and needy;
    Then it was well.
    Is not this to know Me? saith the LORD.
17. But thine eyes and thy heart
    Are not but for thy covetousness,
    And for shedding innocent blood,
    And for oppression, and for violence, to do it.
18. Therefore thus saith the LORD concerning Jehoi-
      akim the son of Josiah, the king of Judah:
    They shall not lament for him:
    'Ah my brother!' or 'Ah sister!'
    They shall not lament for him:
    'Ah lord!' or: 'Ah his glory!'
19. He shall be buried with the burial of an ass,
    Drawn and cast forth beyond the gates of Jeru-
      salem.

22:15 *Shalt thou reign ... excel in cedar?* Your father, Josiah, was granted a long reign because "he judged the cause of the needy" (verse 16). Do you imagine that you too will merit a long reign because of your pretentious building program?

22:18 *They shall not lament ... 'Ah my brother!' ... 'Ah sister!' ... 'Ah lord!'* He shall die "unwept, unhonored, and unsung." Kimchi explains: Neither his relatives will weep for him ("Ah brother!") nor will his subjects weep for him ("Ah lord!").

There is some difficulty in the phrase "Ah sister!" Kimchi explains "Ah sister!" as mourning for the queen, who would die in the same catastrophe. Abarbanel gives another explanation. The words "brother" and "sister" do not apply here to the dead king but to the mourners themselves. A man would weep and say: Ah, I was like a brother to him, and a woman would weep and say: I was like a sister to him.

22:19 *The burial of an ass.* A dead donkey was simply dragged away and dumped outside the city. The phrase used here, "burial of an ass" (*kevurat chamor*), has become a current phrase for the nonreverent burial of apostates.

141

Jeremiah

22

20. Go up to Lebanon, and cry,
    And lift up thy voice in Bashan;
    And cry from Abarim,
    For all thy lovers are destroyed.

21. I spoke unto thee in thy prosperity,
    But thou saidst: 'I will not hear.'
    This hath been thy manner from thy youth,
    That thou hearkenedst not to My voice.

22. The wind shall feed upon all thy shepherds,
    And thy lovers shall go into captivity;
    Surely then shalt thou be ashamed and confounded
    For all thy wickedness.

23. O inhabitant of Lebanon,
    That art nestled in the cedars,
    How gracious shalt thou be when pangs come
      upon thee,
    The pain as of a woman in travail!

24. As I live, saith the LORD, though Coniah the son
    of Jehoiakim king of Judah were the signet upon

22 : 20-23 The prophet now turns to the nation and tells it to weep. Punishments are surely coming because of its lack of faith in God and its trust only in foreign alliances. This searching after allies is frequently described (as here) as Israel, a harlot, wandering around looking for lovers.

22 : 24-30 This is the prophet's reference to the fourth of the kings mentioned in this chapter, namely, the son of Jehoiakim, Coniah, or Jehoiachin, who was captured by the Babylonians and taken to a lifelong captivity in Babylon (verse 27): "But to the land whereunto they long to return, thither shall they not return."

My right hand, yet would I pluck thee thence; 25. and I will give thee into the hand of them that seek thy life, and into the hand of them of whom thou art afraid, even into the hand of Nebuchadrezzar king of Babylon, and into the hand of the Chaldeans. 26. And I will cast thee out, and thy mother that bore thee, into another country, where ye were not born; and there shall ye die. 27. But to the land whereunto they long to return, thither shall they not return.

28. Is this man Coniah a despised, broken image?
Is he a vessel wherein is no pleasure?
Wherefore are they cast out, he and his seed,
And are cast into the land which they know not?

29. O land, land, land,
Hear the word of the LORD.

30. Thus saith the LORD:
Write ye this man childless,
A man that shall not prosper in his days;
For no man of his seed shall prosper,
Sitting upon the throne of David,
And ruling any more in Judah.

22 : 28-30   The chapter ends with a dirge for Jehoiachin (Coniah).

22 : 28   *Is this man Coniah.*   He compares the captive king to a broken vessel that is thrown away.

22 : 30   *No man of his seed . . . upon the throne of David.*   No descendant of Jehoiachin would live to become a king of Judah. Jehoiachin's successor, the last king of Judah, was his uncle, Zedekiah.

23

THE FIRST PART of the chapter, verses 1-8, is addressed to the king, and ends with the promise that someday God will appoint a righteous king in whose days Judah and Israel will be restored. The rest of the chapter is a denunciation of the false prophets, who keep on reassuring the people that in spite of their sins no harm will ever come to them.

Jeremiah

23

1. Woe unto the shepherds that destroy and scatter The sheep of My pasture! saith the LORD.
2. Therefore thus saith the LORD, the God of Israel, against the shepherds that feed My people: Ye have scattered My flock, and driven them away, and have not taken care of them; behold, I will visit upon you the evil of your doings, saith the LORD.
3. And I will gather the remnant of My flock out

23 : 1 *Woe unto the shepherds.* The kings of Judah, who have neglected the people and thus failed in their duties: "Ye have scattered My flock" (verse 2).

23 : 3 *I will gather the remnant of My flock.* Luzzato says this refers to the return from the Babylonian Exile. But Kimchi believes it can hardly be a reference to the return from Babylon because of verse 4, which states that after the return "they shall fear no more, nor be dismayed." The return from Babylon did not usher in such a secure and happy time as here indicated. Kim-

of all the countries whither I have driven them, and
will bring them back to their folds; and they shall
be fruitful and multiply. 4. And I will set up shepherds over them, who shall feed them; and they
shall fear no more, nor be dismayed, neither shall
any be lacking, saith the LORD.

5. Behold, the days come, saith the LORD,
That I will raise unto David a righteous shoot,
And he shall reign as king and prosper,
And shall execute justice and righteousness in the land.

6. In his days Judah shall be saved,
And Israel shall dwell safely;
And this is his name whereby he shall be called,
The LORD is our righteousness.

7. Therefore, behold, the days come, saith the LORD,
that they shall no more say: 'As the LORD
liveth, that brought up the children of Israel out
of the land of Egypt'; 8. but: 'As the LORD liveth,
that brought up and that led the seed of the house
of Israel out of the north country, and from all the

chi therefore says that the return mentioned here means the final gathering of the exiles in messianic days.

Whither I have driven them. First Scripture says that the neglectful shepherds have scattered the flock; now God says it is He Who has scattered them. Luzzato says this means: The evil shepherds have so corrupted them that I had to send the people into exile.

23 : 5 *Unto David a righteous shoot.* The royal family of David is often visualized in Scripture as a living tree, and the righteous king of the future is described as a new shoot, or a new sprout, from the tree. So here the new sprout is described with the Hebrew word *zemach.* Zechariah uses the same word in 6:12. Isaiah in 11:1 uses the word *choter*, "there shall come forth a shoot from the stock of Jesse." But whatever the word used in Scripture, it always means that the Messiah will be the symbol of a new spurt of life coming from the old Davidic tree.

23 : 7-8 *Behold, the days come.* The same verses are found in 16:14-15.

countries whither I had driven them'; and they shall dwell in their own land.

Jeremiah
23

9. Concerning the prophets.
My heart within me is broken,
All my bones shake;
I am like a drunken man,
And like a man whom wine hath overcome;
Because of the LORD,
And because of His holy words.

10. For the land is full of adulterers;
For because of swearing the land mourneth,
The pastures of the wilderness are dried up;
And their course is evil,
And their force is not right.

11. For both prophet and priest are ungodly;
Yea, in My house have I found their wickedness,
Saith the LORD.

12. Wherefore their way shall be unto them as slippery places in the darkness,
They shall be thrust, and fall therein;
For I will bring evil upon them,
Even the year of their visitation,
Saith the LORD.

13. And I have seen unseemliness in the prophets of Samaria:
They prophesied by Baal,
And caused My people Israel to err.

23 : 9 *Concerning the prophets. My heart . . . is broken.* The Hebrew reads "to the prophets," and therefore the sequence is a little difficult. Rashi, Kimchi, and Trani follow the Targum and connect the phrases as follows: It is because of the words of the false prophets that my heart is broken.

23 : 10 *Their force is not right.* They gather their strength for evil purposes.

23 : 13-14 *Prophets of Samaria . . . prophets of Jerusalem.* The sin of the false prophets of the northern kingdom (Samaria) was that they prophesied in the name of Baal. The sin of the false prophets of Jerusalem is a moral sin: "adultery . . . lies . . . strengthen . . . evil-doers."

They . . . as Sodom . . . the inhabitants . . . as Gomorrah.

146

14. But in the prophets of Jerusalem I have seen a
     horrible thing:
    They commit adultery, and walk in lies,
    And they strengthen the hands of evil-doers,
    That none doth return from his wickedness;
    They are all of them become unto Me as Sodom,
    And the inhabitants thereof as Gomorrah.
15. Therefore thus saith the LORD of hosts concerning
     the prophets:
    Behold, I will feed them with wormwood,
    And make them drink the water of gall;
    For from the prophets of Jerusalem
    Is ungodliness gone forth into all the land.
16. Thus saith the LORD of hosts:
    Hearken not unto the words of the prophets that
     prophesy unto you,
    They lead you unto vanity;
    They speak a vision of their own heart,
    And not out of the mouth of the LORD.
17. They say continually unto them that despise Me:
    'The LORD hath said: Ye shall have peace';
    And unto every one that walketh in the stubborn-
     ness of his own heart they say:
    'No evil shall come upon you';
18. For who hath stood in the council of the LORD,
    That he should perceive and hear His word?
    Who hath attended to His word, and heard it?
19. Behold, a storm of the LORD is gone forth in fury,
    Yea, a whirling storm;
    It shall whirl upon the head of the wicked.
20. The anger of the LORD shall not return,

Kimchi says this means that "they," the prophets, are like the
wicked city of Sodom, and "the inhabitants," the people of Jerusalem, are like the wicked city of Gomorrah.

23 : 18   *Who hath stood in the council of the Lord . . . ?*   Rashi
and Kimchi both follow the Targum and take this verse to refer
in derogation to the false prophets, saying of them: Has any one
of these pretenders stood in the council of the Lord? Have they,
then, any right to speak in His name?

23 : 20   *The anger of the Lord shall not return, until He have*

Until He have executed, and till He have performed
the purposes of His heart;
In the end of days ye shall consider it perfectly.

21. I have not sent these prophets, yet they ran;
I have not spoken to them, yet they prophesied.

22. But if they have stood in My council,
Then let them cause My people to hear My words,
And turn them from their evil way,
And from the evil of their doings.

23. Am I a God near at hand, saith the LORD,
And not a God afar off?

24. Can any hide himself in secret places
That I shall not see him? saith the LORD.
Do not I fill heaven and earth?
Saith the LORD.

25. I have heard what the prophets have said,
That prophesy lies in My name, saying;
'I have dreamed, I have dreamed.'

26. How long shall this be?

---

executed. The thought seems to be that the "anger" of the
Lord, or the "word" of the Lord, is a sort of an emissary or agent
who will not return to God, who sent him, before he has fulfilled his mission. The same idea is expressed in Isaiah 55:11: "So
shall My word be that goeth forth out of My mouth: It shall
not return unto Me void, except it accomplish that which I
please."

23 : 22 *If they have stood in My council.* This is connected
with the question in verse 18: "Who hath stood in the council of
the Lord?" God says: If these self-appointed prophets think they
represent Me, let them prove it by turning the people back from
their evil ways.

23 : 23 *Am I a God near at hand . . . ?* Both Kimchi and
Abarbanel take the words "near" and "far" in the sense of time
rather than space. It means: I am eternal, not recently created as
the idols are. The idols are described in Deuteronomy 32:17 as
"new gods that came up of late."

23 : 24 *Can any hide himself . . . ?* As God is Eternal, so He is
Omnipresent. No one can hide from Him.

23 : 26-27 *How long . . . Is it in the heart of the prophets . . .*

148

Is it in the heart of the prophets that prophesy lies,
And the prophets of the deceit of their own heart?
27. That think to cause My people to forget My name
By their dreams which they tell every man to his
neighbour,
As their fathers forgot My name for Baal.
28. The prophet that hath a dream, let him tell a dream;
And he that hath My word, let him speak My word
faithfully.
What hath the straw to do with the wheat?
Saith the Lord.
29. Is not My word like as fire?
Saith the Lord.
And like a hammer that breaketh the rock in
pieces?

That think to cause My people to forget My name. How long
will these false prophets think in their hearts that they can succeed in causing My people to forget Me? (So Luzzato and Tur-
Sinai.)

23 : 28-29 *That hath a dream . . . that hath My word . . . My
word . . . as fire?* Scripture here seems to distinguish between
dreams and the inspired Divine word. This distinction is not acceptable to the classic commentators, for they believe that true
inspiration from God can also come in a dream. In fact, Scripture says that all the prophets, except Moses, received God's
word in dreams. So Numbers 12:6-8: "Hear now My words: If
there be a prophet among you, I the Lord . . . do speak with him
in a dream. My servant Moses is not so; . . . with him do I speak
mouth to mouth." So Kimchi takes the verse as follows: Do not
confuse a mere dream with a prophetic word which may come in
a dream. He connects this explanation with the following verse,
"Is not My word like as fire?" In other words, the true prophetic
word may come in a dream, but it is recognizable by its nature.
It is a burning flame and not smooth words: "peace, peace."
Rashi's explanation is basically the same, namely, that one cannot
confuse an ordinary dream with a prophetic dream. The prophetic dream comes like a fire. So Jeremiah said (20:9): "In my
heart . . . a burning fire." Luzzato follows both these explanations.

30. Therefore, behold, I am against the prophets, saith the LORD, that steal My words every one from his neighbour. 31. Behold, I am against the prophets, saith the LORD, that use their tongues and say: 'He saith.' 32. Behold, I am against them that prophesy lying dreams, saith the LORD, and do tell them, and cause My people to err by their lies, and by their wantonness; yet I sent them not, nor commanded them; neither can they profit this people at all, saith the LORD.

33. And when this people, or the prophet, or a priest, shall ask thee, saying: 'What is the burden of the LORD?' then shalt thou say unto them: 'What burden! I will cast you off, saith the LORD.' 34. And as for the prophet, and the priest, and the people, that shall say: 'The burden of the LORD,' I will even punish that man and his house. 35. Thus shall ye say every one to his neighbour, and every

23 : 30   *The prophets . . . that steal My words . . . every one from his neighbor.*   Rashi and Kimchi (and especially Rashi to verse 36) give this explanation of "stealing God's words": The false prophets would send people to listen to and copy the style of the true prophet, and then they would pervert the prophet's word and use it for their false message. Thus, for example, Jeremiah in 49:35 said: "Behold I will break the bow of Elam," and the false prophet Hananiah ben Azzur borrowed the words and used them to give a reassuring but unreal picture of the destruction of Babylon. He said: "I have broken the yoke of Babylon" (Jeremiah 28:2). This explanation of "stealing God's words" is based on the Talmud (Sanhedrin 89a).

23 : 33   *What is the burden of the Lord?*   The word "burden" (*massa*) is frequently used for a specific prophetic message, most often a message of denunciation against nations. For example, Isaiah 13:1: "Burden of Babylon"; Isaiah 15:1: "Burden of Moab"; Nahum 1:1: "Burden of Nineveh."

one to his brother: 'What hath the LORD answered?'
and: 'What hath the LORD spoken?' 36. And
the burden of the LORD shall ye mention no
more; for every man's own word shall be his
burden; and would ye pervert the words of the
living God, of the LORD of hosts our God? 37. Thus
shalt thou say to the prophet: 'What hath the LORD
answered thee?' and: 'What hath the LORD spoken?'
38. But if ye say: 'The burden of the LORD'; therefore thus saith the LORD: Because ye say this word:
'The burden of the LORD,' and I have sent unto you,
saying: 'Ye shall not say: The burden of the LORD';
39. therefore, behold, I will utterly tear you out,
and I will cast you off, and the city that I gave unto
you and to your fathers, away from My presence;
40. and I will bring an everlasting reproach upon
you, and a perpetual shame, which shall not be
forgotten.

What burden; I will cast you off.   This reading and the
translation are clear enough. However, Rashi translates the
phrase: "Ye are a burden to God." Many modern commentators
give the same meaning to the text ("Ye are a burden"), but they
arrive at it by following the Greek translation, which is apparently based on a regrouping of the letters in this phrase (*atem
hamassa*). They translate it to mean: "Ye (the people) are the
burden." See also Luzzato.

23 : 34-35   The prophet then warns the people not to use the word
"burden" any more; instead, when they consult him, they should
simply say, "What has God answered?" The next verses tell why
the word "burden" should no longer be used.

23 : 36   *Every man's own word shall be his burden.*   Luzzato
says that the word refers to the true prophet, for whom the
solemn task of prophecy is always a heavy burden. He translates
the verse: To him to whom God gives the word (to speak), it
becomes a heavy burden (for he will be hated for saying it).

24

A SERMON given after Nebuchadnezzar had taken King Jehoaichin (Coniah) and the leaders of the people into captivity. Evidently those who remained under Zedekiah, the last king of Judah, must have thought that they had not been taken into captivity because they were more righteous than those who were. Jeremiah therefore tells them that they have misunderstood God's purpose. Those who are now captives will someday be restored, and those remaining in the land will suffer a dire fate.

Jeremiah

24

1. The LORD showed me, and behold two baskets of figs set before the temple of the LORD; after that Nebuchadrezzar king of Babylon had carried away captive Jeconiah the son of Jehoakim, king of Judah, and the princes of Judah, with the craftsmen and smiths, from Jerusalem, and had brought them to Babylon. 2. One basket had very good figs,

24 : 1, 2 *Two baskets of figs.* The good figs represent the captives, who will someday be restored. The bad figs represent the population remaining and their king, Zedekiah. These will be cast away just as worthless figs are discarded.

The craftsmen and smiths. This phrase is used in II Kings 24:14, where the captivity is described, and again in Jeremiah 29:2. Since the passage in Kings seems to include the "craftsmen

152

like the figs that are first-ripe; and the other basket had very bad figs, which could not be eaten, they were so bad. 3. Then said the LORD unto me: 'What seest thou, Jeremiah?' And I said: 'Figs; the good figs, very good; and the bad, very bad, that cannot be eaten, they are so bad.' 4. And the word of the LORD came unto me, saying: 5. 'Thus saith the LORD, the God of Israel: Like these good figs, so will I regard the captives of Judah, whom I have sent out of this place into the land of the Chaldeans, for good. 6. And I will set Mine eyes upon them for good, and I will bring them back to this land; and I will build them, and not pull them down; and I will plant them, and not pluck them up. 7. And I will give them a heart to know Me, that I am the LORD; and they shall be My people, and I will be their God; for they shall return unto Me with their whole heart. 8. And as the bad figs, which cannot be eaten, they are so bad; surely thus saith the LORD: So will I make Zedekiah the king of Judah, and his princes, and the residue of Jerusalem, that remain in this land, and them that dwell in the land of Egypt; 9. I will even make them a horror among all the kingdoms of the earth for evil; a reproach and a proverb, a taunt and a curse, in all places whither I shall drive them. 10. And I will send the sword, the famine, and the pestilence, among them, till they be consumed from off the land that I gave unto them and to their fathers.'

Jeremiah
24

and smiths" among the "mighty men of valor," many of the traditional commentators take "craftsmen and smiths" as referring to eminent citizens rather than artisans. Thus the Talmud (Gittin 88a) says that the craftsmen and smiths were really scholars of outstanding ability. Both Rashi and Kimchi follow this interpretation. Others say that the phrase refers to certain especially skilled soldiers. However, the text as it stands gives an adequate meaning, namely, that Nebuchadnezzar took away all the skilled handworkers since they were especially valuable as slaves.

25

THIS CHAPTER is dated "in the fourth year of king Jehoiakim" (verse 1). In 36:1 we are told that it was in the fourth year of king Jehoiakim that Jeremiah dictated to Baruch "all the words" of his sermons. On the basis of this dating, and also on the basis of the contents of this chapter (25), most modern scholars conclude that it is meant to be the summary chapter of the book which Jeremiah had dictated. Although some of the verses may have been written by an exilic author (according to Duhm), nevertheless the main part of the chapter may well be considered the closing portion of the book as it was dictated by the prophet himself.

The chapter is divided into two parts; 1-14 speaks of the coming rescue of the captives in Babylon and the destruction of Babylon itself; 15-38 is a doom-sermon against various nations.

Jeremiah

. 25

1. The word that came to Jeremiah concerning all the people of Judah in the fourth year of Jehoiakim the son of Josiah, king of Judah, that was the first year of Nebuchadrezzar king of Babylon; 2. which Jeremiah the prophet spoke unto all the people of Judah, and to all the inhabitants of Jerusalem, saying:

3. From the thirteenth year of Josiah the son of Amon, king of Judah, even unto this day, these three and twenty years, the word of the LORD hath come unto me, and I have spoken unto you, speak-

ing betimes and often; but ye have not hearkened. 4. And the LORD hath sent unto you all His servants the prophets, sending them betimes and often —but ye have not hearkened, nor inclined your ear to hear—5. saying: 'Return ye now every one from his evil way, and from the evil of your doings, and dwell in the land that the LORD hath given unto you and to your fathers, for ever and ever; 6. and go not after other gods to serve them, and to worship them, and provoke Me not with the work of your hands; and I will do you no hurt.' 7. Yet ye have not hearkened unto Me, saith the LORD; that ye might provoke Me with the work of your hands to your own hurt. 8. Therefore thus saith the LORD of hosts: Because ye have not heard My words, 9. behold, I will send and take all the families of the north, saith the LORD, and I will send unto Nebuchadrezzar the king of Babylon, My servant, and will bring them against this land, and against the inhabitants thereof, and against all these nations round about and I will utterly destroy them, and make them an astonishment, and a hissing, and perpetual desolations. 10. Moreover

25 : 4 *All His servants the prophets.*   This verse is also found in 7:25, and many scholars consider that chapter 7 is where it properly belongs. Jeremiah speaks here of his personal career and not of the prophets in general. However, Luzzato interprets the verse to give it relevance here. Jeremiah is saying: No wonder you do not listen to me. You never listened to any of the prophets who preceded me.

25 : 9 *All the families of the north.*   Virtually the identical phrase is found in 1:15. The army of Nebuchadnezzar was a conglomerate of the armies of many nations.

   This land . . . and . . . all these nations round about.   The various neighboring nations would from time to time join in resistance against Babylon (as previously against Assyria) and therefore the armies of Babylon would destroy them when they came to destroy Jerusalem.

25 : 10 *The voice of mirth . . . bridegroom . . . bride . . . mill-*

I will cause to cease from among them the voice of mirth and the voice of gladness, the voice of the bridegroom and the voice of the bride, the sound of the millstones, and the light of the lamp. 11. And this whole land shall be a desolation, and a waste; and these nations shall serve the king of Babylon seventy years. 12. And it shall come to pass, when seventy years are accomplished, that I will punish the king of Babylon, and that nation, saith the LORD, for their iniquity, and the land of the Chaldeans; and I will make it perpetual desolations. 13. And I will bring upon that land all My words which I have pronounced against it, even all that is written in this book, which Jeremiah hath

stones, and . . . lamp. This is a favorite phrase of Jeremiah. He uses it in three other places, 7:34, 16:9, 33:11. But here he adds "the sound of the millstones, and the light of the lamp." Rashi, Kimchi, and Trani consider these two additions to the phrase as closely relevant, since when one is preparing for a feast, the grindstone is heard going continually, and the lights are all lit up for the banquet itself. This explanation is based on the Talmud (Sanhedrin 32b).

25 : 11-12 *Seventy years.* Kimchi calculates the length of the reigns of Nebuchadnezzar and his successors in order to prove that the Babylonian dynasty lasted for seventy more years after the prophecy and then the Jews were released by Cyrus the Persian, conqueror of Babylon. Duhm, however, says that it is impossible to arrive chronologically at the number seventy, and therefore the writer of this passage was influenced by Zechariah 1:12. "O Lord of hosts, how long wilt Thou not have compassion on Jerusalem . . . these three score and ten years," and therefore the author of these verses was post-exilic. Tur-Sinai likewise says (without attempting an exact chronology) that this is a prophecy made after the event, thus also indicating that the verse is post-exilic.

25 : 13 *All My words . . . which Jeremiah hath prophesied.* Luzzato observes that it would be strange for God to say, as He is quoted as saying here, I will fulfill what Jeremiah has prophesied. Besides, says Luzzato, this verse is in the midst of

prophesied against all the nations. 14. For many
nations and great kings shall make bondmen of
them also; and I will recompense them according
to their deeds, and according to the work of their
own hands.

15. For thus saith the LORD, the God of Israel, unto
me: Take this cup of the wine of fury at My hand,
and cause all the nations, to whom I send thee, to
drink it. 16. And they shall drink, and reel to and
fro, and be like madmen, because of the sword
that I will send among them.—17. Then took I the
cup at the LORD's hand, and made all the nations
to drink, unto whom the LORD had sent me:
18. Jerusalem, and the cities of Judah, and the
kings thereof, and the princes thereof, to make

Jeremiah's denunciation of Babylon, but his denunciation of the
other nations does not come until further on in the chapter. Actually the Septuagint divides the sentence in a way which removes
this difficulty. The first half of the sentence remains where it is
here and reads: "All My words written in this book." Then the
second half of the sentence—"which Jeremiah had prophesied
against all the nations"—is moved ahead to be an introduction to
the second half of the chapter, beginning with verse 15, which
is actually a prophecy against all the nations.

25 : 15-38   Oracles against the various nations.

25 : 15   *This cup of the wine of fury.*   Kimchi is careful to say
that this description of God handing Jeremiah a cup and Jeremiah handing the cup to various nations is not an objective occur-
ence but a vision of prophecy. So too Abarbanel.

The drinking of a cup of wine is used many times in Scripture as a symbol of the fate of a nation. For example, Isaiah 51:17:
"O Jerusalem, that hast drunk at the hand of the Lord the cup
of His fury." See also verse 22 of the same chapter. Similarly,
indicating that Jerusalem will suffer the same tragic fate that
overtook Samaria, Ezekiel says: "Thou shalt drink of thy sister's
cup, Which is deep and large. . . . Thou shalt be filled with drunkenness and sorrow" (Ezekiel 23:32). The same simile is also used
for a happy fate. Psalm 116:13: "I will lift up the cup of salvation."

them an appalment, an astonishment, a hissing, and a curse; as it is this day; 19. Pharaoh king of Egypt, and his servants, and his princes, and all his people; 20. and all the mingled people; and all the kings of the land of Uz, and all the kings of the land of the Philistines, and Ashkelon, and Gaza, and Ekron, and the remnant of Ashdod; 21. Edom, and Moab, and the children of Ammon; 22. and all the kings of Tyre, and all the kings of Zidon, and the kings of the isle which is beyond the sea; 23. Dedan, and Tema, and Buz, and all that have the corners of their hair polled; 24. and all the kings of Arabia, and all the kings of the mingled people that dwell in the wilderness; 25. and all the kings of Zimri, and all the kings of Elam, and all the kings of the Medes; 26. and all the kings of the north, far and near, one with another; and all the kingdoms of the world, which are upon the face of the earth.—And the king of ªSheshach shall drink after them. 27. And thou shalt say unto them: Thus

25 : 26   *The king of Sheshach.*   The footnote in our translation says: "According to ancient tradition, a cypher for *Babel*" (i.e., Babylon).

There is another such cypher used in Jeremiah (51:1): "I will raise up against Babylon . . . them that dwell in Leb-kamai," to which there is a footnote in our translation, "A cypher for *Casdim*" (that is, Chaldea, i.e., the Babylonians).

Evidently these predictions of doom must have been written at a time when Babylon was still a dominant power and it was necessary, by some sort of a code, to conceal the name of the country, "Babel," and of the people, "Casdim."

The code used here is based upon a rearrangement of the Hebrew alphabet called *at-bash*, which means that the first letter of the alphabet, *a*, is connected with the last letter of the alphabet, *tav*. The second letter of the alphabet, *b*, is connected with the second last letter of the alphabet, *sh*. Hence, *at-bash*. In the encoding the one letter is substituted for the other. So by the system of *at-bash*, *Babel* becomes *Sheshach*, as here in this verse, and *Casdim* becomes *Leb-kamai*, as in 51:1.

ª According to ancient tradition, a cypher for *Babel*.

saith the LORD of hosts, the God of Israel: Drink ye, and be drunken, and spew, and fall, and rise no more, because of the sword which I will send among you. 28. And it shall be, if they refuse to take the cup at thy hand to drink, then shalt thou say unto them: Thus saith the LORD of hosts: Ye shall surely drink. 29. For, lo, I begin to bring evil on the city whereupon My name is called, and should ye be utterly unpunished? Ye shall not be unpunished; for I will call for a sword upon all the inhabitants of the earth, saith the LORD of hosts.

30. Therefore prophesy thou against them all these words, and say unto them:
The LORD doth roar from on high,
And utter His voice from His holy habitation;
He doth mightily roar because of His fold;
He giveth a shout, as they that tread the grapes,
Against all the inhabitants of the earth.

31. A noise is come even to the end of the earth;
For the LORD hath a controversy with the nations,
He doth plead with all flesh;
As for the wicked, He hath given them to the
    sword,
Saith the LORD.

32. Thus saith the LORD of hosts:
Behold, evil shall go forth
From nation to nation,
And a great storm shall be raised up
From the uttermost parts of the earth.

33. And the slain of the LORD shall be at that day from

25 : 30-38   A poetic description of the fate of the nations.

25 : 30   *He giveth a shout, as they that tread the grapes.*   The metaphor is of God destroying His enemies as one treads down the grapes. This metaphor is more greatly elaborated in Isaiah 63: 1-6: "I have trodden the winepress alone. . . . I tread them in Mine anger." This is the source of Julia Ward Howe's theme in the "Battle Hymn of the Republic": "He is trampling out the vintage where the grapes of wrath are stored."

25 : 34-38   The doom of the shepherds, which means, as it often does, the kings and the rulers.

one end of the earth even unto the other end of the earth; they shall not be lamented, neither gathered, nor buried; they shall be dung upon the face of the ground.

34. Wail, ye shepherds, and cry;
And wallow yourselves in the dust, ye leaders of
the flock;
For the days of your slaughter are fully come,
And I will break you in pieces,
And ye shall fall like a precious vessel.

35. And the shepherds shall have no way to flee,
Nor the leaders of the flock to escape.

36. Hark! the cry of the shepherds,
And the wailing of the leaders of the flock!
For the LORD despoileth their pasture.

37. And the peaceable folds are brought to silence
Because of the fierce anger of the LORD.

38. He hath forsaken His covert, as the lion;
For their land is become a waste
Because of the fierceness of the oppressing sword,
And because of His fierce anger.

26

THIS CHAPTER begins a new division of the book, the biographical and historical section. Chapters 1-25 are primarily a collection of the sermons of Jeremiah, although some biographical incidents are mentioned. This section, 26-29, 34-44, with the addition of 45-52, is primarily biographical and historical, with an occasional poem or sermon interspersed. In this section Jeremiah is generally referred to in the third person. The narrator may well be Jeremiah's friend and secretary, Baruch.

The chapter presents an incident in the life of Jeremiah. He preached a sermon at the Temple gate in which he said that God would destroy the Temple, as He had destroyed the sanctuary at Shiloh, if the people did not repent. The priests arrested him, charging that he had incurred the penalty of death for his assertion that God would destroy the Temple. The princes of Judah then came to the Temple to conduct the trial. Jeremiah, in self-defense, said that what he had said was exactly what God had told him to say. On that plea Jeremiah was acquitted. The chapter ends with a narrative about another man, Uriah, perhaps a prophet, who preached a sermon with the same theme as that of Jeremiah's and was put to death for it by the king.

1. In the beginning of the reign of Jehoiakim the son

Jeremiah

26

26 : 1   *In the beginning of the reign of Jehoiakim.*   The preceding chapter is dated four years later than this one. Trani takes note of this, saying it indicates that the book is not in (chronological) order.

Jeremiah
26

of Josiah king of Judah, came this word from the LORD, saying: 2. 'Thus saith the LORD: Stand in the court of the LORD's house, and speak unto all the cities of Judah, which come to worship in the LORD's house, all the word that I command thee to speak unto them; diminish not a word. 3. It may be they will hearken, and turn every man from his evil way; that I may repent Me of the evil, which I purpose to do unto them because of the evil of their doings. 4. And thou shalt say unto them: Thus saith the LORD: If ye will not hearken to Me, to walk in My law, which I have set before you, 5. to hearken to the words of My servants the prophets, whom I sent unto you, even sending them betimes and often, but ye have not hearkened 6. then will I make this house like Shiloh, and will make this city, a curse to all the nations of the earth.'

7. So the priests and the prophets and all the people heard Jeremiah speaking these words in the house of the LORD. 8. Now it came to pass, when Jeremiah had made an end to speaking all that the LORD had commanded him to speak unto all the

26 : 2 *Stand in the court of the Lord's house.*   Chapter 7:2 also begins: "Stand in the gate of the Lord's house." And indeed chapter 7 is the very sermon which Jeremiah preached at the gate of the Temple. This chapter (26) gives only a few sentences from the sermon and concentrates on the events which followed it. It would seem logical, therefore, for this chapter to have followed chapter 7, since we would then have the sermon and its consequences in sequence. Evidently, however, the arrangement of the book was planned as follows: first the collected sermons, and then the biographical and historical incidents.

26 : 7-9   The priests arrested Jeremiah for saying that the Temple would be destroyed and told him he had incurred the penalty of death. Abarbanel, however, says the priests declared that Jeremiah had incurred the death penalty, not because of what he preached, but because they were sure he was not commanded by God to say what he said. Therefore, as a false prophet, he must be put to death.

people, that the priests and the prophets and all the people laid hold on him saying: 'Thou shalt surely die. 9. Why hast thou prophesied in the name of the LORD, saying: This house shall be like Shiloh, and this city shall be desolate, without an inhabitant?' And all the people were gathered against Jeremiah in the house of the LORD.

10. When the princes of Judah heard these things, they came up from the king's house unto the house of LORD; and they sat in the entry of the new gate of the LORD's house. 11. Then spoke the priests and the prophets unto the princes and to

26:10 *Princes . . . came . . . unto the house of the Lord . . . sat in the entry of the new gate.*   The actual administration of justice was carried out by the king and the princes. Since Jeremiah had been arrested at the Temple, the princes came to the gate of the Temple to try the case.

The new gate.   The Targum translates "the eastern gate." Rashi says that the eastern gate was the main gate of the Temple. When Nebuchadnezzar conquered Jerusalem for the first time and took Jehoiachin captive, he destroyed the eastern gate. Zedekiah, the last king of Judah, rebuilt it; so the eastern gate came to be known also as "the new gate." If Rashi's explanation is correct, then to use the words "new gate" here in a narrative set in the reign of Jehoiakim is an anachronism. Evidently the writer (perhaps it was Baruch) wrote this chapter in the time of Zedekiah and used the name of the gate current at the time.

26:11-15 The priests demand Jeremiah's death. Jeremiah defends himself by saying that what he had said about the Temple and its destruction was just what God had told him to say. Therefore, if they put him to death, they will be killing an innocent man. The princes and the people support Jeremiah's argument, reminding the priests that in the time of King Hezekiah (about a hundred years earlier), the Prophet Micah preached a similar sermon and said that the Temple would be destroyed. Yet Hezekiah did not put him to death but entreated God's mercy. So the princes decided to accept the argument (verse 16): "This man is not worthy of death; for he hath spoken to us in the name of the Lord our God." The quotation from Micah is from Micah 3:12 and is precisely as it is found in our present text.

Jeremiah
26

all the people, saying: 'This man is worthy of death; for he hath prophesied against this city, as ye have heard with your ears.' 12. Then spoke Jeremiah unto all the princes and to all the people, saying: 'The LORD sent me to prophesy against this house and against this city all the words that ye have heard. 13. Therefore now amend your ways and your doings, and hearken to the voice of the LORD your God; and the LORD will repent Him of the evil that He hath pronounced against you. 14. But as for me, behold, I am in your hand; do with me as is good and right in your eyes. 15. Only know ye for certain that, if ye put me to death, ye will bring innocent blood upon yourselves, and upon this city, and upon the inhabitants thereof; for of a truth the LORD had sent me unto you to speak all these words in your ears.'

16. Then said the princes and all the people unto the priests and to the prophets: 'This man is not worthy of death; for he hath spoken to us in the name of the LORD our God.' 17. Then rose up certain of the elders of the land, and spoke to all the assembly of the people, saying: 18. 'Micah the Morashtite prophesied in the days of Hezekiah king of Judah; and he spoke to all the people of Judah, saying: Thus saith the LORD of hosts:

Zion shall be plowed as a field,

And Jerusalem shall become heaps,

And the mountain of the house as the high places of a forest.

19. Did Hezekiah king of Judah and all Judah put him at all to death? did he not fear the LORD, and entreat the favour of the LORD, and the LORD repented Him of the evil which He had pronounced against them? Thus might we procure great evil against our own souls.'

20. And there was also a man that prophesied in

26 : 20-23   An additional incident. A man named Uriah, the son of Shemaiah, prophesied, repeating almost the exact words of

164

the name of the LORD Uriah the son of Shemaiah of Kiriathjearim; and he prophesied against this city and against this land according to all the words of Jeremiah; 21. and when Jehoiakim the king, with all his mighty men, and all the princes, heard his words, the king sought to put him to death; but when Uriah heard it, he was afraid, and fled, and went into Egypt; 22. and Jehoiakim the king sent men into Egypt, Elnathan the son of Achbor, and certain men with him, into Egypt; 23. and they fetched forth Uriah out of Egypt, and brought him unto Jehoiakim the king; who slew him with the sword, and cast his dead body into the graves of the children of the people. 24. Nevertheless the hand of Ahikam the son of Shaphan was with Jeremiah, that they should not give him into the hand of the people to put him to death.

Jeremiah. King Jehoiakim sentenced him to death. He fled to Egypt. Jehoiakim had him brought back and put to death. The chapter ends with the following:

26 : 24 *Nevertheless the hand of Ahikam . . . was with Jeremiah, that they should not give him into the hand of the people to put him to death.* There is a difficulty involved in this sentence. Why was it necessary for Ahikam to defend Jeremiah against the people when we note from verse 16 that it was the people and the princes who had defended Jeremiah against the priests? Luzzato says that the incident with Uriah, who was put to death, occurred sometime after the trial of Jeremiah. In the meantime the priests had persuaded the people to turn against Jeremiah.

It is to be noted that the sentence begins with the word "nevertheless," which clearly connects Ahikam's protection of Jeremiah with the story of the execution of Uriah. Rashi, quoting Sifre (Behaalotecha #88), says that after Uriah was killed, the wicked men among the people pointed out that Jeremiah and Uriah had both made the same prophecy, and therefore Jeremiah should be killed just as Uriah had been killed (cf. Yalkut Shimoni, II, #57). This would explain why Ahikam now found it necessary to defend Jeremiah against the people even though they had once defended him.

27

THERE ARE TWO headings in this chapter. The heading in verse 1 gives the first year of Jehoiakim as the date of the incidents described. The heading in verse 12 indicates that what follows was spoken in the time of King Zedekiah. (See comment below on verse 1.)

In spite of the different datings, the chapter has one consistent theme, namely, God's warning through Jeremiah to the nations and to Judah not to resist the armies of Nebuchadnezzar or to hope for his defeat.

Jeremiah 27

1. In the beginning of the reign of Jehoiakim the son of Josiah, king of Judah, came this word unto

27 : 1 *In the beginning of the reign of Jehoiakim.* This heading is hard to understand. The theme of the chapter concerns Nebuchadnezzar. How could he be discussed at the *beginning* of the reign of Jehoiakim, when he did not become king of Babylon until the *fourth* year of Jehoiakim (see 25:1)? Furthermore, in verse 3, we are told that Jeremiah is to confront the various ambassadors who came to Jerusalem to Zedekiah, the king. But Zedekiah's reign was twice removed from that of Jehoiakim. The traditional commentators do not find this apparent contradiction in dates to be a real difficulty. Rashi, Kimchi, and Trani all say that it was in the first year of Jehoiakim (as the heading cor-

166

Jeremiah from the LORD, saying: 2. 'Thus saith the LORD to me: Make thee bands and bars, and put them upon thy neck; 3. and send them to the king of Edom, and to the king of Moab, and to the king of the children of Ammon, and to the king of Tyre, and to the king of Zidon, by the hand of the messengers that come to Jerusalem unto Zedekiah king of Judah; 4. and give them a charge unto their masters, saying: Thus saith the LORD of hosts, the God of Israel: Thus shall ye say unto your masters: 5. I have made the earth, the man and the beast that are upon the face of the earth, by My great power and by My outstretched arm; and I give it unto whom it seemeth right unto Me. 6. And now have I given all these lands into the hand of Nebuchadnezzar the king of Babylon, My servant; and the beasts of the field also have I given him to serve him. 7. And all the nations shall serve him, and his son, and his son's son, until the time of his own land come; and then many nations and great kings shall make him their bondman. 8. And it

rectly says) that God revealed the coming accession of Zedekiah and the reign of Nebuchadnezzar.

However, modern commentators (including Luzzato) note that the first verse of the chapter (dating it in the first year of Jehoiakim) is not found in the Greek and Syriac versions. Clearly the heading was erroneously inserted by some scribe to make it harmonize with the opening of the preceding chapter. We may therefore take it that all the incidents in this chapter occurred in the reign of Zedekiah, the last king of Judah.

27 : 2-11 Jeremiah speaks to the ambassadors from the neighboring nations and tells them it is God's will that "Nebuchadnezzar My servant" (verse 6) shall be the master of all these lands. Those who do not submit to his rule will suffer the Divine wrath.

27 : 2 *Bands and bars.* Again the prophet develops his sermon around a visible object-lesson. The ox-yoke consisted of a wooden bar which was placed across the back of the animal's neck; some of the ropes or bands served to tie the yoke to the animal, and others served as reins.

shall come to pass, that the nation and the kingdom which will not serve the same Nebuchadnezzar king of Babylon, and that will not put their neck under the yoke of the king of Babylon, that nation will I visit, saith the LORD, with the sword, and with the famine, and with the pestilence, until I have consumed them by his hand. 9. But as for you, hearken ye not to your prophets, nor to your diviners, nor to your dreams, nor to your soothsayers, nor to your sorcerers, that speak unto you, saying: Ye shall not serve the king of Babylon; 10. for they prophesy a lie unto you, to remove you far from your land; and that I should drive you out and ye should perish. 11. But the nation that shall bring their neck under the yoke of the king of Babylon, and serve him, that nation will I let remain in their own land, saith the LORD; and they shall till it, and dwell therein.'

12. And I spoke to Zedekiah king of Judah according to all these words, saying: 'Bring your necks under the yoke of the king of Babylon, and serve him and his people, and live. 13. Why will ye die, thou and thy people, by the sword, by the famine, and by the pestilence, as the LORD hath spoken concerning the nation that will not serve the king of Babylon? 14. And hearken not unto the words of the prophets that speak unto you, saying:

27 : 10 *They prophesy a lie . . . to remove you.* Your prophets and soothsayers, who assure you that Nebuchadnezzar can be defeated, are deceiving you. As a consequence of their deception, you will be removed from your homes and taken captive.

Ye shall not serve the king of Babylon, for they prophesy a lie unto you. 15. For I have not sent them, saith the LORD, and they prophesy falsely in My name; that I might drive you out, and that ye might perish, ye, and the prophets that prophesy unto you.'

16. Also I spoke to the priests and to all this people, saying: 'Thus saith the LORD: Hearken not to the words of your prophets that prophesy unto you, saying: Behold, the vessels of the LORD's house shall now shortly be brought back from Babylon; for they prophesy a lie unto you. 17. Hearken not unto them: serve the king of Babylon, and live; wherefore should this city become desolate? 18. But if they be prophets, and if the word of the LORD be with them, let them now make intercession to the LORD of hosts, that the vessels which are left in the house of the LORD, and in the house of the king of Judah, and at Jerusalem, go not to Babylon. 19. For thus saith the LORD of hosts concerning the pillars, and concerning the sea, and concerning the bases, and concerning the residue of the vessels that remain in this city, 20. which Nebuchadnezzar king of Babylon took not, when he carried away captive Jeconiah the son of Jehoiakim, king of Judah, from Jerusalem to Babylon, and all the nobles of Judah and Jerusalem; 21. yea, thus saith the LORD of hosts, the God of Israel, concerning the vessels that remain in the house of the LORD, and in the house of the king of Judah, and at Jerusalem: 22. They shall be carried to Babylon, and there shall they be, until the day that I remember them, saith the LORD, and bring them up, and restore them to this place.'

28

THIS CHAPTER continues the narrative of chapter 27. Hananiah the son of Azzur prophesied that within two years God would break the yoke of Nebuchadnezzar. Jeremiah answered: Would that it were so! If your happy prophecy comes true, we will know that you are a true prophet. Hananiah then broke the yoke which Jeremiah was wearing as a symbol (27:2), and Jeremiah said: I will make a yoke of iron to replace the yoke of wood. You, Hananiah, have spoken untruths, for which you will be punished with death. Hananiah died in that year.

Jeremiah

28

1. And it came to pass the same year, in the beginning of the reign of Zedekiah king of Judah, in the fourth year, in the fifth month that Hananiah the son of Azzur the prophet, who was of Gibeon, spoke unto me in the house of the LORD, in the presence of the priests and of all the people, saying: 2. 'Thus speaketh the LORD of hosts, the God of Israel, saying: I have broken the yoke of the king of Babylon. 3. Within two full years will I bring back into this place all the vessels of the LORD's

28 : 1-5   Hananiah promises that within two years the captive king Jehoiachin and the sacred Temple vessels will come back from Babylon to Jerusalem.

170

house, that Nebuchadnezzar king of Babylon took away from this place, and carried them to Babylon; 4. and I will bring back to this place Jeconiah the son of Jehoiakim, king of Judah, with all the captives of Judah, that went to Babylon, saith the LORD; for I will break the yoke of the king of Babylon.' 5. Then the prophet Jeremiah said unto the prophet Hananiah in the presence of the priests, and in the presence of all the people that stood in the house of the LORD, 6. even the prophet Jeremiah said: 'Amen! the LORD do so! the LORD perform thy words which thou hast prophesied, to bring back the vessels of the LORD's house, and all them that are carried away captive, from Babylon unto this place! 7. Nevertheless hear thou now this word that I speak in thine ears, and in the ears of all the people: 8. The prophets that have been before me and before thee of old prophesied against many countries, and against great kingdoms, of war, and of evil, and of pestilence. 9. The prophet

28 : 5-9 Jeremiah's rejoinder: The prophets before me have all foretold punishments, but you promise happiness. If your promise comes true, then we will know you are a true prophet.

This rejoinder evoked considerable discussion among the classic commentators. Why should the test of Hananiah's genuineness as a prophet have to wait upon the future fulfillment of his roseate promises? And why, then, should not Jeremiah's status as a prophet depend upon the future fulfillment of his dire prophecies and some making happy prophecies, then if any *one* of them is vindicated by the future, both are thus tested; we know "When a prophet speaketh . . . and the thing come not to pass, then the Lord hath not spoken it." Here indeed fulfillment is given as the test of the genuineness of a prophet, but no distinction is made between gloomy and happy prophecy. Then why should not Jeremiah's status as well as the status of Hananiah await the test of the future?

Maimonides, in his introduction to *Zeraim* (new edition by Joseph Kapach, p. 6a), said that the test of Jeremiah's genuineness as a prophet did not depend upon the fulfillment of his dire

Jeremiah

28

that prophesieth of peace, when the word of the prophet shall come to pass, then shall the prophet be known, that the LORD hath truly sent him.'

10. Then Hananiah the prophet took the bar from off the prophet Jeremiah's neck, and broke it. 11. And Hananiah spoke in the presence of all the people, saying: 'Thus saith the LORD: Even so will I break the yoke of Nebuchadnezzar king of Babylon from off the neck of all the nations within two full years.' And the prophet Jeremiah went his way. 12. Then the word of the LORD came unto Jeremiah, after that Hananiah the prophet had broken the bar from off the neck of the prophet Jeremiah, saying: 13. 'Go, and tell Hananiah, saying: Thus saith the

prophecies; because in the meantime, God may have forgiven the sinful. This opinion is also given by Kimchi and Rashi. Abarbanel (cited by Luzzato) solves the problem in another way which makes the test apply to both types of prophecy. He says that in a case where prophets disagree, some making gloomy prophecies and some making happy prophecies, then if any *one* of them is vindicated by the future, both are thus tested; we know that if one prophet is genuine, he who says the opposite is false. Thus Jeremiah is just in saying that Hananiah should be tested by the future, because that test will also be testing Jeremiah. If Hananiah is proved false, Jeremiah, who preached the opposite, will be proved true; and vice versa.

LORD: Thou hast broken the bars of wood; but thou shalt make in their stead bars of iron. 14. For thus saith the LORD of hosts, the God of Israel: I have put a yoke of iron upon the neck of all these nations, that they may serve Nebuchadnezzar king of Babylon; and they shall serve him; and I have given him the beasts of the field also.' 15. Then said the prophet Jeremiah unto Hananiah the prophet: 'Hear now, Hananiah; the LORD hath not sent thee; but thou makest this people to trust in a lie. 16. Therefore thus saith the LORD: Behold, I will send thee away from off the face of the earth; this year thou shalt die, because thou hast spoken perversion against the LORD.' 17. So Hananiah the prophet died the same year in the seventh month.

28 : 10-17   Hananiah breaks the wooden yoke, and Jeremiah says: I will make a yoke of iron to take its place; and you, Hananiah, for misleading the people with false hopes, will die within a year.

28 : 13   *Tell Hananiah . . . thou hast broken . . . wood . . . thou shalt make bars of iron.*   The text sounds as if God is directing Hananiah to make the bars of iron. Kimchi explains that the first half of the verse is directed at Hananiah but the second is directed at Jeremiah, i.e., Jeremiah should make the yoke of iron.

28 : 16   *I will send thee . . . from off the face of the earth.*   Kimchi says this means that Hananiah will die soon. He will be buried, and thus be removed from the *surface* of the earth.

29

JEREMIAH's letter from Jerusalem to the exiles in Babylon. These were the captives whom Nebuchadnezzar had brought to Babylon together with King Jehoiachin after his first conquest of Jerusalem. Jeremiah calls upon the exiles to establish homes in Babylon and to be patient until God restores them to Jerusalem. Two prophets in Babylon object to the pacific tone of Jeremiah's letters and specifically to his statement that the exile will last as long as seventy years. The chapter ends with another self-appointed prophet in Babylon writing to Jerusalem, denouncing Jeremiah's letter, and asking the chief priest of the Temple to imprison him.

Jeremiah

29

1. Now these are the words of the letter that Jeremiah the prophet sent from Jerusalem unto the residue of the elders of the captivity, and to the priests, and to the prophets, and to all the people, whom Nebuchadnezzar had carried away captive

29 : 1   *The words of the letter that Jeremiah . . . sent . . . unto the captivity.*   There is a considerable tradition with regard to correspondence between Jeremiah and the first group of Babylonian exiles. The Aramaic sentence in Jeremiah 10:11 is taken by the commentators to be part of a letter sent by Jeremiah to the exiles. The sixth chapter of the apocryphal Book of Baruch is also described as a letter of Jeremiah to the captivity. The letter in the Apocrypha and the sentence in 10:11 are both a warning to the

174

from Jerusalem to Babylon, 2. after that Jeconiah the king, and the queen-mother, and the officers, and the princes of Judah and Jerusalem, and the craftsmen, and the smiths, were departed from Jerusalem; 3. by the hand of Elasah the son of Shaphan, and Gemariah the son of Hilkiah, whom Zedekiah king of Judah sent unto Babylon to Nebuchadnezzar king of Babylon, saying:

4. Thus saith the LORD of hosts, the God of Israel, unto all the captivity, whom I have caused to be carried away captive from Jerusalem unto Babylon:

5. Build ye houses, and dwell in them, and plant gardens, and eat the fruit of them; 6. take ye wives, and beget sons and daughters; and take wives for your sons, and give your daughters to husbands, that they may bear sons and daughters; and multiply ye there, and be not diminished. 7. And seek the peace of the city whither I have caused you to be carried away captive, and pray unto the LORD for it; for in the peace thereof shall ye have peace.

8. For thus saith the LORD of hosts, the God of Israel: Let not your prophets that are in the midst of you, and your diviners, beguile you, neither hearken ye to your dreams which ye cause to be dreamed. 9. For they prophesy falsely unto you in My name; I have not sent them, saith the LORD.

exiles to resist the temptations of idolatry. The letter here has another theme. It is a warning to them against impatience and rebellion.

29 : 2 *The craftsmen, and the smiths.*   See comment to 24:1.
29 : 5-8 *Build ye houses . . . seek the peace of the city . . . let not your prophets . . . beguile you.*   Do not believe those prophets among you who tell you that you will return home very soon. Seventy years will pass before God restores you, so make Babylon your home and pray for its peace. You will be there for three generations. Your sons and your daughters will be married and have their children in Babylon.

Jeremiah
29

10. For thus saith the LORD: After seventy years are accomplished for Babylon, I will remember you and perform My good word toward you, in causing you to return to this place. 11. For I know the thoughts that I think toward you, saith the LORD, thoughts of peace, and not of evil to give you a future and a hope. 12. And ye shall call upon Me, and go, and pray unto Me, and I will hearken unto you. 13. And ye shall seek Me, and find Me, when ye shall search for Me with all your heart. 14. And I will be found of you, saith the LORD, and I will turn your captivity, and gather you from all the nations, and from all the places whither I have driven you, saith the LORD; and I will bring you back unto the place whence I caused you to be carried away captive. 15. For ye have said: 'The LORD hath raised us up prophets in Babylon.' 16. For thus saith the LORD concerning the king that sitteth upon the throne of David, and concerning all the people that dwell in this city, your brethren that are not gone forth with you into captivity; 17. thus saith the LORD of hosts: Behold,

29 : 10-14   God's promise to restore them, if they repent and seek Him. If "Ye shall seek Me . . . with all your heart" (verse 13), then "I will bring you back" (verse 14).

29 : 15-23   Denouncing the false prophets among the captives in Babylon and calling down punishment upon them. He names two of them, Ahab and Zedekiah.

29 : 15   *Prophets in Babylon.*   The transition seems abrupt here following God's command to the exiles to be at home in Babylon. Kimchi and Luzzato connect the text as follows: Jeremiah says, I tell you to be at home there and wait for the seventy years to pass, but the false prophets in Babylon tell you that you will be redeemed at once.

29 : 16   *The king . . . and . . . the people.*   Do not listen to your false prophets who tell you that your suffering will soon be over and you will return to the land of Judah. It is not safe for your return, for I will yet send punishment to the remnants of the people still in Jerusalem.

29 : 17   *Like vile figs.*   The description of the remnant in Jeru-

176

I will send upon them the sword, the famine, and the pestilence, and will make them like vile figs, that cannot be eaten, they are so bad. 18. And I will pursue after them with the sword, with the famine, and with the pestilence, and will make them a horror unto all the kingdoms of the earth, a curse, and an astonishment, and a hissing, and a reproach, among all the nations whither I have driven them; 19. because they have not hearkened to My words, saith the LORD, wherewith I sent unto them My servants the prophets, sending them betimes and often; but ye would not hear, saith the LORD. 20. Hear ye therefore the word of the LORD, all ye of the captivity, whom I have sent away from Jerusalem to Babylon: 21. Thus saith the LORD of hosts, the God of Israel, concerning Ahab the son of Kolaiah, and concerning Zedekiah the son of Maaseiah, who prophesy a lie unto you in My name: Behold, I will deliver them into the hand of Nebuchadrezzar king of Babylon; and he shall slay them before your eyes; 22. and of them shall be taken up a curse by all the captivity of Judah that are in Babylon, saying: 'The LORD make thee like Zedekiah and like Ahab, whom the king of Babylon roasted in the fire'; 23. because they have wrought vile deeds in Israel, and have committed adultery with their neighbours' wives, and have spoken words in My name falsely, which I commanded them not; but I am He that knoweth, and am witness, saith the LORD.

24. And concerning Shemaiah the Nehelamite

salem as "vile figs" is repeated here in almost the exact language of 24:8 ff.

29:22 *Taken up [as] a curse.* The two false prophets will have so awful a fate that when one person wants to curse another, he will say: "May you have the fate of Ahab and Zedekiah, whom the king of Babylon killed by burning" (verse 22).

Neither these two men nor their fate are mentioned anywhere else in Scripture.

29:24-32 Another episode, also dealing with communication be-thou shalt speak, saying: 25. Thus speaketh the LORD of hosts, the God of Israel, saying: Because thou hast sent letters in thine own name unto all the people that are at Jerusalem, and to Zephaniah the son of Maaseiah the priest, and to all the priests, saying: 26. 'The LORD hath made thee priest in the stead of Jehoiada the priest, that there should be officers in the house of the LORD for every man that is mad, and maketh himself a prophet, that thou shouldest put him in the stocks and in the collar. 27. Now therefore, why hast thou not rebuked Jeremiah of Anathoth, who maketh himself a prophet to you, 28. foreasmuch as he hath sent unto us in Babylon, saying: The captivity is long; build ye houses, and dwell in them; and plant gardens, and eat the fruit of them?' 29. And Zephaniah the priest read this letter in the ears of Jeremiah the prophet. 30. Then came the word of the LORD unto Jeremiah, saying: 31. Send to all them of the captivity, saying: Thus saith the LORD concerning Shemaiah the Nehelamite: Because that Shemaiah hath prophesied unto you, and I sent him not, and he hath caused you to trust in a lie; 32. therefore thus saith the LORD: Behold, I will punish Shemaiah the Nehelamite, and his seed; he shall not have a man to dwell among this people, neither shall he behold the good that I will do unto My people, saith the LORD; because he hath spoken perversion against the LORD.

tween Jerusalem and Babylon, and citing the theme of Jeremiah's letter (verse 28). Shemaiah, evidently a prominent member of the exile, writes to Zephaniah, the chief priest in Jerusalem, urging him to imprison Jeremiah. Jeremiah's response.

29 : 26 *In the stead of Jehoiada.*   Jehoiada was the chief priest in the time of King Josiah. Shemaiah, writing to Zephaniah the priest, reminds him of his responsibility as the successor of an illustrious man.

The stocks and in the collar.   Kimchi defines the word translated here as "collar" as a "vessel" that locks up the hands.

30

CHAPTERS 30 AND 31 are a unit. They both voice a mood of consolation. The dating of these chapters has evoked considerable discussion. Earlier scholars dated their composition after the time of
Jeremiah, and they found very little by Jeremiah himself in them.
There are two reasons for this opinion. First, the language in which
the consolations are couched closely resembles the language of the
Second Isaiah, who lived during the exile. Second, the early critics
generally doubted that Jeremiah ever had any thoughts of consolation. More recent scholars are inclined to believe that Jeremiah
did harbor and voice thoughts of consolation for his people; as for
the resemblance to Deutero-Isaiah, they tend to feel that the author
of Jeremiah 30-31 and the author of Deutero-Isaiah were both
utilizing a style of literary expression that had become popular for
certain kinds of prophetic writing. Bright (p. 284) says: "Now it is
impossible to doubt that Jeremiah held some sort of hope for the
future of his people, and few scholars today would be inclined to
do so [i.e., to doubt it]. . . . Stylistic similarities to Second Isaiah
are explained on the supposition that both prophets made use of the
same conventional forms of address."

The two chapters are addressed primarily to the exile of the
Ten Tribes, the northern kingdom; and it is assumed, because of
their optimistic mood, that the chapters were composed during a
comparatively happy period in the reign of King Josiah.

1. The word that came to Jeremiah from the LORD, **Jeremiah**
saying: 2. 'Thus speaketh the LORD, the God of   **30**

Jeremiah
30

Israel, saying: Write thee all the words that I have spoken unto thee in a book. 3. For, lo, the days come, saith the LORD, that I will turn the captivity of My people Israel and Judah, saith the LORD; and I will cause them to return to the land that I gave to their fathers, and they shall possess it.'

4. And these are the words that the LORD spoke concerning Israel and concerning Judah. 5. For thus saith the LORD:

We have heard a voice of trembling,
Of fear, and not of peace.

6. Ask ye now, and see
Whether a man doth travail with child;
Wherefore do I see every man
With his hands on his loins, as a woman in travail,
And all faces are turned into paleness?

7. Alas! for that day is great,
So that none is like it;

---

30 : 2 *Write thee all the words ... in a book.* Why should these particular messages be written down and not delivered orally, as were most of the prophet's messages? Kimchi explains it as follows: Do not voice these consolations at present because this is a time for punishment. These words are to be kept for the future; so write them down to be read later. Luzzato gives a similar explanation.

30 : 4-7 The passage describes the agonies of the time which will precede the restoration. The metaphor used is that of a woman in the pains of childbirth. So it will be a time of "trembling and fear" (verse 5); everybody will seem to be writhing with pain.

But when will that be? Rashi is inclined to say that it will be during the time of terror which will come in the war against Babylon. The fall of Babylon will precede the return to Jerusalem. But Rashi mentions that others say this refers to the time of danger before the coming of the Messiah. Those days will be darkened by the great wars of Gog and Magog (see Ezekiel 38), which were to precede the coming of the Messiah. This opinion is held by Joseph Nachmias and Isaiah of Trani. Kimchi also says that "the time of terror" means the pre-messianic days.

30 : 7 *Alas! for that day is great.* The day is ominously great. *Jacob ... shall be saved.* After that awful day of great

180

And it is a time of trouble unto Jacob,
But out of it shall he be saved.

8. And it shall come to pass in that day,
Saith the LORD of hosts,
That I will break his yoke from off thy neck,
And will burst thy bands;
And strangers shall no more make him their bond-
man;

9. But they shall serve the LORD their God,
And David their king,
Whom I will raise up unto them.

10. Therefore fear thou not, O Jacob My servant, saith
the LORD;
Neither be dismayed, O Israel;
For, lo, I will save thee from afar,
And thy seed from the land of their captivity;
And Jacob shall again be quiet and at ease,
And none shall make him afraid.

11. For I am with thee, saith the LORD, to save thee,
For I will make a full end of all the nations whither
I have scattered thee,
But I will not make a full end of thee;
For I will correct thee in measure,
And will not utterly destroy thee.

12. For thus saith the LORD:

terror, Israel will be saved. Trani calls attention to almost the same thought in Daniel 12:1: "There shall be a time of trouble that never was since there was the nation . . . at that time thy people shall be delivered."

30 : 9 *David their king.* Kimchi says this may mean David him-self after the resurrection, or David's descendant, the Messiah. The Targum simply says the Messiah, son of David.

30 : 10 *Therefore fear thou not, O Jacob My servant.* The same phrase is found in Isaiah 44:2. The whole passage resembles the language of Deutero-Isaiah.

30 : 12-17 Zion is sorely wounded. Her enemies consider her finished, yet God will restore her.

30 : 12 *Thy hurt is incurable.* The word translated here as "incurable" means "serious" or "grievous."

Thy hurt is incurable,
And thy wound is grievous.

Jeremiah 30

13. None deemeth of thy wound that it may be bound up;
   Thou hast no healing medicines.
14. All thy lovers have forgotten thee,
   They seek thee not;
   For I have wounded thee with the wound of an enemy,
   With the chastisement of a cruel one;
   For the greatness of thine iniquity,
   Because thy sins were increased.
15. Why criest thou for thy hurt,
   That thy pain is incurable?
   For the greatness of thine iniquity, because thy sins were increased,
   I have done these things unto thee.
16. Therefore all they that devour thee shall be devoured,
   And all thine adversaries, every one of them, shall go into captivity;
   And they that spoil thee shall be a spoil,
   And all that prey upon thee will I give for a prey.
17. For I will restore health unto thee,
   And I will heal thee of thy wounds, saith the LORD;
   Because they have called thee an outcast:
   'She is ᵃZion, there is none that careth for her.'
18. Thus saith the LORD:
   Behold, I will turn the captivity of Jacob's tents,
   And have compassion on his dwelling-places;

30 : 14 *All thy lovers.* Metaphorical for "all thy allies." They have all deserted you in your trouble. Kimchi says this refers specifically to Assyria and Egypt, to whom you used to go for help.

30 : 18-22 The coming restoration. The captives will be brought home again, and Israel will be once more God's people.

30 : 21 *For who . . . hath pledged his heart to approach unto Me?* According to Rashi (followed by Luzzato), the two uses of the word "approach" in this verse have opposite meanings. The first

ᵃWith a play on the meaning, *a dry land.*

And the city shall be builded upon her own mound,
And the palace shall be inhabited upon its wonted place.

19. And out of them shall proceed thanksgiving
And the voice of them that make merry;
And I will multiply them, and they shall not be diminished,
I will also increase them, and they shall not dwindle away.

20. Their children also shall be as aforetime,
And their congregation shall be established before Me,
And I will punish all that oppress them.

21. And their prince shall be of themselves,
And their ruler shall proceed from the midst of them;
And I will cause him to draw near, and he shall approach unto Me;
For who is he that hath pledged his heart
To approach unto Me? saith the Lord.

22. And ye shall be My people,
And I will be your God.

23. Behold, a storm of the Lord is gone forth in fury,
A sweeping storm;
It shall whirl upon the head of the wicked.

24. The fierce anger of the Lord shall not return,
Until He have executed, and till He have performed
The purposes of His heart;
In the end of days ye shall consider it.

one refers to Israel and means "to draw nigh in worship." The second refers to the enemy and means "to draw nigh in battle." But Trani says both parts of the sentence refer to Israel, and the second half of the verse means: Who but Israel would draw (approach) near to God, and therefore Israel will be Thy people.

30:23-25 God will punish the wicked and in the end will be worshiped by all the families of Israel. The phrase "all the families of Israel" indicates that the chapter was addressed chiefly to the exiles of the northern kingdom.

31

THIS CHAPTER continues the theme of chapter 30 and presents visions of the future restoration.

Jeremiah

31

1. At that time, saith the LORD,
   Will I be the God of all the families of Israel,
   And they shall be My people.
2. Thus saith the LORD:
   The people that were left of the sword
   Have found grace in the wilderness,
   Even Israel, when I go to cause him to rest.
3. 'From afar the LORD appeared unto me.'
   'Yea, I have loved thee with an everlasting love;
   Therefore with affection have I drawn thee.

31 : 1 *At that time, saith the Lord.* In most Hebrew Bibles this verse is the last verse of the preceding chapter.

31 : 2 *People that were left of the sword.* The Targum applies this verse to the exodus from Egypt, thus: The people escaped from the sword of Pharaoh, were shielded by God's grace in the wilderness, and He led them to their rest in the land of Canaan. Most of the classic commentators accept this interpretation.

31 : 3 *From afar the Lord appeared unto me.* Rashi, following the Targum, takes the word "afar" to mean far back in time, and therefore understands the verse to mean: God, Who had ap-

4. Again will I build thee, and thou shalt be built,
   O virgin of Israel;
   Again shalt thou be adorned with thy tabrets,
   And shalt go forth in the dances of them that make
      merry.

5. Again shalt thou plant vineyards upon the moun-
      tains of Samaria;
   The planters shall plant, and shall have the use
      thereof.
6. For there shall be a day,
   That the watchmen shall call upon the mount
      Ephraim:
   Arise ye, and let us go up to Zion,
   Unto the LORD our God.'
7. For thus saith the LORD:
   Sing with gladness for Jacob,
   And shout at the head of the nations;
   Announce ye, praise ye, and say:
   'O LORD, save Thy people,
   The remnant of Israel.'
8. Behold, I will bring them from the north country,
   And gather them from the uttermost parts of the
      earth,
   And with them the blind and the lame,

peared to our fathers long ago, continues His love to us, "with everlasting love." But Kimchi says that the verse refers to the Babylonian exile and is a dialogue between Israel complaining and God reassuring. Israel says: It is so long ago that You revealed Yourself to us, and God answers: Nevertheless My love for you is everlasting.

31:6 *Mount Ephraim . . . go up to Zion.* Ephraim is a term frequently used for the northern kingdom because the tribe of Ephraim was by far the largest of the Ten Tribes. The verse means that when the redemption comes, the northern tribes will once more make their pilgrimages to Jerusalem. The nation will be unified again.

31:8 *The blind and the lame.* Kimchi: God will lead them so gently and on such a straight road (see verse 9) that even the blind and the lame will not lag behind.

Jeremiah
31

The woman with child and her that travaileth with
    child together;
A great company shall they return hither.
9. They shall come with weeping,
And with supplications will I lead them;
I will cause them to walk by rivers of waters,
In a straight way wherein they shall not stumble;
For I am become a father to Israel,
And Ephraim is My first-born.
10. Hear the word of the LORD, O ye nations,
And declare it in the isles afar off, and say:
'He that scattered Israel doth gather him,
And keep him, as a shepherd doth his flock.'
11. For the LORD hath ransomed Jacob,
And He redeemeth him from the hand of him that
    is stronger than he.
12. And they shall come and sing in the height of Zion,
And shall flow unto the goodness of the LORD,
To the corn, and to the wine, and to the oil,
And to the young of the flock and of the herd;
And their soul shall be as a watered garden,
And they shall not pine any more at all.
13. Then shall the virgin rejoice in the dance,
And the young men and the old together;

31:9 *They shall come with weeping.* Rashi says this means the tears of prayer and repentance, but Kimchi says it means tears of joy.

A father to Israel, and Ephraim is My first-born. The Targum, as usual, tries to avoid too human a description of God and therefore translates the verse: My word will be as a guide to Israel, and Ephraim will be dear to Me as to a father.

Ephraim . . . first-born. Ephraim was not the first-born of the tribes. Kimchi says the verse means: Ephraim is as dear to me as a first-born is to his father. A similar usage is: Israel is My first-born (Exodus 4:22), i.e., Israel is dear to Me.

31:12 *Flow unto the goodness.* They will stream like a flowing river; they will come in multitudes. The same verb is used in Isaiah 2:2: "The mountain of the Lord's house . . . and all nations shall flow unto it."

186

For I will turn their mourning into joy,

And will comfort them, and make them rejoice
  from their sorrow.

14. And I will satiate the soul of the priests with fatness,

  And My people shall be satisfied with My goodness,

  Saith the LORD:

15. Thus saith the LORD:

  A voice is heard in Ramah,

  Lamentation, and bitter weeping,

  Rachel weeping for her children;

  She refuseth to be comforted for her children,

  Because they are not.

16. Thus saith the LORD:

  Refrain thy voice from weeping,

  And thine eyes from tears;

  For thy work shall be rewarded, saith the LORD;

  And they shall come back from the land of the
  enemy.

17. And there is hope for thy future, saith the LORD;

  And thy children shall return to their own border.

Jeremiah

31

31 : 14 *Satiate . . . the priests with fatness.* Kimchi says that in
those days the Temple will be restored, and so many offerings
will be brought that the priests will be satiated.

31 : 15-20 The restoration of the north (Ephraim).

31 : 15 *A voice . . . in Ramah . . . Rachel weeping.* Rachel was
the mother of Joseph, and thus the grandmother of Ephraim, so
in a sense she is the ancestress of the northern kingdom. Now
that the kingdom is destroyed and the tribes are in exile, she is
weeping for them: "She refuseth to be comforted for her children." Luzzato calls attention to the fact that the town of Ramah
is in Benjamin near the tomb of Rachel. The Prophet Samuel,
who lived in Ramah, said to Saul: "When thou art departed from
me, thou shalt find two men by the tomb of Rachel in the border
of Benjamin" (I Samuel 10:2).

31 : 16 *Refrain thy . . . weeping . . . they shall come back.* God
reassures Rachel that the tribe of Ephraim, her descendants, will
be restored.

Jeremiah

31

18. I have surely heard Ephraim bemoaning himself:
    'Thou hast chastised me, and I was chastised,
    As a calf untrained;
    Turn thou me, and I shall be turned,
    For Thou art the LORD my God.

19. Surely after that I was turned, I repented,
    And after that I was instructed, I smote upon my
        thigh;
    I was ashamed, yea, even confounded,
    Because I did bear the reproach of my youth.'

20. Is Ephraim a darling son unto Me?
    Is he a child that is dandled?
    For as often as I speak of him,
    I do earnestly remember him still;
    Therefore My heart yearneth for him,
    I will surely have compassion upon him, saith the
        LORD.

21. Set thee up waymarks,
    Make thee guide-posts;
    Set thy heart toward the highway,
    Even the way by which thou wentest;
    Return, O virgin of Israel,
    Return to these thy cities.

22. How long wilt thou turn away coyly,
    O thou backsliding daughter?
    For the LORD hath created a new thing in the
        earth:
    A woman shall court a man.

31 : 18-20   A dialogue between Ephraim and God. Ephraim bemoans his exile. He says God has punished him but now he has repented of his sins. God says: Ephraim is dear to Me: "My heart yearneth for him and I will have compassion upon him" (verse 20).

31 : 19   *I smote upon my thigh.*   A gesture of shame and mourning.

31 : 21-25   God summons the exiles to begin their march back to Zion.

31 : 22   *A new thing ... a woman shall court a man.*   The Second Isaiah frequently uses the metaphor in which God is de-

23. Thus saith the LORD of hosts, the God of Israel:
Yet again shall they use this speech
In the land of Judah and in the cities thereof,
When I shall turn their captivity:
'The LORD bless thee, O habitation of righteousness.
O mountain of holiness.'
24. And Judah and all the cities thereof
Shall dwell therein together:
The husbandmen, and they that go forth with
flocks.
25. For I have satiated the weary soul.
And every pining soul have I replenished.
26. Upon this I awaked, and beheld;
And my sleep was sweet unto me.
27. Behold, the days come, saith the LORD, that I will
sow the house of Israel and the house of Judah
with the seed of man, and with the seed of beast.
28. And it shall come to pass, that like as I have
watched over them to pluck up and to break down,
and to overthrow and to destroy, and to afflict; so
will I watch over them to build and to plant, saith
the LORD.
29. In those days they shall say no more:
'The fathers have eaten sour grapes,

scribed as the husband and Zion as His wife. God says here to
Zion: Just forget your shyness; go now and seek after Me. Rashi
says simply: Do not be ashamed to seek after Me.

31 : 26   *I awaked . . . and my sleep was sweet unto me.*   Kimchi
says that to most of the prophets the prophecies come in a dream.
So Jeremiah says here: When I awoke from the dream and
prophecy of redemption, I knew that my sleep was sweet. So
too Trani. But Luzzato quotes two Italian scholars who say that it
is Israel who is speaking. It has awakened from the sleep of exile.

31 : 27-40   Mostly a prose elaboration of the various steps in the
coming redemption.

31 : 27   *The seed of man, and . . . the seed of beast.*   Israel will
be blessed in their families and in their flocks.

31 : 29, 30   *Fathers have eaten sour grapes, and the children's teeth*

And the children's teeth are set on edge.'

30. But every one shall die for his own iniquity; every man that eateth the sour grapes, his teeth shall be set on edge.

Jeremiah
31

31. Behold, the days come, saith the LORD, that I will make a new covenant with the house of Israel, and with the house of Judah; 32. not according to the covenant that I made with their fathers in the day that I took them by the hand to bring them out of the land of Egypt; forasmuch as they broke My covenant, although I was a lord over them, saith the LORD. 33. But this is the covenant that I will make with the house of Israel after those days, saith the LORD, I will put My law in their inward parts, and in their heart will I write it; and I will be their God, and they shall be My people; 34. and they shall teach no more every man his brother, saying: 'Know the LORD'; for they shall all know Me, from the least of them unto the greatest of them, saith the LORD; for I will forgive their iniquity, and their sin will I remember no more.

35. Thus saith the LORD,
Who giveth the sun for a light by day,

are set on edge. This popular proverb meant that the fathers have sinned but the children must suffer for it. The prophet continues (verse 30) that this proverb will no longer be true. Each person will be rewarded or punished for his own actions. The same proverb is used and developed by Ezekiel (chapter 18).

31 : 30-34 A new covenant will take the place of the old one, which was made when Israel left Egypt, and which Israel has

And the ordinances of the moon and of the stars
  for a light by night
Who stirreth up the sea, that the waves thereof
  roar,
The LORD of hosts is His name:
36. If these ordinances depart from before Me,
  Saith the LORD,
  Then the seed of Israel also shall cease
  From being a nation before Me for ever.
37. Thus saith the LORD:
  If heaven above can be measured,
  And the foundations of the earth searched out be-
    neath,
  Then will I also cast off all the seed of Israel
  For all that they have done, saith the LORD.
38. Behold, the days come, saith the LORD, that the
city shall be built to the LORD from the tower of
Hananel unto the gate of the corner. 39. And the
measuring line shall yet go out straight forward
unto the hill Gareb, and shall turn about unto
Goah. 40. And the whole valley of the dead bodies,
and of the ashes, and all the fields unto the brook
Kidron, unto the corner of the horse gate toward
the east, shall be holy unto the LORD; it shall not be
plucked up, nor thrown down any more for ever.

broken. God's special blessing now in the redemption is that the
renewed covenant will be written on their hearts. It will be part
of their nature. So verse 34: "For they shall all know Me, from
the least . . . unto the greatest."

31 : 35-37   As the universe is eternal, so Israel will be. As the
universe can never be measured, so Israel will never be cast off.

31 : 38-40   The future dimensions of the new Jerusalem.

32

CHAPTERS 26 TO 29 recount historical events and biographical incidents in the life of Jeremiah. Chapters 30 and 31 are consolatory, presenting visions of the messianic time. This chapter has both types of material. It mentions a biographical incident in the life of Jeremiah, namely, that Jeremiah bought land in his native village; this incident is then taken as a symbol, or promise, of the future redemption from Babylon.

Jeremiah

32

1. The word that came to Jeremiah from the LORD in the tenth year of Zedekiah king of Judah, which was the eighteenth year of Nebuchadrezzar. 2. Now at that time the king of Babylon's army was besieging Jerusalem; and Jeremiah the prophet was shut up in the court of the guard, which was in the king

32 : 1-5   These verses set the scene for the chapter. The events take place in the tenth year of Zedekiah's reign. The Babylonian armies are besieging the city. The siege will last for a year and a half, then the city will be captured and the nation's independence come to an end. Jeremiah had preached that the city would be captured, and for that gloomy prediction the king had him imprisoned. The prison seems to be the one used by the palace guard and is situated in the palace precincts. Thus, as will be seen in later chapters, Zedekiah and Jeremiah could be in frequent communication.

of Judah's house. 3. For Zedekiah king of Judah had shut him up, saying: 'Wherefore dost thou prophesy, and say: Thus saith the LORD: Behold, I will give this city into the hand of the king of Babylon, and he shall take it; 4. and Zedekiah king of Judah shall not escape out of the hand of the Chaldeans, but shall surely be delivered into the hand of the king of Babylon, and shall speak with him mouth to mouth, and his eyes shall behold his eyes; 5. and he shall lead Zedekiah to Babylon, and there shall he be until I remember him, saith the LORD; though ye fight with the Chaldeans, ye shall not prosper?'

6. And Jeremiah said: 'The word of the LORD came unto me, saying; 7. Behold, Hanamel, the son of Shallum thine uncle, shall come unto thee, saying: Buy thee my field that is in Anathoth; for the right of redemption is thine to buy it.' 8. So Hanamel mine uncle's son came to me in the court of the guard according to the word of the LORD, and said unto me: 'Buy my field, I pray thee, that is in Anathoth, which is in the land of Benjamin; for the right of inheritance is thine, and the redemption is thine; buy it for thyself.' Then I knew that this

32 : 6-15   The central incident of the chapter: Jeremiah buys land in his native village of Anathoth. The purchase has a symbolic meaning, as will be explained later on in the chapter.

32 : 7   *For the right of redemption is thine.*   The land belonging to any tribe was never to be permanently alienated. Therefore if a man was compelled by poverty to sell his land, his closest relative had the right (and duty) to buy it first or to rebuy it from the purchaser. Leviticus 25:25: "Then shall his kinsmen who is next to him . . . redeem that which his brother has sold." Thus in Ruth 4:1-10, Boaz tells the nearest kinsman of Elimelech, Ruth's father-in-law, that he has the right to redeem the land first, and only if this closest relative refuses to buy it (which he did), could it be purchased by Boaz, who was also a relative. Jeremiah was the closest relative of the man who sold the land, and therefore the right of redemption (i.e., purchase) was his.

Jeremiah
32

was the word of the LORD. 9. And I bought the field that was in Anathoth of Hanamel mine uncle's son, and weighed him the money, even seventeen shekels of silver. 10. And I subscribed the deed, and sealed it, and called witnesses, and weighed him the money in the balances. 11. So I took the deed of the purchase, both that which was sealed, containing the terms and conditions, and that which was open; 12. and I delivered the deed of the purchase unto Baruch the son of Neriah, the son Mahseiah, in the presence of Hanamel mine uncle['s son], and in the presence of the witnesses that subscribed the deed of the purchase, before all the Jews that sat in the court of the guard. 13. And I charged Baruch before them, saying: 14. 'Thus saith the LORD of hosts, the God of Israel: Take these deeds, this deed of the purchase, both that which is sealed, and this deed which is open, and put them in an earthen vessel; that they may continue many days. 15. For thus saith the LORD of hosts, the God of Israel: Houses and fields and vineyards shall yet again be bought in this land.'

16. Now after I had delivered the deed of the

32 : 11 *The deed of the purchase . . . that which was sealed . . . that which was open.* There were two copies of the deed. The sealed copy was signed by the purchaser. The other copy, the open one, was given into the possession of the court (Rashi).

32 : 12 *I delivered the deed . . . unto Baruch the son of Neriah.* This is the first mention of Baruch, Jeremiah's friend and scribe.

32 : 14 *That they may continue many days.* That they may last for a long time and be consulted in the future.

32 : 15 *Vineyards shall yet again be bought.* The symbolic meaning of Jeremiah's land-purchase is here explained: After the inevitable destruction of Jerusalem, God will restore the people to their home. Then land will again be bought and cultivated.

32 : 16-25 Jeremiah's prayer asking God to reveal to him the reason why he was commanded to buy the land. But verse 15 has already given the reason! It is evident either that verse 15 is misplaced and should come further on in the chapter or that the

purchase unto Baruch the son of Neriah, I prayed unto the LORD, saying 17. 'Ah Lord GOD! behold, Thou hast made the heaven and the earth by Thy great power and by Thy outstretched arm; there is nothing too hard for Thee; 18. who showest mercy unto thousands, and recompensest the iniquity of the fathers into the bosom of their children after them; the great, the mighty God, the LORD of hosts is His name; 19. great in counsel, and mighty in work; whose eyes are open upon all the ways of the sons of men, to give every one according to his ways, and according to the fruit of his doings; 20. who didst set signs and wonders in the land of Egypt, even unto this day, and in Israel and among other men; and madest Thee a name, as at this day; 21. and didst bring forth Thy people Israel out of the land of Egypt with signs, and with wonders, and with a strong hand, and with an outstretched arm, and with great terror; 22. and gavest them this land, which Thou didst swear to their fathers to give them, a land flowing with milk and honey; 23. and they came in, and possessed it; but they hearkened not to Thy voice, neither walked in Thy law; they have done nothing of all that Thou commandedst them to do; therefore Thou hast caused all this evil to befall them; 24. behold the mounds, they are come unto the city to take it; and the city is given into the hand of the Chaldeans that fight against it, because of the sword, and of the famine, and of the pestilence; and what Thou hast spoken is come to pass; and, behold, Thou seest it. 25. Yet Thou hast said unto me, O Lord GOD: Buy thee the field for money, and call witnesses; whereas the city is given into the hand of the Chaldeans.'

following prayer was a later addition. In this prayer Jeremiah speaks of God's kindness to Israel in the past, but now, he says, the Chaldean earthworks are high enough to shoot down into the city, and it is evident that the city will soon be captured. Then why did God say to him: "Buy thee the field . . . and call witnesses" (verse 25)?

Jeremiah
32

26. Then came the word of the LORD unto Jeremiah, saying: 27. 'Behold, I am the LORD, the God of all flesh; is there any thing too hard for Me? 28. Therefore thus saith the LORD: Behold, I will give this city into the hand of the Chaldeans, and into the hand of Nebuchadrezzar king of Babylon, and he shall take it; 29. and the Chaldeans, that fight against this city, shall come and set this city on fire, and burn it, with the houses, upon whose roofs they have offered unto Baal, and poured out drink-offerings unto other gods, to provoke Me. 30. For the children of Israel and the children of Judah have only done that which was evil in My sight from their youth; for the children of Israel have only provoked Me with the work of their hands, saith the LORD. 31. For this city hath been to Me a provocation of Mine anger and of My fury from the day that they built it even unto this day, that I should remove it from before My face; 32. because of all the evil of the children of Israel and of the children of Judah, which they have done to provoke Me, they, their kings, their princes, their priests, and their prophets, and the men of Judah, and the inhabitants of Jerusalem. 33. And they have turned unto Me the back, and not the face; and though I taught them, teaching them betimes and often, yet they have not hearkened to receive instruction. 34. But they set their abominations in the house whereupon My name is called, to defile it. 35. And they built the high places of Baal, which are in the valley of the son of Hinnom, to set apart their sons and their daughters unto Molech; which I commanded them not, neither came it into My mind, that they should do this

32 : 26-44   God's answer: The city will indeed be destroyed because of the sins of the people, but I shall restore them and the

abomination; to cause Judah to sin. 36. And now therefore thus saith the LORD, the God of Israel, concerning this city, whereof ye say: It is given into the hand of the king of Babylon by the sword, and by the famine, and by the pestilence: 37. Behold, I will gather them out of all the countries, whither I have driven them in Mine anger, and in My fury, and in great wrath; and I will bring them back unto this place, and I will cause them to dwell safely; 38. and they shall be My people, and I will be their God; 39. and I will give them one heart and one way, that they may fear Me for ever; for the good of them, and of their children after them; 40. and I will make an everlasting covenant with them, that I will not turn away from them, to do them good; and I will put My fear in their hearts, that they shall not depart from Me. 41. Yea, I will rejoice over them to do them good, and I will plant them in this land in truth with My whole heart and with My whole soul. 42. For thus saith the LORD: Like as I have brought all this great evil upon this people, so will I bring upon them all the good that I have promised them. 43. And fields shall be bought in this land, whereof ye say: It is desolate, without man or beast; it is given into the hand of the Chaldeans. 44. Men shall buy fields for money, and subscribe the deeds, and seal them, and call witnesses, in the land of Benjamin, and in the places about Jerusalem, and in the cities of Judah, and in the cities of the hill-country, and in the cities of the Lowland, and in the cities of the South; for I will cause their captivity to return, saith the LORD.'

land will resume its normal life. "Men shall buy fields . . . and call witnesses" (as I have bid you do now as a prophetic symbol).

33

THIS CHAPTER continues the mood of consolation with a description of the coming redemption. The message came during the siege while Jeremiah was still in the prison of the palace guard.

Jeremiah

33

1. Moreover the word of the LORD came unto Jeremiah the second time, while he was yet shut up in the court of the guard, saying:
2. Thus saith the LORD the Maker thereof,
   The LORD that formed it to establish it,
   The LORD is His name:
3. Call unto Me, and I will answer thee,
   And will tell thee great things, and hidden, which thou knowest not.
4. For thus saith the LORD, the God of Israel, concerning the houses of this city, and concerning the houses of the kings of Judah, which are broken down for mounds, and for ramparts; 5. whereon they come to fight with the Chaldeans, even to fill

33 : 2 *The Lord that formed it.* Exactly what God is described as having formed is not clear since there is no antecedent noun for "it." Kimchi says the verse must be understood as meaning: God, Who formed this city of Jerusalem and glorified it, will now cause it to be destroyed.

them with the dead bodies of men, whom I have
slain in Mine anger and in My fury, and for all
whose wickedness I have hid My face from this
city; 6. Behold, I will bring it healing and cure,
and I will cure them; and I will reveal unto them
the abundance of peace and truth. 7. And I will
cause the captivity of Judah and the captivity of
Israel to return, and will build them, as at the first.
8. And I will cleanse them from all their iniquity,
whereby they have sinned against Me; and I will
pardon all their iniquities, whereby they have
sinned against Me, and whereby they have transgressed against Me. 9. And this city shall be to Me
for a name of joy, for a praise and for a glory, before all the nations of the earth, which shall hear all
the good that I do unto them, and shall fear and
tremble for all the good and for all the peace that
I procure unto it.

10. Thus saith the LORD: Yet again there shall be
heard in this place, whereof ye say: It is waste,
without man and without beast, even in the cities
of Judah, and in the streets of Jerusalem, that are
desolate, without man and without inhabitant and
without beast, 11. the voice of joy and the voice
of gladness, the voice of the bridegroom and the
voice of the bride, the voice of them that say: 'Give
thanks to the LORD of hosts, for the LORD is good,
for His mercy endureth for ever,' even of them
that bring offerings of thanksgiving into the house
of the LORD. For I will cause the captivity of the
land to return as at the first, saith the LORD.

12. Thus saith the LORD of hosts: Yet again shall there
be in this place, which is waste, without man and
without beast, and in all the cities thereof, a
habitation of shepherds causing their flocks to lie
down. 13. In the cities of the hill-country, in the

---

33 : 7 *Captivity of Judah and the captivity of Israel.*   As in the
preceding two chapters of consolation, both Judah and Israel
(the northern kingdom) will be restored and the nation reunited.

cities of the Lowland, and in the cities of the South, and in the land of Benjamin, and in the places about Jerusalem, and in the cities of Judah, shall the flocks again pass under the hands of him that counteth them, saith the LORD.

14. Behold, the days come, saith the LORD, that I will perform that good word which I have spoken concerning the house of Israel and concerning the house of Judah. 15. In those days, and at that time,
Will I cause a shoot of righteousness to grow up unto David;
And he shall execute justice and righteousness in the land.

16. In those days shall Judah be saved,
And Jerusalem shall dwell safely;
And this is the name whereby she shall be called,
The LORD is our righteousness.

17. For thus saith the LORD: There shall not be cut off unto David a man to sit upon the throne of the house of Israel; 18. neither shall there be cut off unto the priests the Levites a man before Me to offer burnt-offerings, and to burn meal-offerings, and to do sacrifice continually.

19. And the word of the LORD came unto Jeremiah, saying: 20. Thus saith the LORD:
If ye can break My covenant with the day,

33 : 13 *Shall the flocks again pass under the hands.* When the day is over, the sheep return to the fold. They pass one by one under the hands of the shepherd, who counts to see if any are lost.

33 : 15 *Shoot of righteousness . . . unto David.* The classic commentators agree that this refers to the messianic king. Thus the promise of the redemption from Babylon is enlarged into a vision of the final redemption in the days of the Messiah. For commentary on "shoot" or "sprout," see 23:5.

And My covenant with the night,
So that there should not be day and night in their
season;

21. Then may also My covenant be broken with David
My servant,
That he should not have a son to reign upon his
throne;
And with the Levites the priests, My ministers.

22. As the host of heaven cannot be numbered.
Neither the sand of the sea measured;
So will I multiply the seed of David My servant,
And the Levites that minister unto Me.

23. And the word of the LORD came to Jeremiah,
saying: 24. 'Considerest thou not what this people
have spoken, saying: The two families which the
LORD did choose, He hath cast them off? and they
contemn My people, that they should be no more a
nation before them. 25. Thus saith the LORD: If
My covenant be not with day and night, if I have
not appointed the ordinances of heaven and earth;
26. then will I also cast away the seed of Jacob,
and of David My servant, so that I will not take of
his seed to be rulers over the seed of Abraham,
Isaac, and Jacob; for I will cause their captivity to
return, and will have compassion on them.'

33 : 19-22   This is almost the same conclusion as in 31:35-36,
namely, that just as God's covenant with the heavens maintains
them through eternity, so will the house of David endure.

33 : 24   *The two families which the Lord did choose.*   Rashi:
This refers to the families of David and Aaron, i.e., the royalty
and the priesthood.

33 : 25 f.   Repeats the promise of the eternity of the Davidic line
and of the people of Israel, descendants of the patriarchs.

34

THIS CHAPTER resumes the presentation of historical and biographical material, such as were given in chapters 26-29. Jeremiah in-
forms King Zedekiah that the Babylonian armies will surely take
the city and that the king himself will not escape. Then Jeremiah
denounces the people for reenslaving their Hebrew bondsmen,
whom they had previously set free.

Jeremiah

34

1. The word which came unto Jeremiah from the
LORD, when Nebuchadrezzar king of Babylon, and
all his army, and all the kingdoms of the land of his
dominion, and all the peoples, fought against Jerusalem, and against all the cities thereof, saying:

2. Thus saith the LORD, the God of Israel: Go,
and speak to Zedekiah king of Judah, and tell him:
Thus saith the LORD: Behold, I will give this city
into the hand of the king of Babylon, and he shall
burn it with fire; 3. and thou shalt not escape out
of his hand, but shalt surely be taken, and delivered into his hand; and thine eyes shall behold
the eyes of the king of Babylon, and he shall speak
with thee mouth to mouth, and thou shalt go to
Babylon. 4. Yet hear the word of the LORD, O
Zedekiah king of Judah: Thus saith the LORD concerning thee: Thou shalt not die by the sword;

5. thou shalt die in peace; and with the burnings of thy fathers, the former kings that were before thee, so shall they make a burning for thee; and they shall lament thee: 'Ah lord!' for I have spoken the word, saith the LORD.

6. Then Jeremiah the prophet spoke all these words unto Zedekiah king of Judah in Jerusalem,
7. when the king of Babylon's army fought against Jerusalem, and against all the cities of Judah that were left, against Lachish and against Azekah; for these alone remained of the cities of Judah as fortified cities.

8. The word that came unto Jeremiah from the

34 : 5 *Thou shalt die in peace; . . . they make a burning for thee.* According to the Talmud (Avodah Zarah 11a), when a king died they made a bonfire at his funeral of the articles of his personal use, his bed, etc. Others say that they burned great amounts of incense. At all events, this bonfire was part of the solemn and dignified funeral for a king, in contrast to the shameful funeral which his predecessor, Jehoiakim, was to have: "the burial of a donkey." And he was not to be lamented: "Ah my lord" (Jeremiah 22:18 f.).

34 : 8-22 The biblical law (Exodus 21:2) provided that if a Hebrew sold himself as an indentured servant, he could serve only for seven years and then must go free. During the siege, at Zedekiah's command, the people had freed all their Hebrew bondsmen, possibly to help in the siege (so Luzzato to verse 9). Then they reenslaved them, perhaps because Nebuchadnezzar had lifted the siege for a while. For this sin the prophet pronounces their punishment.

34 : 8 *Zedekiah had made a covenant . . . to proclaim liberty.* How could he have done this? Each Hebrew indentured bondsman had his own term and could go free only when *his* seven years were up. How, then, could they all be freed at the same time? Trani said that all Zedekiah meant was that each bondsman was to be freed when his seven years were up. So, too, Rashi. But Luzzato said they could all be freed at once because by this time they had all been compelled to serve much more than seven years.

Jeremiah
34

LORD, after that the king Zedekiah had made a covenant with all the people that were at Jerusalem, to proclaim liberty unto them; 9. that every man should let his man-servant, and every man his maid-servant, being a Hebrew man or a Hebrew woman, go free; that none should make bondmen of them, even of a Jew his brother; 10. and all the princes and all the people hearkened, that had entered into the covenant to let every one his man-servant, and every one his maid-servant, go free, and not to make bondmen of them any more; they hearkened, and let them go; 11. but afterwards they turned, and caused the servants and the handmaids, whom they had let go free, to return, and brought them into subjection for servants and for handmaids; 12. therefore the word of the LORD came to Jeremiah from the LORD, saying:

13. Thus saith the LORD, the God of Israel: I made a covenant with your fathers in the day that I brought them forth out of the land of Egypt, out of the house of bondage, saying: 14. 'At the end of seven years ye shall let go every man his brother that is a Hebrew, that hath been sold unto thee, and hath served thee six years, thou shalt let him go free from thee'; but your fathers hearkened not unto Me, neither inclined their ear. 15. And ye were now turned, and had done that which is right in Mine eyes, in proclaiming liberty every man to his neighbour; and ye had made a covenant before Me in the house whereon My name is called; 16. but ye turned and profaned My name, and

34 : 17   *I proclaim for you a liberty . . . unto the sword.*   I will give the sword complete liberty to work its will against you.

34 : 22   *I will command . . . them to return.*   Evidently the siege had been lifted. The Babylonian armies had marched away in order to reduce the fortresses of Lachish and Azeka (see verse 6).

caused every man his servant, and every man his handmaid, whom ye had let go free at their pleasure, to return; and ye brought them into subjection, to be unto you for servants and for handmaids. 17. Therefore thus saith the LORD: Ye have not hearkened unto Me, to proclaim liberty, every man to his brother, and every man to his neighbour; behold, I proclaim for you a liberty, saith the LORD, unto the sword, unto the pestilence, and unto the famine; and I will make you a horror unto all the kingdoms of the earth. 18. And I will give the men that have transgressed My covenant, that have not performed the words of the covenant which they made before Me, when they cut the calf in twain and passed between the parts thereof; 19. the princes of Judah, and the princes of Jerusalem, the officers, and the priests, and all the people of the land, that passed between the parts of the calf; 20. I will even give them into the hand of their enemies, and into the hand of them that seek their life; and their dead bodies shall be for food unto the fowls of the heaven, and to the beasts of the earth. 21. And Zedekiah king of Judah and his princes will I give into the hand of their enemies, and into the hand of them that seek their life, and into the hand of the king of Babylon's army, that are gone up from you. 22. Behold, I will command, saith the LORD, and cause them to return to this city; and they shall fight against it, and take it, and burn it with fire; and I will make the cities of Judah a desolation, without inhabitant.

In 37:7 ff., another reason is given for the lifting of the siege. Apparently an Egyptian army was approaching, and the Babylonians marched off to meet them. Perhaps it was because the siege had been lifted that the leaders of the people, thinking all danger had now passed, reenslaved their Hebrew bondsmen.

35

A CONTINUATION of the narrative portion of the book, with each narrative used as the basis for a preachment to the people.

Here the tribe of the Rechabites is the theme of Jeremiah's message. The Rechabites, according to some scholars, were descendants of the father-in-law of Moses; but according to Luzzato, they were descendants of the tribe of Judah. They refused to settle down as farmers, remaining nomadic, and they also refrained from drinking wine. Jeremiah brings their leaders into the Temple and offers them wine, but they refuse, saying that they had made a promise to Jonadab, the son of Rechab, their ancestor, never to drink wine.

Thereupon Jeremiah contrasts the loyal obedience of the Rechabites to a promise made in the past with Israel's violation of their covenant with God. The descent of the Rechabites is mentioned in I Chronicles 2:55, and their ancestor, Jonadab ben Rechab, is mentioned as a co-worker with Jehu in destroying the dynasty of Ahab and the worship of Baal (II Kings 10:15 ff.) .

Jeremiah 1. The word which came unto Jeremiah from the
35   LORD in the days of Jehoiakim the son of Josiah,

35 : 1 *The days of Jehoiakim.* The chapters in this book do not follow a chronological order. The events recounted in the preceding chapter took place in the closing days of the siege of Jerusalem. This chapter is dated a number of years earlier.

206

king of Judah, saying: 2. 'Go unto the house of the Rechabites, and speak unto them, and bring them into the house of the LORD, into one of the chambers, and give them wine to drink.' 3. Then I took Jaazaniah the son of Jeremiah, the son of Habazziniah, and his brethren, and all his sons, and the whole house of the Rechabites; 4. and I brought them into the house of the LORD, into the chamber of the sons of Hanan the son of Igdaliah, the man of God, which was by the chamber of the princes, which was above the chamber of Maaseiah the son of Shallum, the keeper of the door; 5. and I set before the sons of the house of the Rechabites goblets full of wine, and cups, and I said unto them: 'Drink ye wine.' 6. But they said: 'We will drink no wine; for Jonadab the son of Rechab our father commanded us, saying: Ye shall drink no wine, neither ye, nor your sons, for ever; 7. neither shall ye build house, nor sow seed, nor plant vineyard, nor have any; but all your days ye shall dwell in tents, that ye may live many days in the land wherein ye sojourn. 8. And we have hearkened to the voice of Jonadab the son of Rechab our father in all that he charged us, to drink no wine all our days, we, our wives, our sons, nor our daughters; 9. nor to build houses for us to dwell in, neither to have vineyard, or field, or seed; 10. but we have dwelt in tents, and have hearkened, and done according to all that Jonadab our father commanded us. 11. But

Jeremiah
35

35 : 2 *The house of the Rechabites.* The household. So in verse 3: "the whole house of the Rechabites." While the Rechabites were generally nomadic, they had moved into Jerusalem to escape the Babylonian army.

35 : 6 *Ye shall drink no wine.* A man who had taken a Nazirite vow was not permitted to drink wine or cut his hair (Numbers 6:1-21). The vow was usually for thirty days, but Samson was a lifelong Nazirite. The Rechabites lived as perpetual Nazirites, at least with regard to abstaining from wine. Some scholars theorize that the Nazirite vow originated with the Rechabites.

it came to pass, when Nebuchadrezzar king of Babylon came up against the land, that we said: Come, and let us go to Jerusalem for fear of the army of the Chaldeans, and for fear of the army of the Arameans; so we dwell at Jerusalem.' 12. Then came the word of the LORD unto Jeremiah, saying: 13 'Thus saith the LORD of hosts, the God of Israel: Go, and say to the men of Judah and the inhabitants of Jerusalem: Will ye not receive instruction to hearken to My words? saith the LORD. 14. The words of Jonadab the son of Rechab, that he commanded his sons, not to drink wine, are performed, and unto this day they drink none, for they hearken to their father's commandment; but I have spoken unto you, speaking betimes and often, and ye have not hearkened unto Me. 15. I have sent also unto you all My servants the prophets, sending them betimes and often, saying: Return ye now every man from his evil way, and amend your doings, and go not after other gods to serve them, and ye shall dwell in the land

35 : 12-17 Jeremiah tells the people of Jerusalem to note how the Rechabites have kept a promise made in ancient times; yet Israel has not kept God's ordinances or observed the covenant.

which I have given to you and to your fathers; but ye have not inclined your ear, nor hearkened unto Me. 16. Because the sons of Jonadab the son of Rechab have performed the commandment of their father which he commanded them, but this people hath not hearkened unto Me; 17. therefore thus saith the LORD, the God of hosts, the God of Israel: Behold, I will bring upon Judah and upon all the inhabitants of Jerusalem all the evil that I have pronounced against them; because I have spoken unto them, but they have not heard, and I have called unto them, but they have not answered.'

18. And unto the house of the Rechabites Jeremiah said: Thus saith the LORD of hosts, the God of Israel: Because ye have hearkened to the commandment of Jonadab your father, and kept all his precepts, and done according unto all that he commanded you; 19. therefore thus saith the LORD of hosts, the God of Israel: There shall not be cut off unto Jonadab the son of Rechab a man to stand before Me for ever.

35 : 18-19   God blesses the Rechabites for their loyalty to the tradition of their fathers.

36

ANOTHER NARRATIVE dating from the reign of Jehoiakim. Jeremiah dictates his sermons to Baruch and tells Baruch to read the scroll of the sermons to the people gathered in the Temple. Baruch does so; and he also reads it to the princes who are so impressed that they inform the king. King Jehoiakim has the scroll read and then burned up. Jeremiah takes another scroll and again dictates all that was in the first scroll, and more. "And there were added besides unto them many like words" (verse 32).

Jeremiah

36

1. And it came to pass in the fourth year of Jehoiakim the son of Josiah, king of Judah, that this word came unto Jeremiah from the LORD, saying: 2. 'Take thee a roll of a book, and write therein all the words that I have spoken unto thee against Israel, and against Judah, and against all the nations, from the day I spoke unto thee, from the days of Josiah, even unto this day. 3. It may be that the house of Judah will hear all the evil which I purpose to do unto them; that they may return every man from his evil way, and I may forgive their iniquity and their sin.'

36 : 2-3   God instructs Jeremiah to record "the words I have spoken to thee against Israel and Judah," the purpose being that the people may yet repent and be forgiven.

4. Then Jeremiah called Baruch the son of Neriah; and Baruch wrote from the mouth of Jeremiah all the words of the LORD, which He had spoken unto him, upon a roll of a book. 5. And Jeremiah commanded Baruch, saying: 'I am detained, I cannot go into the house of the LORD; 6. therefore go thou, and read in the roll, which thou hast written from my mouth, the words of the LORD in the ears of the people in the LORD's house upon a fast-day; and also thou shalt read them in the ears of all Judah that come out of their cities. 7. It may be they will present their supplication before the LORD, and will return every one from his evil way; for great is the anger and the fury that the LORD hath pronounced against this people.' 8. And Baruch the son of Neriah did according to all that Jeremiah the prophet commanded him, reading in the book the words of the LORD in the LORD's house.

9. Now it came to pass in the fifth year of Jehoiakim the son of Josiah, king of Judah, in the ninth month, that they proclaimed a fast before the LORD, all the people in Jerusalem, and all the people that came from the cities of Judah unto Jerusalem. 10. Then did Baruch read in the book

36 : 4-8   Jeremiah dictates the scroll and instructs Baruch to read it to the people when they gather in the Temple. Baruch does so.

36 : 5   *I am detained.*   The Targum translates: I cannot go to the Temple. Rashi says that Jehoiakim had had Jeremiah imprisoned.

36 : 6   *Upon a fast-day.*   When the people of Jerusalem and the countryside would gather in the Temple: "Judah that come out of their cities."

36 : 9-19   Baruch reads the scroll to the people. The princes then tell Baruch to bring the scroll and read it to them. When they heard the dire prophecies, they "turned in fear to one another" (verse 16). They said that they must show the scroll to the king. Meantime, anticipating the king's wrath, they advised Baruch and Jeremiah to go into hiding.

the words of Jeremiah in the house of the LORD, in the chamber of Gemariah the son of Shaphan the scribe, in the upper court, at the entry of the new gate of the LORD's house, in the ears of all the people. 11. And when Micaiah the son of Gemariah, the son of Shaphan, had heard out of the book all the words of the LORD, 12. he went down into the king's house, into the scribe's chamber; and, lo, all the princes sat there, even Elishama the scribe, and Delaiah the son of Shemaiah, and Elnathan the son of Achbor, and Gemariah the son of Shaphan, and Zedekiah the son of Hananiah, and all the princes. 13. Then Micaiah declared unto them all the words that he had heard, when Baruch read the book in the ears of the people. 14. Therefore all the princes sent Jehudi the son of Nethaniah, the son of Shelemiah, the son of Cushi, unto Baruch, saying: 'Take in thy hand the roll wherein thou hast read in the ears of the people, and come.' So Baruch the son of Neriah took the roll in his hand, and came unto them. 15. And they said unto him: 'Sit down now, and read it in our ears.' So Baruch read it in their ears. 16. Now it came to pass, when they had heard all the words, they turned in fear one toward another, and said unto Baruch: 'We will surely tell the king of all these words.' 17. And they asked Baruch, saying: 'Tell us now: How didst thou write all these words at his mouth?' 18. Then Baruch answered them: 'He

36 : 17-18 *How didst thou write all these words . . . ? Baruch answered . . . he pronounced all these words unto me.* Why should the princes care to know just how the dictation was carried out? Abarbanel gives the following explanation. They asked Baruch: Did Jeremiah simply suggest the general thoughts of these prophecies, and did you then work out the wording yourself? To this Baruch answered: No, I took it down from his dictation word by word. (The princes then realized that these words were not the words of Baruch but the words of Jeremiah himself and thus were genuine prophecies.)

pronounced all these words unto me with his mouth, and I wrote them with ink in the book.' 19. Then said the princes unto Baruch: 'Go, hide thee, thou and Jeremiah; and let no man know where ye are.' 20. And they went in to the king into the court; but they had deposited the roll in the chamber of Elishama the scribe; and they told all the words in the ears of the king. 21. So the king sent Jehudi to fetch the roll; and he took it out of the chamber of Elishama the scribe. And Jehudi read it in the ears of the king, and in the ears of all the princes that stood beside the king. 22. Now the king was sitting in the winter-house in the ninth month; and the brazier was burning before him. 23. And it came to pass, when Jehudi had read three or four columns, that he cut it with the penknife, and cast it into the fire that was in the brazier, until all the roll was consumed in the fire that was in the brazier. 24. Yet they were not afraid, nor rent their garments, neither the king, nor any of his servants that heard all these words. 25. Moreover Elnathan and Delaiah and Gemariah had entreated the king not to burn the roll; but he would not hear them. 26. And the king commanded Jerahmeel the king's son, and Seraiah the son of Azriel, and Shelemiah the son of Abdeel, to take Baruch the scribe and Jeremiah the prophet; but the LORD hid them.

27. Then the word of the LORD came to Jeremiah, after that the king had burned the roll, and the words which Baruch wrote at the mouth of Jeremiah, saying: 28 'Take thee again another roll,

36 : 20-26   Jehoiakim hears the scroll read and has it burned. He then orders the arrest of Baruch and Jeremiah. But "the Lord hid them" (verse 26).

36 : 27-31   Doom is pronounced against Jehoiakim, with the additional disgrace that his body will not even be brought to decent burial. The same imprecation was given more elaborately in 22:18-19.

Jeremiah
36

and write in it all the former words that were in the first roll, which Jehoiakim the king of Judah hath burned. 29. And concerning Jehoiakim king of Judah thou shalt say: Thus saith the LORD: Thou hast burned this roll, saying: Why hast thou written therein, saying: The king of Babylon shall certainly come and destroy this land, and shall cause to cease from thence man and beast? 30. Therefore thus saith the LORD concerning Jehoiakim king of Judah: He shall have none to sit upon the throne of David; and his dead body shall be cast out in the day to the heat, and in the night to the frost. 31. And I will visit upon him and his seed and his servants their iniquity; and I will bring upon them, and upon the inhabitants of Jerusalem, and upon the men of Judah, all the evil that I have pronounced against them, but they hearkened not.'

32. Then took Jeremiah another roll, and gave it to Baruch the scribe, the son of Neriah; who wrote therein from the mouth of Jeremiah all the words of the book which Jehoiakim king of Judah had burned in the fire; and there were added besides unto them many like words.

36 : 32 Jeremiah dictates another scroll and adds to it more than was in the first scroll.

37

THE NARRATIVE now moves forward to the reign of Zedekiah, the last king of Judah. Zedekiah asks Jeremiah to pray for the nation, but Jeremiah repeats his somber predictions. Meanwhile the Babylonians (Chaldeans) have temporarily lifted the siege. Taking advantage of that fact, Jeremiah sets out to visit his native town. He is accused of deserting to the Chaldeans and put into a dungeon. The king sends for him. Jeremiah pleads with the king to free him from the dungeon. Zedekiah does so and has him confined in the court of the palace guards and provides food for him.

1. And Zedekiah the son of Josiah reigned as king, instead of Coniah the son of Jehoiakim, whom Nebuchadrezzar king of Babylon made king in the land of Judah. 2. But neither he, nor his servants, nor the people of the land, did hearken unto the words of the LORD, which He spoke by the prophet Jeremiah.

Jeremiah

37

3. And Zedekiah the king sent Jehucal the son of Shelemiah, and Zephaniah the son of Maaseiah the priest, to the prophet Jeremiah, saying: 'Pray now unto the LORD our God for us.' 4. Now Jere-

37 : 1-15   The king asks Jeremiah to pray for him and the people, but Jeremiah pronounces the doom that is to come. Jeremiah is accused of desertion. He denies it but is put into prison.

Jeremiah
37

miah came in and went out among the people; for they had not put him into prison. 5. And Pharaoh's army was come forth out of Egypt; and when the Chaldeans that besieged Jerusalem heard tidings of them, they broke up from Jerusalem. 6. Then came the word of the LORD unto the prophet Jeremiah, saying: 7. 'Thus saith the LORD, the God of Israel: Thus shall ye say to the king of Judah, that sent you unto Me to inquire of Me: Behold, Pharaoh's army, which is come forth to help you, shall return to Egypt into their own land. 8. And the Chaldeans shall return, and fight against this city; and they shall take it, and burn it with fire. 9. Thus saith the LORD: Deceive not yourselves, saying: The Chaldeans shall surely depart from us; for they shall not depart. 10. For though ye had smitten the whole army of the Chaldeans that fight against you, and there remained but wounded men among them, yet would they rise up every man in his tent, and burn this city with fire.'

11. And it came to pass, that when the army of the Chaldeans was broken up from Jerusalem for fear of Pharaoh's army, 12. then Jeremiah went forth out of Jerusalem to go into the land of Benjamin, to receive his portion there, in the midst of the people. 13. And when he was in the gate of Benjamin, a captain of the ward was there, whose name was Irijah, the son of Shelemiah, the son of Hananiah; and he laid hold on Jeremiah the prophet, saying: 'Thou fallest away to the Chaldeans.' 14. Then said Jeremiah: 'It is false; I fall

37 : 12 *To receive his portion there, in the midst of the people.* This translation follows the Targum, but Kimchi (and Luzzato after him) says the verse means that Jeremiah went to hide himself among his own kinfolk.

37 : 18-19 *Wherein have I sinned against thee . . . ? Where . . . are your prophets?* I am accused of discouraging the people in their struggle against the Chaldeans. It is true that I have predicted an unhappy future for the city, but wherein is this a sin?

not away to the Chaldeans'; but he hearkened not to him; so Irijah laid hold on Jeremiah, and brought him to the princes. 15. And the princes were wroth with Jeremiah, and smote him, and put him in prison in the house of Jonathan the scribe; for they had made that the prison.

16. When Jeremiah was come into the dungeon-house, and into the cells, and Jeremiah had remained there many days; 17. then Zedekiah the king sent, and fetched him; and the king asked him secretly in his house, and said: 'Is there any word from the LORD?' And Jeremiah said: 'There is.' He said also: 'Thou shalt be delivered into the hand of the king of Babylon.' 18. Moreover Jeremiah said unto king Zedekiah: 'Wherein have I sinned against thee, or against thy servants, or against this people, that ye have put me in prison? 19. Where now are your prophets that prophesied unto you, saying: The king of Babylon shall not come against you, nor against this land? 20. And now hear, I pray thee, O my lord the king; let my supplication, I pray thee, be presented before thee; that thou cause me not to return to the house of Jonathan the scribe, lest I die there.' 21. Then Zedekiah the king commanded, and they committed Jeremiah into the court of the guard, and they gave him daily a loaf of bread out of the bakers' street, until all the bread in the city was spent. Thus Jeremiah remained in the court of the guard.

You have other prophets who have predicted peace for you. But here are the Chaldeans, ready to capture the city. My unhappy prophecies are not a sin because I have spoken only what God has told me to say. This is the same defense that Jeremiah makes in 26: 12 ff., when, after his Temple sermon, he is accused of having made a treasonable utterance and therefore incurs the penalty of death. But there, too, he answers: I have not committed a sin or a crime. What I have said is exactly what God told me to say.

38

THIS CHAPTER deals with the final days of the city of Jerusalem before its fall to the Babylonian besiegers. Jeremiah has been thrown into a muddy pit. He is prevented from perishing there when Ebed Melech, an Ethiopian officer, gets permission from King Zedekiah to rescue him. Then follows one of the last interviews between prophet and king.

Jeremiah

38

1. And Shephatiah the son of Mattan, and Gedaliah the son of Pashhur, and Jucal the son of Shelemiah, and Pashhur the son of Malchiah, heard the words that Jeremiah spoke unto all the people, saying: 2 'Thus saith the LORD: He that remaineth in this city shall die by the sword, by the famine, and by the pestilence; but he that goeth forth to the Chaldeans shall live, and his life shall be unto him for a prey, and he shall live. 3. Thus saith the

38 : 1-6   The princes charge that Jeremiah, by saying that resistance is hopeless, is undermining the fighting spirit of the people. The king permits them to imprison the prophet, and they throw him into the muddy pit. In chapter 26, when the Temple was the issue, the priests accused Jeremiah and the princes defended him. Here where the question at issue is the fighting spirit of the soldiers, the princes attack Jeremiah and no one defends him.

LORD: This city shall surely be given into the land of the army of the king of Babylon, and he shall take it.' 4. Then the princes said unto the king: 'Let this man, we pray thee, be put to death; forasmuch as he weakeneth the hands of the men of war that remain in this city, and the hands of all the people, in speaking such words unto them; for this man seeketh not the welfare of this people, but the hurt.' 5. Then Zedekiah the king said: 'Behold, he is in your hand; for the king is not he that can do any thing against you.' 6. Then took they Jeremiah, and cast him into the pit of Malchiah the king's son, that was in the court of the guard; and they let down Jeremiah with cords. And in the pit there was no water, but mire; and Jeremiah sank in the mire.

7. Now when Ebed-melech the Ethiopian, an officer, who was in the king's house, heard that they had put Jeremiah in the pit; the king then sitting in the gate of Benjamin; 8. Ebed-melech went forth out of the king's house, and spoke to the king, saying: 9. 'My lord the king, these men have done evil in all that they have done to Jeremiah the prophet, whom they have cast into the pit; and he is like to die in the place where he is because of the famine; for there is no more bread in the city.' 10. Then the king commanded Ebed-melech the Ethiopian, saying: 'Take from hence thirty men with thee, and take up Jeremiah the prophet out of the pit, before he die.' 11. So Ebed-melech took

38 : 5 *For the king is not he that can do any thing.* The king is helpless against you in this matter at this time.

38 : 7-12 Ebed Melech, an Ethiopian officer in Zedekiah's service, tells the king that Jeremiah will starve to death in the pit if nothing is done to help him. The king orders Ebed Melech to rescue Jeremiah.

38 : 11 *Under the treasury . . . clouts and . . . rags.* Apparently old, worn-out objects were kept in the cellar under the royal treasury. The commentators vary in their rendering of the words

Jeremiah
38

the men with him, and went into the house of the king under the treasury, and took thence worn clouts and worn rags, and let them down by cords into the pit to Jeremiah. 12. And Ebed-melech the Ethiopian said unto Jeremiah: 'Put now these worn clouts and rags under thine armholes under the cords.' And Jeremiah did so. 13. So they drew up Jeremiah with the cords, and took him up out of the pit; and Jeremiah remained in the court of the guard.

14. Then Zedekiah the king sent, and took Jeremiah the prophet unto him into the third entry that was in the house of the LORD; and the king said unto Jeremiah: 'I will ask thee a thing; hide nothing from me.' 15. Then Jeremiah said unto Zedekiah: 'If I declare it unto thee, wilt thou not surely put me to death? and if I give thee counsel, thou wilt not hearken unto me.' 16. So Zedekiah the king swore secretly unto Jeremiah, saying: 'As the LORD liveth, that made us this soul, I will not put thee to death, neither will I give thee into the hand of these men that seek thy life.'

17. Then said Jeremiah unto Zedekiah: 'Thus saith the LORD, the God of hosts, the God of Israel: If thou wilt go forth unto the king of Babylon's princes, then thy soul shall live, and this city shall not be burned with fire; and thou shalt live, thou, and thy house; 18. but if thou wilt not go forth to

translated here as "rags and clouts." In general the phrase seems to mean worn-out clothes and old ropes.

38 : 14-23 Zedekiah sends for Jeremiah and asks him about the future of the city; Jeremiah tells the king that Jerusalem will be taken and he will be made captive. The only possible way in which the city might be saved would be if the king surrenders to the Chaldeans. Zedekiah says if he does that, he would have to endure the abuse of those Jews who have already gone over to the camp of the Chaldeans. Jeremiah then answers: If you do not surrender, you will be captured, and the women will sing songs of derision against you, and the city will be burned.

the king of Babylon's princes, then shall this city be given into the hand of the Chaldeans, and they shall burn it with fire, and thou shalt not escape out of their hand.' 19. And Zedekiah the king said unto Jeremiah: 'I am afraid of the Jews that are fallen away to the Chaldeans, lest they deliver me into their hand, and they mock me.' 20. But Jeremiah said: 'They shall not deliver thee. Hearken, I beseech thee, to the voice of the LORD, in that which I speak unto thee; so it shall be well with thee, and thy soul shall live. 21. But if thou refuse to go forth, this is the word that the LORD hath shown me: 22. Behold, all the women that are left in the king of Judah's house shall be brought forth to the king of Babylon's princes, and those women shall say:

Thy familiar friends have set thee on,
And have prevailed over thee;
Thy feet are sunk in the mire,
And they are turned away back.

23. And they shall bring out all thy wives and thy children to the Chaldeans; and thou shalt not escape out of their hand, but shalt be taken by the hand of the king of Babylon; and thou shalt cause this city to be burned with fire.'

24. Then said Zedekiah unto Jeremiah: 'Let no man know of these words, and thou shalt not die. 25. But if the princes hear that I have talked with thee, and they come unto thee, and say unto thee:

38 : 22 *Thy familiar friends have set thee on.* Thy friends have led thee astray. Almost the exact words are used in Obadiah 7. Evidently the phrase must have been a familiar taunt. The commentators explain it to mean: Your false prophets kept on telling you that the Chaldeans would be defeated. See now how they have deceived you, now that "thy feet are sunk in the mire" (verse 22).

38 : 24-28 Zedekiah warns Jeremiah not to repeat this unhappy conversation to the princes, for in their frustration they would put him (Jeremiah) to death.

Jeremiah

38

Declare unto us now what thou hast said unto the king; hide it not from us, and we will not put thee to death; also what the king said unto thee; 26. then thou shalt say unto them: I presented my supplication before the king, that he would not cause me to return to Jonathan's house, to die there.' 27. Then came all the princes unto Jeremiah, and asked him; and he told them according to all these words that the king had commanded. So they left off speaking with him; for the matter was not reported. 28. So Jeremiah abode in the court of the guard until the day that Jerusalem was taken.

38 : 27 *They left off speaking with him . . . the matter was not reported.* Jeremiah is careful not to report to the princes the actual contents of his conversation with Zedekiah. He says only that he was pleading with the king to set him free. So the princes lost interest in the matter: "They left off speaking with him" (ibid.).

39

THIS CHAPTER deals with the fall of Jerusalem.

And it came to pass, when Jerusalem was taken— 1. in the ninth year of Zedekiah king of Judah, in the tenth month, came Nebuchadrezzar king of Babylon and all his army against Jerusalem, and besieged it; 2. in the eleventh year of Zedekiah, in the fourth month, the ninth day of the month, a breach was made in the city—3. that all the princes of the king of Babylon came in, and sat in the middle gate, even Nergal-sarezer, Samgar-nebo, Sarsechim ᵃRab-saris, Nergal-sarezer ᵃRab-mag, with all the residue of the princes of the king of Babylon. 4. And it came to pass, that when Zedekiah the king of Judah and all the men of war saw them, then they fled, and went forth out of the city by night, by the way of the king's garden, by the gate betwixt the two walls; and he went out

39 : 1-7 The Chaldeans breach the walls. Zedekiah flees. He is overtaken, blinded, and carried away captive to Babylon.

39 : 1 *Came Nebuchadnezzar . . . and all his army.* The siege was temporarily lifted when the Babylonians marched away from Jerusalem to confront the Egyptian army (37:5), but now the final siege has begun.

ᵃ Titles of officers.

the way of the Arabah. 5. But the army of the Chaldeans pursued after them, and overtook Zedekiah in the plains of Jericho; and when they had taken him, they brought him up to Nebuchadrezzar king of Babylon to Riblah in the land of Hamath, and he gave judgment upon him. 6. Then the king of Babylon slew the sons of Zedekiah in Riblah before his eyes; also the king of Babylon slew all the nobles of Judah. 7. Moreover he put out Zedekiah's eyes, and bound him in fetters, to carry him to Babylon. 8. And the Chaldeans burned the king's house, and the house of the people, with fire, and broke down the walls of Jerusalem. 9. Then Nebuzaradan the captain of the guard carried away captive into Babylon the remnant of the people that remained in the city, the deserters also, that fell away to him, with the rest of the people that remained. 10. But Nebuzaradan the captain of the guard left of the poor of the people, that had nothing, in the land of Judah, and gave them vineyards and fields in that day. 11. Now Nebuchadrezzar king of Babylon gave charge concerning Jeremiah to Nebuzaradan the captain of

39 : 5 *He gave judgment.*   The Targum translates: He spoke words of law. But what possible law or justice could give Nebuchadnezzar the legal right to blind Zedekiah and lead him off in chains? Rashi and Kimchi answer this question as follows: It was indeed a matter of law. It concerned a broken oath. Nebuchadnezzar himself had put Zedekiah on the throne, and Zedekiah swore that he would be a vassal of Nebuchadnezzar, but now he had violated his oath and rebelled.

39 : 8-10 The Chaldeans burn Jerusalem and carry the people captive to Babylon, leaving only "the poor of the people, that had nothing" (verse 10).

39 : 8 *The Chaldeans burned . . . the house of the people.*   This sounds as if there might have been a sort of town hall for popular assembly. And in fact the Talmud (Megilla 27a) says it was a *bet haknesset,* a synagogue. But Kimchi explains the phrase simply; he says that "the house of the people" was simply a generalized term for the houses in which people lived. In fact, in

the guard, saying: 12. 'Take him, and look well to him, and do him no harm; but do unto him even as he shall say unto thee.' 13. So Nebuzaradan the captain of the guard sent, and Nebushazban Rab-saris, and Nergal-sarezer Rab-mag, and all the chief officers of the king of Babylon; 14. they sent, and took Jeremiah out of the court of the guard, and committed him unto Gedaliah the son of Ahikam, the son of Shaphan, that he should carry him home; so he dwelt among the people.

15. Now the word of the LORD came unto Jeremiah, while he was shut up in the court of the guard, saying: 16. 'Go, and speak to Ebed-melech the Ethiopian, saying: Thus saith the LORD of hosts, the God of Israel: Behold, I will bring My words upon this city for evil, and not for good; and they shall be accomplished before thee in that day. 17. But I will deliver thee in that day, saith the LORD; and thou shalt not be given into the hand of the men of whom thou art afraid. 18. For I will surely deliver thee, and thou shalt not fall by the sword, but thy life shall be for a prey unto thee; because thou hast put thy trust in Me, saith the LORD.'

the account given in II Kings 25:9, instead of the words "the house of the people," it says "the houses of Jerusalem."

39 : 11-14   Nebuchadnezzar tells his general to protect Jeremiah from harm, so Jeremiah is put into the care of Gedaliah ben Ahikam, who is to be the viceroy.

39 : 14   *He should carry him home.*   Gedaliah, who lived in Mizpah, should take Jeremiah away from the burning city to his home (Luzzato).

39 : 15-18   This goes back to the time just before the fall of the city when Jeremiah was still in the prison of the palace guard. He utters a blessing and a promise of safety to Ebed Melech, the Ethiopian.

39 : 16   *Go, and speak to Ebed Melech.*   Since Jeremiah was now confined in the court of the palace guard, Ebed Melech could visit him often, and Jeremiah was able to give him assurances of his safe future.

40

THE EVENTS immediately following the fall of the city. Gedaliah, appointed to be the king's representative, is told that Baalis, the king of the Ammonites, is sending Ishmael ben Nethaniah to assassinate him. Gedaliah refuses to believe it.

Jeremiah

40

1. The word which came to Jeremiah from the LORD, after that Nebuzaradan the captain of the guard had let him go from Ramah, when he had taken him being bound in chains among all the captives of Jerusalem and Judah, that were carried away cap-

40 : 1-6   Jeremiah is offered the choice of being well treated in Babylon or of remaining here in the land.

40 : 1   *Being bound in chains among all the captives.*   This description contradicts the account in the previous chapter, where Nebuchadnezzar gave strict orders that Jeremiah be protected and provided with sustenance. The Midrash (Pesikta d'Rav Kahana 13:54) says that when Jeremiah saw young Jews bound in chains, he voluntarily joined them and had himself shackled. Luzzato says the explanation must be that some Babylonian officers, ignorant of the royal orders protecting Jeremiah, put him in chains with the other people. Then, possibly when the royal order came through, the captain of the guard said to Jeremiah: "I loose thee this day from the chains which are upon thy hand" (verse 4).

226

tive unto Babylon. 2. And the captain of the guard took Jeremiah, and said unto him: 'The LORD thy God pronounced this evil upon this place; 3. and the LORD hath brought it, and done according as He spoke; because ye have sinned against the LORD, and have not hearkened to His voice, therefore this thing is come upon you. 4. And now, behold, I loose thee this day from the chains which are upon thy hand. If it seem good unto thee to come with me into Babylon, come, and I will look well unto thee; but if it seem ill unto thee to come with me into Babylon, forbear; behold, all the land is before thee; whither it seemeth good and right unto thee to go, thither go.—5. Yet he would not go back.—Go back then to Gedaliah the son of Anikam, the son of Shaphan, whom the king of Babylon hath made governor over the cities of Judah, and dwell with him among the people; or go wheresoever it seemeth right unto thee to go.' So the captain of the guard gave him an allowance and a present, and let him go. 6. Then went Jeremiah unto Gedaliah the son of Ahikam to Mizpah, and dwelt with him among the people that were left in the land.

7. Now when all the captains of the forces that

Jeremiah

40

40 : 5 *Yet he would not go back . . . Go back then.*   A difficult verse. While the commentators agree that the words "Yet he would not go back" refer to Jeremiah, they disagree as to *why* he would not go back. They also disagree as to who said the words "Go back then." Rashi says that Jeremiah was uncertain whether to go back to the people left in Judah or to go on to Babylon to join the main captivity. But God said to him: Go back to Gedaliah here in Judah. Trani says it is the officer who said to Jeremiah: Go back (to Gedaliah). Ehrlich (also Tur-Sinai) emends the text to read as follows: "Yet he did not *answer*. Thereupon the officers said to him 'Go back.'"

40 : 7 *Captains of the forces that were in the fields.*   The scattered companies of the Judean army. Their officers decided to join Gedaliah. Also, many Jews who had fled to Moab and Edom came back to be with Gedaliah (verse 11).

227

were in the fields, even they and their men, heard that the king of Babylon had made Gedaliah the son of Ahikam governor in the land, and had committed unto him men, and women, and children, and of the poorest of the land, of them that were not carried away captive to Babylon; 8. then they came to Gedaliah to Mizpah, even Ishmael the son of Nethaniah, and Johanan and Jonathan the sons of Kareah, and Seraiah the son of Tanhumeth, and the sons of Ephai the Netophathite, and Jezeniah the son of the Maacathite, they and their men. 9. And Gedaliah the son of Ahikam the son of Shaphan swore unto them and to their men, saying: 'Fear not to serve the Chaldeans; dwell in the land, and serve the king of Babylon, and it shall be well with you. 10. As for me, behold, I will dwell at Mizpah, to stand before the Chaldeans that may come unto us; but ye, gather ye wine and summer fruits and oil, and put them in your vessels, and dwell in your cities that ye have taken.' 11. Likewise when all the Jews that were in Moab, and among the children of Ammon, and in Edom, and that were in all the countries, heard that the

40 : 10   *To stand before the Chaldeans.*   To be your contact with the emissaries of the king of Babylon.

king of Babylon had left a remnant of Judah, and
that he had set over them Gedaliah the son of
Ahikam, the son of Shaphan; 12. then all the Jews
returned out of all places whither they were driven,
and came to the land of Judah, to Gedaliah, unto
Mizpah, and gathered wine and summer fruits in
great abundance.

13. Moreover Johanan the son of Kareah, and
all the captains of the forces that were in the fields,
came to Gedaliah to Mizpah, 14. and said unto
him: 'Dost thou know that Baalis the king of the
children of Ammon hath sent Ishmael the son of
Nethaniah to take thy life?' But Gedaliah the son
of Ahikam believed them not. 15. Then Johanan
the son of Kareah spoke of Gedaliah in Mizpah
secretly, saying: 'Let me go, I pray thee, and I will
slay Ishmael the son of Nethaniah, and no man
shall know it; wherefore should he take thy life,
that all the Jews that are gathered unto thee should
be scattered, and the remnant of Judah perish?'
16. But Gedaliah the son of Ahikam said unto
Johanan the son of Kareah: 'Thou shalt not do
this thing; for thou speakest falsely of Ishmael.'

40 : 13-16   Gedaliah is told of Ishmael ben Nethaniah's conspiracy
to assassinate him, but he refuses to believe that Ishmael would
be capable of such treachery.

41

THE EVENTS following the fall of Jerusalem. Gedaliah, appointed by the Chaldeans to govern the people, is assassinated by Ishmael ben Nethaniah. Then Ishmael, pursued by Jochanan ben Kareah, flees to the land of the Ammonites.

Jeremiah

41

1. Now it came to pass in the seventh month, that Ishmael the son of Nethaniah, the son of Elishama, of the seed royal, and one of the chief officers of the king, and ten men with him, came unto Gedaliah the son of Ahikam to Mizpah; and there they did eat bread together in Mizpah. 2. Then arose Ishmael the son of Nethaniah, and the ten men that were with him, and smote Gedaliah the son of Ahikam the son of Shaphan with the sword, and slew him, whom the king of Babylon had made

41 : 1-10 Ishmael, having slain Gedaliah, plans to take the remnants of the people into captivity in the land of Ammon.

41 : 1 *The seventh month.* Kimchi concludes that the assassination took place on the day of the New Year, but when the fast of Gedaliah was ordained in memory of Gedaliah (Rosh Hashonah 18b), it was postponed to the third of Tishri because of the holiday. This is the fast of the seventh month referred to in Zechariah 8:19.

governor over the land. 3. Ishmael also slew all the Jews that were with him, even with Gedaliah, at Mizpah, and the Chaldeans that were found there, even the men of war.

4. And it came to pass the second day after he had slain Gedaliah, and no man knew it, 5. that there came certain men from Shechem, from Shiloh, and from Samaria, even fourscore men, having their beards shaven and their clothes rent, and having cut themselves, with meal-offerings and frankincense in their hand to bring them to the house of the LORD. 6. And Ishmael the son of Nethaniah went forth from Mizpah to meet them, weeping all along as he went; and it came to pass, as he met them, he said unto them: 'Come to Gedaliah the son of Ahikam.' 7. And it was so, when they came into the midst of the city, that Ishmael the son of Nethaniah slew them, and cast them into the midst of the pit, he, and the men that were with him. 8. But ten men were found among them that said unto Ishmael: 'Slay us not; for we have stores hidden in the field, of wheat,

41 : 5 *Men from Shechem . . . Samaria . . . their clothes rent, and . . . with meal-offerings.*   If these pilgrims had their garments torn, etc., as a mark of mourning for the destruction of the Temple (see Moed Katan 26a), then why were they bringing offerings "to bring to the house of the Lord" (verse 5)? Kimchi solves the apparent contradiction, saying that when they started out from the north, they had not yet heard that the Temple was destroyed and so they brought their offerings. On the way south they heard that the Temple was destroyed and tore their garments as a mark of mourning. But Abarbanel (cited by Luzzato) says that this explanation is impossible. The Temple was destroyed on the ninth of Av, virtually two months before this event, which took place on the New Year. The whole land, even the regions furthest north, must have known by then that the Temple was destroyed. But, he says, although they were mourning for the Temple, they nevertheless brought meal-offerings and frankincense to offer within the ruins of the Temple.

Jeremiah

41

and of barley, and of oil, and of honey.' So he forbore, and slew them not among their brethren. 9. Now the pit wherein Ishmael cast all the dead bodies of the men whom he had slain by the side of Gedaliah was that which Asa the king had made for fear of Baasa king of Israel; the same Ishmael the son of Nethaniah filled with them that were slain. 10. Then Ishmael carried away captive all the residue of the people that were in Mizpah, even the king's daughters, and all the people that remained in Mizpah, whom Nebuzaradan the captain of the guard had committed to Gedaliah the son of Ahikam; Ishmael the son of Nethaniah carried them away captive, and departed to go over to the children of Ammon.

11. But when Johanan the son of Kareah, and all the captains of the forces that were with him, heard of all the evil that Ishmael the son of Nethaniah had done, 12. then they took all the men, and went to fight with Ishmael the son of Nethaniah, and found him by the great waters that are in

41 : 9 *Which Asa the king made for fear of Baasa king of Israel.* The Targum explains that this pit was made (perhaps for storage of food) when Baasa, the king of Israel, besieged Asa, the king of Judah.

41 : 10 *To go over to the children of Ammon.* It was Baalis, the king of Ammon, who had sent Ishmael to murder Gedaliah (40: 14). So Ishmael was now returning to the safety of the land of Ammon.

Gibeon. 13. Now it came to pass, that when all the people that were with Ishmael saw Johanan the son of Kareah, and all the captains of the forces that were with him, then they were glad. 14. So all the people that Ishmael had carried away captive from Mizpah cast about and returned, and went unto Johanan the son of Kareah. 15. But Ishmael the son of Nethaniah escaped from Johanan with eight men, and went to the children of Ammon.

16. Then took Johanan the son of Kareah, and all the captains of the forces that were with him, all the remnant of the people whom he had recovered from Ishmael the son of Nethaniah, from Mizpah, after that he had slain Gedaliah the son of Ahikam, the men, even the men of war, and the women, and the children, and the officers, whom he had brought back from Gibeon; 17. and they departed, and dwelt in Geruth Chimham, which is by Beth-lehem, to go to enter into Egypt, 18. because of the Chaldeans; for they were afraid of them, because Ishmael the son of Nethaniah had slain Gedaliah the son of Ahikam, whom the king of Babylon made governor over the land.

41 : 11-18   Jochanan ben Kareah defeats Ishmael and takes the remnants of the people with him southward toward Egypt.

41 : 18   *For they were afraid of them.*   They were afraid of what the Chaldeans might do because of the murder of Gedaliah, their representative. Even though they were not the ones guilty of the murder, they thought it safer to leave the country.

42

THE EVENTS following the assassination of Gedaliah. Johanan ben Kareah asks Jeremiah to inquire of God what the people now should do. God's answer: Do not go down to Egypt. If you do, the sword of the Chaldeans, from which you think you are running away, will pursue you there (verse 16) and you will perish in Egypt.

Jeremiah

42

1. Then all the captains of the forces, and Johanan the son of Kareah, and Jezaniah the son of Hoshaiah, and all the people from the least even unto the greatest, came near, 2. and said unto Jeremiah the prophet: 'Let, we pray thee, our supplication be accepted before thee, and pray for us unto the LORD thy God, even for all this remnant; for we are left but a few of many, as thine eyes do behold us; 3. that the LORD thy God may tell us the way wherein we should walk, and the thing that we should do.' 4. Then Jeremiah the prophet said unto them: 'I have heard you; behold, I will pray unto the LORD your God according to your words; and it shall come to pass, that whatsoever thing the LORD shall answer you, I will declare it unto you; I will keep nothing back from you.' 5. Then they said to Jeremiah: 'The LORD be a true and faithful witness against us, if we do not even according to all the word wherewith the LORD thy God shall

send thee to us. 6. Whether it be good, or whether it be evil, we will hearken to the voice of the LORD our God, to whom we send thee that it may be well with us, when we hearken to the voice of the LORD our God.'

7. And it came to pass after ten days, that the word of the LORD came unto Jeremiah. 8. Then called he Johanan the son of Kareah, and all the captains of the forces that were with him, and all the people from the least even to the greatest, 9. and said unto them: 'Thus saith the LORD, the God of Israel, unto whom ye sent me to present your supplication before Him: 10. If ye will still abide in this land, then will I build you, and not pull you down, and I will plant you, and not pluck you up; for I repent Me of the evil that I have done unto you. 11. Be not afraid of the king of Babylon, of whom ye are afraid; be not afraid of him, saith the LORD; for I am with you to save you, and to deliver you from his hand. 12. And I will grant you compassion, that he may have compassion upon you, and cause you to return to your own land. 13. But if ye say: We will not abide in this land; so that ye hearken not to the voice of the LORD your God; 14. saying: No; but we will go into the land of Egypt, where we shall see no war, nor hear the sound of the horn, nor have hunger of bread; and there will we abide; 15. now therefore hear ye the word of the LORD, O remnant of Judah: Thus saith the LORD of hosts, the God of Israel: If ye wholly set your faces to enter into Egypt, and go to sojourn there; 16. then it shall come to pass, that the sword, which ye fear, shall overtake you there in the land of Egypt, and the famine, whereof ye are afraid, shall follow hard after you there in Egypt; and there ye shall die. 17. So shall it be with all the men that set their faces to go into Egypt to sojourn there; they shall die by the sword, by the famine, and by the pestilence; and none of them shall remain or escape from the evil that I

Jeremiah
42

will bring upon them. 18. For thus saith the LORD of hosts, the God of Israel: As Mine anger and My fury hath been poured forth upon the inhabitants of Jerusalem, so shall My fury be poured forth upon you, when ye shall enter into Egypt; and ye shall be an execration, and an astonishment, and a curse, and a reproach; and ye shall see this place no more. 19. The LORD hath spoken concerning you, O remnant of Judah: Go ye not into Egypt; know certainly that I have forewarned you this day. 20. For ye have dealt deceitfully against your own souls; for ye sent me unto the LORD your God, saying: Pray for us unto the LORD our God; and according unto all that the LORD our God shall say, so declare unto us, and we will do it; 21. and I have this day declared it to you; but ye have not hearkened to the voice of the LORD your God in any thing for which He hath sent me unto you. 22. Now therefore know certainly that ye shall die by the sword, by the famine, and by the pestilence, in the place whither ye desire to go to sojourn there.'

42 : 20 *For ye have dealt deceitfully against your own souls.* Jeremiah says to them: Even though you promised to do whatever God would tell you, nevertheless you have already made up your mind that whatever God might say, you will go down to Egypt. You have deceived me and you have done great harm to yourselves by your deceit.

43

CONTINUATION OF the events following the assassination of Gedaliah. The people, led by Azariah and Johanan ("the proud men," verse 2), deny that the command not to go down to Egypt is truly the word of God. They insist that Jeremiah has been influenced by Baruch ben Neriah, who wants them to go to Babylon instead. So the people go down to Egypt, taking Jeremiah and Baruch with them. Then follows the pronouncement of doom by Jeremiah against the land of Egypt.

1. And it came to pass, that when Jeremiah had made an end of speaking unto all the people all the words of the LORD their God, wherewith the LORD their God had sent him to them, even all these words. 2. then spoke Azariah the son of Hoshaiah, and Johanan the son of Kareah, and all the proud men, saying unto Jeremiah: 'Thou speakest falsely; the LORD our God hath not sent thee to say: Ye shall not go into Egypt to sojourn there; 3. but Baruch the son of Neriah setteth thee on against

Jeremiah

43

43 : 3 *That they may put us to death.* This can hardly mean that Johanan and Azariah accused Baruch of wanting them to be killed. They meant that Baruch wanted them to go to Babylon; and there, they were sure, they would be killed.

us, to deliver us into the hand of the Chaldeans, that they may put us to death, and carry us away captives to Babylon.' 4. So Johanan the son of Kareah, and all the captains of the forces, and all the people, hearkened not to the voice of the LORD, to dwell in the land of Judah. 5. But Johanan the son of Kareah, and all the captains of the forces, took all the remnant of Judah, that were returned from all the nations whither they had been driven to sojourn in the land of Judah: 6. the men, and the women, and the children, and the king's daughters, and every person that Nebuzaradan the captain of the guard had left with Gedaliah the son of Ahikam, the son of Shaphan, and Jeremiah the prophet, and Baruch the son of Neriah; 7. and they came into the land of Egypt; for they hearkened not to the voice of the LORD; and they came even to Tahpanhes.

8. Then came the word of the LORD unto Jeremiah in Tahpanhes, saying: 9. 'Take great stones

43 : 8-13   An oracle against Egypt declaring that Nebuchadnezzar would overrun and despoil the entire land.

43 : 9   *Take . . . stones . . . hide them in the mortar in the framework . . . at the entry of Pharaoh's house.*   The word translated here as "framework" is sometimes said to mean "brick forms" or "a brick kiln." But in general the translation given here follows the interpretation of most of the commentators. The difficulty with this interpretation is that the rest of the sentence speaks of "the entry of Pharaoh's house." It is hardly possible that there would be a brick kiln at the gate of Pharaoh's palace.

in thy hand, and hide them in the mortar in the framework, which is at the entry of Pharaoh's house in Tahpanhes, in the sight of the men of Judah; 10. and say unto them: Thus saith the LORD of hosts, the God of Israel: Behold, I will send and take Nebuchadrezzar the king of Babylon, My servant, and will set his throne upon these stones that I have hid; and he shall spread his royal pavilion over them. 11. And he shall come, and shall smite the land of Egypt; such as are for death to death, and such as are for captivity to captivity, and such as are for the sword to the sword. 12. And I will kindle a fire in the houses of the gods of Egypt; and he shall burn them, and carry them away captives; and he shall fold up the land of Egypt, as a shepherd foldeth up his garment; and he shall go forth from thence in peace. 13. He shall also break the pillars of Beth-shemesh, that is in the land of Egypt; and the houses of the gods of Egypt shall he burn with fire.'

Tur-Sinai, sensing the difficulty, notices that the Septuagint leaves out the references to cement and brick forms and simply says: Put the stones at the gateway entrance of Pharaoh's palace. The stones put at the entrance of Pharaoh's palace would certainly be a noticeable symbol.

43 : 11 *Death . . . captivity . . . sword.* Jeremiah used the same sequence in 15:2.

43 : 12 *Go forth . . . in peace.* After Nebuchadnezzar has conquered Egypt, he will not occupy the country but will carry away its treasures and depart.

44

THE CHAPTER following this one is dated to the fourth year of Jehoiakim—in other words, about twenty years earlier than this chapter. The series of oracles against the nations, comprising chapters 46-51, is undated. Chapter 52 is a historical appendix. Thus this chapter contains the last utterance of Jeremiah. The remaining chapters of the book offer no record of any words he may have spoken subsequent to this utterance. In fact they contain no further reference to him at all. Evidently he died in Egypt.

Jeremiah

44

1. The word that came to Jeremiah concerning all the Jews that dwelt in the land of Egypt, that dwelt at Migdol, and at Tahpanhes, and at Noph, and in the country of Pathros, saying: 2. 'Thus saith the LORD of hosts, the God of Israel: Ye have seen all the evil that I have brought upon Jerusalem, and upon all the cities of Judah; and behold, this day they are a desolation, and no man dwelleth therein;

44 : 1-14   Jeremiah denounces the people for their persistent idolatry. He reminds them that it was the sins of the king and the people of Judah which were punished by the overthrow of the kingdom. Nevertheless, he continues: You exiles in Egypt have learned no lesson from these events which you yourselves have experienced. You are still idolaters and will surely be punished.

3. because of their wickedness which they have committed to provoke Me, in that they went to offer, and to serve other gods, whom they knew not, neither they, nor ye, nor your fathers. 4. Howbeit I sent unto you all My servants the prophets, sending them betimes and often, saying: Oh, do not this abominable thing that I hate. 5. But they hearkened not, nor inclined their ear to turn from their wickedness, to forbear offering unto other gods. 6. Wherefore My fury and Mine anger was poured forth, and was kindled in the cities of Judah and in the streets of Jerusalem; and they are wasted and desolate, as at this day. 7. Therefore now thus saith the LORD, the God of hosts, the God of Israel: Wherefore commit ye this great evil against your own souls, to cut off from you man and woman, infant and suckling out of the midst of Judah, to leave you none remaining; 8. in that ye provoke Me with the works of your hands, offering unto other gods in the land of Egypt, whither ye are gone to sojourn; that ye may be cut off, and that ye may be a curse and a reproach among all the nations of the earth? 9. Have ye forgotten the wicked deeds of your fathers, and the wicked deeds of the kings of Judah, and the wicked deeds of their wives, and your own wicked deeds, and the wicked deeds of your wives, which they committed in the land of Judah, and in the streets of Jerusalem? They are not humbled even unto this day, neither have they feared, nor walked in My law, nor in My statutes, that I set before you and before your fathers. 11. Therefore thus saith the LORD of hosts, the God of Israel: Behold, I will set My face against you for evil, even to cut off all Judah. 12. And I will take the remnant of Judah, that have set their faces to go into the land of Egypt to sojourn there, and they shall all be consumed; in the land of Egypt shall they fall; they shall be consumed by the sword and by the famine; they shall die, from the least even unto the greatest, by the

Jeremiah
44

sword and by the famine: and they shall be an ex-ecration, and an astonishment, and a curse, and a reproach. 13. For I will punish them that dwell in the land of Egypt, as I have punished Jerusalem, by the sword, by the famine, and by the pestilence; 14. so that none of the remnant of Judah, that are gone into the land of Egypt to sojourn there, shall escape or remain, that they should return into the land of Judah, to which they have a desire to return to dwell there; for none shall return save such as shall escape.'

15. Then all the men who knew that their wives offered unto other gods, and all the women that stood by, a great assembly, even all the people that dwelt in the land of Egypt, in Pathros, answered Jeremiah, saying: 16. 'As for the word that thou hast spoken unto us in the name of the LORD, we will not hearken unto thee. 17. But we will cer-tainly perform every word that is gone forth out of our mouth, to offer unto the queen of heaven, and to pour out drink-offerings unto her, as we have done, we and our fathers, our kings and our princes, in the cities of Judah, and in the streets of Jerusalem; for then had we plenty of food, and were well, and saw no evil. 18. But since we let off to offer to the queen of heaven, and to pour out drink-offerings unto her, we have wanted all things, and have been consumed by the sword and by the famine. 19. And is it we that offer to the queen of heaven, and pour out drink-offerings unto her? did we make her cakes in her image, and pour out

44 : 15-19   The response of the people to Jeremiah. This seems to be the only time that the people actually argued in defense of their idolatry. They said that as long as they offered sacrifices to the queen of heaven, they had "plenty of food and were well and saw no evil" (verse 17).

44 : 19   *Queen of heaven . . . cakes.*   The cakes that were baked and offered were part of the ritual of moon or star worship. See comment on 7:18.

drink-offerings unto her, without our husbands?'

20. Then Jeremiah said unto all the people, to the men, and to the women, even to all the people that had given him that answer, saying: 21 'The offering that ye offered in the cities of Judah, and in the streets of Jerusalem, ye and your fathers, your kings and your princes, and the people of the land, did not the Lord remember them, and came it not into His mind? 22. so that the Lord could no longer bear, because of the evil of your doings, and because of the abominations which ye have committed; therefore is your land become a desolation, and an astonishment, and a curse, without an inhabitant, as at this day. 23. Because ye have offered, and because ye have sinned against the Lord, and have not hearkened to the voice of the Lord, nor walked in His law, nor in His statutes, nor in His testimonies; therefore this evil is happened unto you, as at this day.'

24. Moreover Jeremiah said unto all the people, and to all the women: 'Hear the word of the Lord, all Judah that are in the land of Egypt: 25. Thus saith the Lord of hosts, the God of Israel, saying: Ye and your wives have both spoken with your mouths, and with your hands have fulfilled it, saying: We will surely perform our vows that we have vowed, to offer to the queen of heaven, and to pour out drink-offerings unto her; ye shall surely establish your vows, and surely perform your vows. 26. Therefore hear ye the word of the Lord, all Judah that dwell in the land of Egypt: Behold, I have sworn by My great name, saith the Lord, that My name shall no more be named in the mouth of any man of Judah in all the land of Egypt, saying: As the Lord God liveth. 27. Behold, I watch

Jeremiah

44

44 : 20-30   Jeremiah's rejoinder, warning the people that they will be punished for their idolatry. As proof that the punishment is coming, Hophra, the Pharaoh of Egypt, will be defeated by his enemies, just as Zedekiah was.

over them for evil, and not for good; and all the men of Judah that are in the land of Egypt shall be consumed by the sword and by the famine, until there be an end of them. 28. And they that escape the sword shall return out of the land of Egypt into the land of Judah, few in number; and all the remnant of Judah, that are gone into the land of Egypt to sojourn there, shall know whose word shall stand, Mine, or theirs. 29. And this shall be the sign unto you, saith the LORD, that I will punish you in this place, that ye may know that My words shall surely stand against you for evil; 30. thus saith the LORD: Behold, I will give Pharaoh Hophra king of Egypt into the hand of his enemies, and into the hand of them that seek his life; as I gave Zedekiah king of Judah into the hand of Nebuchadrezzar king of Babylon, his enemy, and that sought his life.'

44 : 30 *Pharaoh Hophra king of Egypt.* The Targum translates "Pharaoh Hophra" as the "lame Pharaoh." In other words, it does not take Hophra actually to be a proper name. So, too, Trani says that Hophra is not a proper name at all, but is a mocking anagram of the word "Pharaoh."

45

THIS BRIEF chapter is the counsel that Jeremiah gave to Baruch, his companion and scribe, when he was dictating his prophecies to him.

1. The word that Jeremiah the prophet spoke unto Baruch the son of Neriah, when he wrote these words in a book at the mouth of Jeremiah, in the fourth year of Jehoiakim the son of Josiah, king of Judah, saying: 2. 'Thus saith the LORD, the God of Israel, concerning thee, O Baruch: Thou didst say:
3. Woe is me now!
   For the LORD hath added sorrow to my pain;
   I am weary with my groaning,
   And I find no rest.

Jeremiah

45

45 : 1 *Fourth year of Jehoiakim.* As stated also in 36:1, this was the year that Jeremiah dictated his prophecies.

45 : 3 *The Lord hath added sorrow to my pain.* Trani says that Baruch's grief and pain came to him when he wrote down the prophecies and thus learned of the coming sufferings of his people. However, according to the Midrash, his sorrows were not due to pity for the people but to self-pity. His complaint was that the servants of earlier prophets had been rewarded with the gift of prophecy; thus Joshua, who served Moses, and Gehazi, who served Elisha. Then: Why am I not given the same gift? (Mekilta *Bo*, end of the introduction, edition Weiss, 2b)

Jeremiah

45

4. Thus shalt thou say unto him:
Thus saith the LORD:
Behold, that which I have built will I break down,
And that which I have planted I will pluck up;
And this in the whole land.

5. And seekest thou great things for thyself?
Seek them not;
for, behold, I will bring evil upon all flesh, saith
the LORD; but thy life will I give unto thee for a
prey in all places whither thou goest.'

The Targum evidently had this Midrash in mind when it translated as follows: God has added to my sorrow and I found no prophecy.

45 : 4 *This in the whole land.* The word "this" refers to the punishment that God will send. The phrase therefore means: This punishment will be thoroughgoing. It will reach the whole country.

45 : 5 *Seekest thou great things?* Trani consistently says that this means: Do you seek to persuade Me to change My decree of punishment? This is too great a thing for you to attain. I will not change it. An analogous explanation is given by Luzzato. It is too great a thing for you to expect to be spared of sorrow.

But Rashi and Kimchi both follow the midrashic explanation of verse 3, namely: It is too great a thing for you to expect to be made a prophet. They call attention to the term "great things" used in II Kings 8:4, where the king asks Gehazi to tell him "the great things" that Elisha had done. There the phrase is taken to mean "the prophecies" of Elisha.

Thy life will I give unto thee for a prey. "Prey" here means "loot" or "booty," i.e., the invaders will come and loot the land and take everything away; but you will be able to take your own life away in safety.

246

46

THE FIRST IN a series of nine oracles against various nations. Similar oracles are frequently found in the prophetic literature. The first chapter of the Prophet Amos is really a series of brief oracles against various sinful nations. In Isaiah the oracles occupy chapters 13-25, and in Ezekiel, 25-32. The oracle in this chapter is against Egypt and is in the form of a dramatic dialogue. There are various speakers: Pharaoh marshaling his troops, the prophet mocking the fate of his army, the cries of the various soldiers in flight, and the Babylonians making scornful reference to the defeated Egyptian army. The chapter ends with God reassuring the remnants of Israel in Egypt that they will not be destroyed but will someday be restored to their home.

The chapter contains two oracles against Egypt. The first (1-12) taunts Egypt for its defeat at Carchemish; the second oracle (13-26) depicts the coming invasion of Egypt by Nebuchadnezzar.

1. The word of the LORD which came to Jeremiah the prophet concerning the nations.
2. Of Egypt: concerning the army of Pharaoh-neco king of Egypt, which was by the river Euphrates in Carchemish, which Nebuchadrezzar king of

Jeremiah

46

46 : 2 *Carchemish.* At Carchemish on the Euphrates River, in the year 605 B.C.E., the Egyptian armies were routed by the Babylonians. This is often counted among the decisive battles of the world.

Jeremiah
46

Babylon smote in the fourth year of Jehoiakim the son of Josiah, king of Judah.

3. Make ready buckler and shield,
   And draw near to battle.
4. Harness the horses, and mount, ye horsemen,
   And stand forth with your helmets;
   Furbish the spears, put on the coats of mail.
5. Wherefore do I see them dismayed and turned backward?
   And their mighty ones are beaten down,
   And they are fled apace, and look not back;
   Terror is on every side, saith the LORD.
6. The swift cannot flee away,
   Nor the mighty man escape;
   In the north by the river Euphrates
   Have they stumbled and fallen.
7. Who is this like the Nile that riseth up,
   Like the rivers whose waters toss themselves?
8. Egypt is like the Nile that riseth up,
   And like the rivers whose waters toss themselves;
   And he saith: 'I will rise up, I will cover the earth,
   I will destroy the city and the inhabitants thereof.'
9. Prance, ye horses, and rush madly, ye chariots;
   And let the mighty men go forth:
   Cush and Put, that handle the shield,
   And the Ludim, that handle and bend the bow.
10. For the Lord GOD of hosts shall have on that day

46 : 3-6 First the array of the armies before battle, then their disarray after the defeat.

46 : 3-4 Orders by the Egyptian officers mobilizing their army.

46 : 5-6 The headlong flight after the defeat.

46 : 7-12 A poetic elaboration of the battle array and the disarray of the flight.

46 : 7 *Who is this like the Nile.* The annual rising of the Nile floods the surrounding fields. This fact is taken as a symbol of Egypt's boasting that, like the Nile in flood, "I will rise up and I will cover the earth" (verse 8).

46 : 9 *Cush . . . Put . . . and the Ludim.* The various districts and nations that were part of the Egyptian army.

248

A day of vengeance, that He may avenge Him of
His adversaries;
And the sword shall devour and be satiate,
And shall be made drunk with their blood;
For the Lord GOD of hosts hath a sacrifice
In the north country by the river Euphrates.

11. Go up into Gilead, and take balm,
O virgin daughter of Egypt;
In vain dost thou use many medicines;
There is no cure for thee.

12. The nations have heard of thy shame,
And the earth is full of thy cry;
For the mighty man hath stumbled against the
mighty,
They are fallen both of them together.

13. The word that the LORD spoke to Jeremiah the
prophet, how that Nebuchadrezzar king of Babylon
should come and smite the land of Egypt.

14. Declare ye in Egypt, and announce in Migdol,
And announce in Noph and in Tahpanhes;
Say ye: 'Stand forth, and prepare thee,
For the sword hath devoured round about thee.'

15. Why is thy strong one overthrown?
He stood not, because the LORD did thrust him
down.

16. He made many to stumble;
Yea, they fell one upon another,
And said: 'Arise, and let us return to our own
people,

46 : 12 *The mighty man hath stumbled . . . fallen . . . together.*
When they marched to battle it was in orderly fashion, each
soldier in his place. But when they fled it was in wild disorder;
the soldiers stumbled and bumped against each other until they
fell down together.

46 : 13-28 The second oracle, describing the coming invasion of
Egypt.

46 : 16 *To the land of our birth.* The Egyptian armies will be
quickly defeated, and their various allies will rush back to their
native lands.

And to the land of our birth,
From the oppressing sword.'

17. They cried there: 'Pharaoh king of Egypt is but
    a noise;
    He hath let the appointed time pass by.'

18. As I live, saith the King,
    Whose name is the LORD of hosts,
    Surely like Tabor among the mountains,
    And like Carmel by the sea, so shall he come.

19. O thou daughter that dwellest in Egypt,
    Furnish thyself to go into captivity;
    For Noph shall become a desolation,
    And shall be laid waste, without inhabitant.

20. Egypt is a very fair heifer;
    But the gadfly out of the north is come, it is come.

21. Also her mercenaries in the midst of her
    Are like calves of the stall,
    For they also are turned back, they are fled away
        together,
    They did not stand;
    For the day of their calamity is come upon them,
    The time of their visitation.

22. The sound thereof shall go like the serpent's;

46 : 17 *Pharaoh . . . is but a noise; he hath let the appointed times pass by.* It is not certain who says this. It could be the words of the various mercenary soldiers, now contemptuous of their former Egyptian leaders. It could also mean that the Babylonians, as they invade Egypt, are saying: Pharaoh is just a loud boaster. He did not come to meet us in battle.

46 : 18 *Like Tabor . . . and like Carmel . . . so shall he come.* As clearly as these mountains are seen, so it is clear and certain that the Babylonian invaders will come.

46 : 20 *A fair heifer . . . gadfly.* The word translated here as "gadfly" (to sting the heifer) can also be translated "ox-goad."

46 : 21 *Mercenaries . . . like calves of the stall.* Egypt's mercenaries were of no help. All they were good for was to stuff themselves with food. When it came to battle, they turned and fled.

46 : 22 *Sound . . . like the serpent's . . . they march.* Judging

For they march with an army,
And come against her with axes,
As hewers of wood.

23. They cut down her forest, saith the LORD,
Though it cannot be searched;
Because they are more than the locusts,
And are innumerable.

24. The daughter of Egypt is put to shame;
She is delivered into the hand of the people of the
north.

25. The LORD of hosts, the God of Israel, saith:
Behold, I will punish Amon of No, and Pharaoh,
and Egypt, with her gods, and her kings; even
Pharaoh, and them that trust in him; 26. and I will
deliver them into the hand of those that seek their
lives, and into the hand of Nebuchadrezzar king of
Babylon, and into the hand of his servants; and
afterwards, it shall be inhabited, as in the days of
old, saith the LORD.

27. But fear not thou, O Jacob My servant,
Neither be dismayed, O Israel;
For, lo, I will save thee from afar,
And thy seed from the land of their captivity;
And Jacob shall again be quiet and at ease,
And none shall make him afraid.

Jeremiah
46

by the second half of the verse, "sound like the serpent's" means
the continuous hiss and hum of the advancing Babylonian army.

46 : 23 *It cannot be searched.* There is no clear antecedent for
"it." Most commentators say "it" refers to the Babylonian army,
which is so numerous that it cannot be counted. This explanation
harmonizes with the second half of the verse: "they are innumerable."

46 : 25 *Amon of No, and Pharaoh, and Egypt.* I will punish
the gods, the king, and the nation.

46 : 27-28 This chapter, foretelling the doom of Egypt, ends with
a reassurance to the Jewish exiles in Egypt. They shall not be
destroyed. God will gather them and bring them back.

46 : 27 *Fear not thou, O Jacob My servant.* Isaiah uses the same
phrase (44:2). Jeremiah used it also in 30:10.

Jeremiah
46

28. Fear not thou, O Jacob My servant, saith the LORD,
    For I am with thee;
    For I will make a full end of all the nations whither
      I have driven thee,
    But I will not make a full end of thee;
    And I will correct thee in measure,
    But will not utterly destroy thee.

47

THE ORACLE against the Philistines is the subject of this chapter.

1. The word of the LORD that came to Jeremiah the
   prophet concerning the Philistines, before that
   Pharaoh smote Gaza.
2. Thus saith the LORD:
   Behold, waters rise up out of the north,
   And shall become an overflowing stream,

47 : 1   *Before that Pharaoh smote Gaza.*   It is not certain to
which Egyptian campaign this refers. Gaza must have been
captured by the Egyptians frequently when they marched
north. Rashi's explanation seems reasonable: When Nebuchadnezzar was besieging Jerusalem, the Egyptian army invaded
Palestine (Jeremiah 37:5). During their march north, they captured Gaza.

But the prophet speaks of Pharaoh's capture of Gaza merely
as a means of fixing the date. The invasion of Gaza and the other
Philistine cities, which he now predicts, will be an invasion by
the Chaldeans from the north.

47 : 2   *Waters rise up out of the north.*   A frequent simile, comparing an invading army to an irresistible flood. In Jeremiah 46:8
the Egyptian army is compared to the flooding of the Nile. In
Isaiah 8:7-8 the Assyrian army is compared to the flooding of the
Euphrates.

And they shall overflow the land and all that is
therein,
The city and them that dwell therein;
And the men shall cry,
And all the inhabitants of the land shall wail.

3. At the noise of the stamping of the hoofs of his
strong ones,
At the rushing of his chariots, at the rumbling of
his wheels,
The fathers look not back to their children
For feebleness of hands;

4. Because of the day that cometh
To spoil all the Philistines,
To cut off from Tyre and Zidon

47 : 3 *Fathers look not back to their children.* The people will
be so enfeebled and panic-stricken by the invasion that fathers
fleeing the enemy will not even look back to see whether their
children are safe.

47 : 4 *Tyre and Zidon every helper.* These great Phoenician
cities were in frequent alliance with Gaza and the other Philistine
cities; but now the Chaldeans, coming down from the north, will
capture them first, and the Philistines will have no ally, "no
helper," left.

Every helper that remaineth;
For the LORD will spoil the Philistines,
The remnant of the isle of Caphtor.
5. Baldness is come upon Gaza,
Ashkelon is brought to nought, the remnant of
their valley;
How long wilt thou cut thyself?
6. O thou sword of the LORD,
How long will it be ere thou be quiet?
Put up thyself into thy scabbard,
Rest, and be still.
7. How canst thou be quiet?
For the LORD hath given it a charge;
Against Ashkelon, and against the sea-shore,
There hath He appointed it.

Isle of Caphtor. This is usually taken to mean the island of Crete, the homeland of the Philistines.

47 : 5 *Baldness . . . cut thyself.* The usual self-mutilations as marks of mourning. The Torah forbids such practices (Leviticus 19:28, 21:5).

47 : 6-7 The prophet now addresses the sword of the Lord, which cannot be sheathed again until it fulfills its task against Ashkelon and the other Philistine cities.

48

A PROPHECY of doom against Moab. Largely the same material is found in the Moab prophecy in Isaiah 15-16. Many of the verses are identical. Mention is made here of the various Moabite cities that were being destroyed: Kiriathaim, Misgab, Heshbon, Madmen, etc.

Jeremiah

48

1. Of Moab.
   Thus saith the LORD of hosts, the God of Israel:
   Woe unto Nebo! for it is spoiled;
   Kiriathaim is put to shame, it is taken;
   Misgab is put to shame and dismayed.
2. The praise of Moab is no more;
   In Heshbon they have devised evil against her:
   'Come, and let us cut her off from being a nation.'
   Thou also, O Madmen, shalt be brought to silence;
   The sword shall pursue thee.

48 : 2 *In Heshbon they have devised evil . . . O Madmen.* In the Hebrew text, the name of the city and the verb used to describe its destruction are alliterative. The effect of this is similar to that in Isaiah in 5:7: "For justice . . . violence, for righteousness . . . a cry." There too the Hebrew of "justice" and "violence" are alliterative, as also "righteousness" and "a cry." The strong effect of this alliteration has not been rendered in the translations of Isaiah or of this passage in Jeremiah.

3. Hark! a cry from Horonaim,
   Spoiling and great destruction!
4. Moab is destroyed;
   Her little ones have caused a cry to be heard.
5. For by the ascent of Luhith
   With continual weeping shall they go up;
   For in the going down of Horonaim
   They have heard the distressing cry of destruction.
6. Flee, save your lives,
   And be like a tamarisk in the wilderness.
7. For, because thou hast trusted
   In thy works and in thy treasures,
   Thou also shalt be taken;
   And Chemosh shall go forth into captivity,
   His priests and his princes together.
8. And the spoiler shall come upon every city,
   And no city shall escape;
   The valley also shall perish, and the plain shall be
       destroyed;
   As the LORD hath spoken.
9. Give wings unto Moab,
   For she must fly and get away;
   And her cities shall become a desolation,
   Without any to dwell therein.
10. Cursed be he that doeth the work of the LORD with
    a slack hand,
    And cursed be he that keepeth back his sword from
        blood.
11. Moab hath been at ease from his youth,

48 : 6 *Tamarisk in the wilderness.* Jeremiah uses the same
  thought in 17:6: "He shall be like a tamarisk in the desert and shall
  not see when good cometh." The tree, growing where abundant
  water is lacking, lives a marginal existence and can easily die.

48 : 7 *Chemosh . . . into captivity.* The chief god of Moab
  (I Kings 11:33).

48 : 10 *His sword from blood.* An interruption calling upon
  the sword to fulfill its appointed task. See also 47:6-7.

48 : 11-12 *Settled on his lees . . . not been emptied from vessel to*

And he hath settled on his lees,
And hath not been emptied from vessel to vessel,
Neither hath he gone into captivity;
Therefore his taste remaineth in him,
And his scent is not changed.

12. Therefore, behold, the days come,
Saith the LORD,
That I will send unto him them that tilt up,
And they shall tilt him up;
And they shall empty his vessels,
And break their bottles in pieces.

13. And Moab shall be ashamed of Chemosh,
As the house of Israel was ashamed
Of Beth-el their confidence.

14. How say ye: 'We are mighty men,
And valiant men for the war'?

15. Moab is spoiled, and they are gone up into her cities,
And his chosen young men are gone down to the slaughter,
Saith the King,
Whose name is the LORD of hosts.

16. The calamity of Moab is near to come,
And his affliction hasteth fast.

vessel.   The simile used here is that of wine which, once it has fermented, is allowed to stay in the original barrel and not poured "from vessel to vessel." So its dregs (the "lees") slowly settle down to the bottom of the barrel and the wine continues to draw strength and flaver from them.

So Edam has been undisturbed, uninvaded, for a long time, and its life went on in its accustomed ways. But now the "bottles will be tilted, emptied and broken."

48 : 13   *Moab ... Chemosh ... Israel ... Beth-el.*   Jeroboam had set up golden calves to be worshiped in Beth-el (I Kings 12:28). But when Israel's calamity came, the idols proved worthless and Israel grew to be ashamed of them. So Moab will grow to be ashamed of its god, Chemosh, who will prove helpless to save them in the coming calamity.

17. Bemoan him, all ye that are round about him,
    And all ye that know his name;
    Say: 'How is the strong staff broken,
    The beautiful rod!'
18. O thou daughter that dwellest in Dibon,
    Come down from thy glory, and sit in thirst;
    For the spoiler of Moab is come up against thee,
    He hath destroyed thy strongholds.
19. O inhabitant of Aroer,
    Stand by the way, and watch;
    Ask him that fleeth, and her that escapeth;
    Say: 'What hath been done?'
20. Moab is put to shame, for it is dismayed;
    Wail and cry;
    Tell ye it in Arnon,
    That Moab is spoiled.
21. And judgment is come upon the country of the
    Plain; upon Holon, and upon Jahzah, and upon
    Mephaath; 22. and upon Dibon, and upon Nebo,
    and upon Beth-diblathaim; 23. and upon Kiriath-
    aim, and upon Beth-gamul, and upon Beth-meon;
    24. and upon Kerioth, and upon Bozrah, and upon
    all the cities of the land of Moab, far or near.
25. The horn of Moab is cut off,
    And his arm is broken,
    Saith the LORD.
26. Make ye him drunken,
    For he magnified himself against the LORD;
    And Moab shall wallow in his vomit,
    And he also shall be in derision.

48 : 17 *The beautiful rod.* That is, the glorious scepter. The
  Targum translates: "the rule of the oppressors."
48 : 25 *The horn of Moab . . . is broken.* The wild ox, in his
  strength and pride, raises his horns high; but when he is wounded
  and dying, his head sinks and his horns trail in the dust. This
  figure is frequently used in Scripture as a metaphor for human
  pride. Thus when Hannah rejoices, she says: "God gives strength
  and exalts the horn of His anointed" (I Samuel 2:10). In a warning to the wicked not to be too proud, the psalmist says: "I say

Jeremiah
48

259

27. For was not Israel a derision unto thee?
    Was he found among thieves?
    For as often as thou speakest of him,
    Thou waggest the head.
28. O ye that dwell in Moab,
    Leave the cities, and dwell in the rock;
    And be like the dove that maketh her nest
    In the sides of the pit's mouth.
29. We have heard of the pride of Moab;
    He is very proud;
    His loftiness, and his pride, and his haughtiness,
    And the assumption of his heart.
30. I know his arrogancy, saith the LORD,
    That it is ill-founded;
    His boastings have wrought nothing well-founded.
31. Therefore will I wail for Moab;
    Yea, I will cry out for all Moab;
    For the men of Kir-heres shall my heart moan.
32. With more than the weeping of Jazer will I weep
    for thee,
    O vine of Sibmah;

unto the arrogant . . . lift not up the horn" (Psalm 75:5). So here the simile means that Moab will be humbled. This sentence must be read together with verses 29 and 30. "Moab . . . is very proud."

48 : 27   *Was not Israel a derision?*   Moab mocked Israel in the time of its trouble. Now in turn Moab will become a mockery. See verse 39: "So shall Moab become a derision."

48 : 28   *The dove . . . her nest . . . In the sides of the pit's mouth.* Rashi says that when the river subsides, the dove selects the hollowed-out bank (under the overhang) to conceal its nest. Other commentators have other explanations for the phrase "sides of the pit's mouth." But all the explanations express the same idea—that the dove hides its nest where it will be either invisible or inaccessible.

48 : 32   *More than the weeping of Jazer.*   The city of Jazer had been destroyed sometime previously, and its destruction was greatly mourned.

48 : 33   *The shouting shall be no shouting.*   The word for

Thy branches passed over the sea,
They reached even to the sea of Jazer;
Upon thy summer fruits and upon thy vintage
The spoiler is fallen.

33. And gladness and joy is taken away
From the fruitful field, and from the land of Moab;
And I have caused wine to cease from the wine-
    presses;
None shall tread with shouting;
The shouting shall be no shouting.

34. From the cry of Heshbon even unto Elealeh,
Even unto Jahaz have they uttered their voice,
From Zoar even unto Horonaim,
A heifer of three years old;
For the Waters of Nimrim also
Shall be desolate.

35. Moreover I will cause to cease in Moab,
Saith the LORD,
Him that offereth in the high place,
And him that offereth to his gods.

36. Therefore my heart moaneth for Moab like pipes,
And my heart moaneth like pipes for the men of
    Kir-heres;
Therefore the abundance that he hath gotten is
    perished.

37. For every head is bald,

"shouting" (*hedad*) means "the cry of joy of the harvesters." It is used three times in close succession at the end of the verse. Our translation follows that of Abarbanel: "If they do shout, it will no longer be the joyous harvest shout."

48 : 34 *A heifer of three years old.* The same phrase is used in the parallel sentence in Isaiah 15:5. It seems to mean that just as a heifer is at its best when it is three years old, so this calamity will come to Moab when it is at the very height of its strength (Kimchi).

48 : 37 *Head . . . bald . . . beard . . . clipped . . . hands . . . cuttings.* The customary mourning practices involved these various self-mutilations (see comment on 47:5).

And every beard clipped;
Upon all the hands are cuttings,
And upon the loins sackcloth.

38. On all the housetops of Moab and in the broad
places thereof
There is lamentation every where;
For I have broken Moab like a vessel wherein
is no pleasure,
Saith the LORD.

39. 'How is it broken down!' wail ye!
'How hath Moab turned the back with shame!'
So shall Moab become a derision and a dismay
To all that are round about him.

40. For thus saith the LORD:
Behold, he shall swoop as a vulture,
And shall spread out his wings against Moab.

41. The cities are taken.
And the strongholds are seized,
And the heart of the mighty men of Moab at that
day
Shall be as the heart of a woman in her pangs.

42. And Moab shall be destroyed from being a people,
Because he hath magnified himself against the
LORD.

43. Terror, and the pit, and the trap,
Are upon thee, O inhabitant of Moab,
Saith the LORD.

44. He that fleeth from the terror
    Shall fall into the pit;
    And he that getteth up out of the pit
    Shall be taken in the trap;
    For I will bring upon her, even upon Maob,
    The year of their visitation, saith the LORD.
45. In the shadow of Heshbon the fugitives
    Stand without strength;
    For a fire is gone forth out of Heshbon,
    And a flame from the midst of Sihon,
    And it devoureth the corner of Moab,
    And the crown of the head of the tumultuous ones.
46. Woe unto thee, O Moab!
    The people of Chemosh is undone;
    For thy sons are taken away captive,
    And thy daughters into captivity.
47. Yet will I turn the captivity of Moab
    In the end of days, saith the LORD.
    Thus far is the judgment of Moab.

48 : 47 *Yet will I turn the captivity of Moab.*   Someday God
will restore Moab. Kimchi says this means in the messianic time.
But Abarbanel says: It means before that, but in the rather distant
future.

49

THE CHAPTER contains prophecies of doom against five nations: the Ammonites, Edom, Damascus, Keda (i.e., the Arab tribes), and Elam.

Jeremiah

49

1. Of the children of Ammon.
   Thus saith the LORD.
   Hath Israel no sons?
   Hath he no heir?
   Why then doth Malcam take possession of Gad,
   And his people dwell in the cities thereof?
2. Therefore, behold, the days come, saith the LORD,
   That I will cause an alarm of war to be heard
   Against Rabbah of the children of Ammon;

49 : 1-6   Prophecy against the Ammonites.

49 : 1   *Hath Israel no sons? . . . doth Malcam take . . . Gad.*   Malcam, or Milcom, was the chief idol of the Ammonites (II Kings 23:13). The verse refers to the fact that the Ammonites had captured the lands of the tribe of Gad, which were on the east side of the Jordan.

49 : 2   *Rabbah . . . her daughters shall be burned.*   Rabbah was the chief city of the Ammonites. "Her daughters" means the daughter towns around the capital city. All of them, Rabbah and her "daughter" towns, will be burned.

264

And it shall become a desolate mound,
And her daughters shall be burned with fire;
Then shall Israel dispossess them that did dis-
possess him,
Saith the LORD.

3. Wail, O Heshbon, for Ai is undone;
Cry, ye daughters of Rabbah, gird you with sack-
cloth;
Lament, and run to and fro among the folds;
For Malcam shall go into captivity,
His priests and his princes together.

4. Wherefore gloriest thou in the valleys,
Thy flowing valley, O backsliding daughter?
That didst trust in thy treasures:
'Who shall come unto me?'

5. Behold, I will bring a terror upon thee,
Saith the Lord GOD of hosts,
From all that are round about thee;
And ye shall be driven out every man right forth,
And there shall be none to gather up him that
wandereth.

6. But afterward I will bring back the captivity of the
children of Ammon,
Saith the LORD

7. Of Edom.
Thus saith the LORD of hosts:

49 : 3 *Among the folds.*   Among the sheepfolds. Kimchi translates it: Hide among the villages.

Malcam shall go into captivity.   When an ancient nation
was defeated, its gods, as well as its people, were taken into captivity (see also 48:7).

49 : 4 *Thy flowing valley.*   Thy rich and fruitful valley (as
"flowing with milk and honey"). However, Joseph Nachmias
says the verse means: Thy fertile valley will soon be flowing with
the blood of the slain.

49 : 6 *I will bring back the captivity.*   See also 48:47.

49 : 7-22 Prophecy against Edom.   There is disagreement
among the classic commentators as to what nation is really meant
here by "Edom." Ibn Ezra (cited by Abarbanel) says the proph-

Jeremiah 49

Is wisdom no more in Teman?
Is counsel perished from the prudent?
Is their wisdom vanished?

8. Flee ye, turn back, dwell deep,
O inhabitants of Dedan;
For I do bring the calamity of Esau upon him,
The time that I shall punish him.

9. If grape-gatherers came to thee,
Would they not leave some gleaning grapes?
If thieves by night,
Would they not destroy till they had enough?

10. But I have made Esau bare,
I have uncovered his secret places,
And he shall not be able to hide himself;
His seed is spoiled, and his brethren,
And his neighbours; and he is not.

11. Leave thy fatherless children, I will rear them,
And let thy widows trust in Me.

ecy means literally what it says. It predicts the doom of the neighboring Trans-Jordanian country of Edom. But Kimchi says it is a prophecy of the more distant future. It refers to the fall of Rome (also called "Edom" in later Jewish literature). Abarbanel says that the first part of the prophecy literally deals with the neighboring land of Edom; the second part of it may deal with Rome.

49 : 8 *Flee . . . dwell deep.*   Hide in the deepest valleys (Rashi).

Calamity of Esau.   Esau's other name was "Edom" (Genesis 25:30). The Edomites were Esau's descendants.

49 : 10 *His seed is spoiled.*   Despoiled, looted.

He is not.   "He" (the nation of Edom) is no longer here; he is done for.

49 : 11 *Leave thy fatherless children, I will rear them.*   It is not clear who is speaking this sentence. The Targum connects it with the following verse, "Thus saith the Lord," and therefore understands the sentence to mean that God says to Israel: Do not fear for your orphans; leave them in My charge, I will rear them. But this interpretation does not fit into the prophecy of the doom of Edom. Kimchi connects the verse with the preceding one, Thy neighbors and thy brothers are gone; and he understands the

266

12. For thus saith the Lord: Behold, they to whom it
pertained not to drink of the cup shall assuredly
drink; and art thou he that shall altogether go unpunished? thou shalt not go unpunished, but thou
shalt surely drink. 13. For I have sworn by Myself,
saith the Lord, that Bozrah shall become an astonishment, a reproach, a waste, and a curse; and
all the cities thereof shall be perpetual wastes.

14. I have heard a message from the Lord,
And an ambassador is sent among the nations:
'Gather yourselves together, and come against her,
And rise up to the battle.'

15. For, behold, I make thee small among the nations,
And despised among men.

16. Thy terribleness hath deceived thee,
Even the pride of thy heart,
O thou that dwellest in the clefts of the rock,
That holdest the height of the hill;
Though thou shouldest make thy nest as high as
the eagle,
I will bring thee down from thence, saith the Lord.

17. And Edom shall become an astonishment;
Every one that passeth by it

**Jeremiah
49**

verse to mean as follows (and presumably it is the prophet speaking): Since your brothers and neighbors are all gone, there is no
one left to say to the captives or to the slain: Leave your orphans
to me. In other words, there is no one left to take care of them.

49 : 12 *To whom it pertained not to drink . . . art thou . . . unpunished?*   The simile here refers to the cup of destruction as
mentioned in Jeremiah 25:15. The commentators agree that this
passage speaks of the various degrees of guilt of the different
nations who have attacked Israel. Edom is, after all, a brother
(i.e., Esau to Jacob). Therefore he is more guilty than other nations for his cruelty to the people of Israel. The verse therefore
means: The other nations, who are not as guilty as you, will drink
the cup of destruction. So surely you will not go unpunished.

49 : 16 *Thy terribleness hath deceived thee.*   Your ability to
strike terror in the heart of others has deceived you into believing
that you are invulnerable.

Shall be astonished and shall hiss at all the plagues thereof.

Jeremiah
49

18. As in the overthrow of Sodom and Gomorrah
And the neighbour cities thereof, saith the Lord,
No man shall abide there,
Neither shall any son of man dwell therein.

19. Behold, he shall come up like a lion from the thickets of the Jordan
Against the strong habitation;
For I will suddenly make him run away from it,
And whoso is chosen, him will I appoint over it;
For who is like Me? and who will appoint Me a time?
And who is that shepherd that will stand before Me?

20. Therefore hear ye the counsel of the Lord,
That He hath taken against Edom;
And His purposes, that He hath purposed against the inhabitants of Teman:
Surely the least of the flock shall drag them away,
Surely their habitation shall be appalled at them.

21. The earth quaketh at the noise of their fall;
There is a cry, the noise whereof is heard in the Red Sea.

22. Behold, he shall come up and swoop down as the vulture,
And spread out his wings against Bozrah;
And the heart of the mighty men of Edom at that day
Shall be as the heart of a woman in her pangs.

---

49 : 19   The verse means: The invader whom I shall appoint will make Edom flee in panic, but no one can summon Me to an appointment. No shepherd, i.e., no king, can stand against me.

49 : 20   *The least of the flock shall drag them.*   The Edomites will be so broken in defeat that the weakest of nations will be able to drag them away (Trani).

Their habitation . . . appalled.   Trani translates "desolate" instead of "appalled." Their former habitations shall now be desolate.

23. Of Damascus.
    Hamath is ashamed, and Arpad;
    For they have heard evil tidings, they are melted
        away;
    There is trouble in the sea;
    It cannot be quiet.

24. Damacus is waxed feeble, she turneth herself to flee,
    And trembling hath seized on her;
    Anguish and pangs have taken hold of her, as a
        woman in travail.
25. 'How is the city of praise left unrepaired,
    The city of my joy?'
26. Therefore her young men shall fall in her broad
    places,
    And all the men of war shall be brought to silence
        in that day,
    Saith the LORD of hosts.
27. And I will kindle a fire in the wall of Damascus,
    And it shall devour the palaces of Ben-hadad.
28. Of Kedar, and of the kingdoms of Hazor, which
    Nebuchadrezzar king of Babylon smote.
    Thus saith the LORD:
    Arise ye, go up against Kedar,
    And spoil the children of the east.

49: 23-27   Prophecy against Damascus.
49 : 23   *Hamath . . . and Arpad.*   Cities belonging to Damascus.
        Trouble in the sea; it cannot be quiet.   But Damascus is
inland, far from the sea. The commentators therefore consider the
phrase to be a figure of speech: The heart is as troubled as the
sea; it cannot rest. Tur-Sinai, however, notes that the word "sea"
is not found in the Septuagint. Therefore the text simply means:
Their heart is worried; it cannot find rest.
49 : 25   *The city of praise left unrepaired.*   Our translation here
follows Rashi. But Kimchi says the verb (translated here "unrepaired") means "left alone," and therefore says that the people
of Damascus are referring to the enemy and wondering: Why
did they not leave this beautiful city alone and spare it?
49 : 25-33   Prophecy of doom against the Arab tribes (Kedar and
Hazor).

29. Their tents and their flocks shall they take,
    They shall carry away for themselves their curtains,
    And all their vessels, and their camels;
    And they shall proclaim against them a terror on
      every side.
30. Flee ye, flit far off, dwell deep,
    O ye inhabitants of Hazor, saith the LORD;
    For Nebuchadrezzar king of Babylon hath taken
      counsel against you,
    And hath conceived a purpose against you.
31. Arise, get you up against a nation that is at ease,
    That dwelleth without care, saith the LORD;
    That have neither gates nor bars,
    That dwell alone.
32. And their camels shall be a booty,
    And the multitude of their cattle a spoil;
    And I will scatter unto all winds them that have the
      corners polled;
    And I will bring their calamity from every side
      of them, saith the LORD.
33. And Hazor shall be a dwelling-place of jackals,
    A desolation for ever;
    No man shall abide there,
    Neither shall any son of man dwell therein.

49 : 31   *That have neither gates nor bars.*   The Arabs do not dwell in walled cities but in their desert tents.

49 : 32   *That have the corners polled.*   The Arabs keep their hair cut short. The "corners" mean here the "corners" of the hair.

49 : 34-39   Doom against Elam.   Elam was a nation east of Babylon. It is therefore difficult to see what possible contact they

34. The word of the LORD that came to Jeremiah the
prophet concerning Elam in the beginning of the
reign of Zedekiah king of Judah, saying:

35. Thus saith the LORD of hosts:
Behold, I will break the bow of Elam,
The chief of their might.
36. And I will bring against Elam the four winds
From the four quarters of heaven,
And will scatter them toward all those winds;
And there shall be no nation whither the dispersed
of Elam shall not come.
37. And I will cause Elam to be dismayed before their
enemies,
And before them that seek their life;
And I will bring evil upon them,
Even My fierce anger, saith the LORD;
And I will send the sword after them,
Till I have consumed them;
38. And I will set My throne in Elam,
And will destroy from thence king and princes,
saith the LORD.
39. But it shall come to pass in the end of days,
That I will bring back the captivity of Elam, saith
the LORD.

could have had with Israel. There must have been some contact,
however, or they would not have been included in this prophecy.
49 : 35 *Bow of Elam.* The Elamites must have been famous as
archers. See Isaiah 22:6: "Elam bore the quiver."
49 : 39 *Bring back the captivity.* Elam will someday be restored; as Moab will be (48:47) and Ammon (49:6).

50

THIS CHAPTER and the following one are a unit, a prophecy of doom against Babylonia.

Jeremiah

50

1. The word that the LORD spoke concerning Babylon, concerning the land of the Chaldeans, by Jeremiah the prophet.
2. Declare ye among the nations and announce,
   And set up a standard;
   Announce, and conceal not;
   Say: 'Babylon is taken,
   Bel is put to shame, Merodach is dismayed;
   Her images are put to shame, her idols are dismayed.'
3. For out of the north there cometh up a nation against her,
   Which shall make her land desolate,

50 : 2 *Declare ye among the nations.*   Since Babylon had conquered and despoiled many nations, the news of its fall will be welcome in many lands.

Set up a standard.   Around which the people can gather to hear the news (Rashi).

Bel . . . Merodach.   These are two names of the chief deity of Babylon. He is now proved to be helpless to save the city, and so he is "put to shame."

50 : 3 *Out of the north.*   The Medes and the Persians.

272

And none shall dwell therein;
They are fled, they are gone, both man and beast.

4. In those days, and in that time, saith the LORD,
The children of Israel shall come,
They and the children of Judah together;
They shall go on their way weeping,
And shall seek the LORD their God.

5. They shall inquire concerning Zion
With their faces hitherward:
'Come ye, and join yourselves to the LORD
In an everlasting covenant that shall not be for-
gotten.'

6. My people hath been lost sheep;
Their shepherds have caused them to go astray,
They have turned them away on the mountains;
They have gone from mountain to hill,
They have forgotten their restingplace.

7. All that found them have devoured them;
And their adversaries said: 'We are not guilty';
Because they have sinned against the LORD, the
habitation of justice,
Even the LORD, the hope of their fathers.

8. Flee out of the midst of Babylon,
And go forth out of the land of the Chaldeans,
And be as the he-goats before the flocks.

50 : 4   *Israel . . . Judah.*   Both the northern kingdom and the southern will now leave their captivity, return home, and become a united nation "in an everlasting covenant" (verse 5).

Go on their way weeping.   Tears of joy (Kimchi). See also the note to 31:9.

50 : 6   *My people . . . lost sheep.*   The same thought is more fully expressed in Jeremiah 23:1 ff.

50 : 7   *The habitation of justice.*   This refers to God who was a true habitation for them when they obeyed His will (Kimchi). But the Targum, wishing to avoid, as it generally does, any material simile used for God, adds the words "they have left," meaning they have left God's dwelling place, i.e., the Temple.

50 : 8   *He-goats before the flocks.*   The he-goat leads the flock. So Israel should now lead the exodus of the many captive nations out of Babylon.

9. For, lo, I will stir up and cause to come up against
   Babylon
   An assembly of great nations from the north
   country;
   And they shall set themselves in array against her,
   From thence she shall be taken;
   Their arrows shall be as of a mighty man that
   maketh childless;
   None shall return in vain.
10. And Chaldea shall be a spoil;
   All that spoil her shall be satisfied, saith the LORD.
11. Because ye are glad, because ye rejoice,
   O ye that plunder My heritage,
   Because ye gambol as a heifer at grass,
   And neigh as strong horses;
12. Your mother shall be sore ashamed,
   She that bore you shall be confounded;
   Behold, the hindermost of the nations
   Shall be a wilderness, a dry land, and a desert.
13. Because of the wrath of the LORD it shall not be
   inhabited,
   But it shall be wholly desolate;
   Every one that goeth by Babylon
   Shall be appalled and hiss at all her plagues.

50:9 *Maketh childless.* The word translated "childless" here
is *maskil*, which really means "to make wise." But most commentators read the word as *mashkil*, meaning "to bereave." So
Trani explains the sentence to mean: The arrows which will bereave the mothers of their sons.

50:11 *Because ye rejoice.* Babylon deserves to be destroyed,
not because it had destroyed the Temple in Jerusalem, since that
was done at God's command, but because of the Babylonians'
delight at the destruction they cause.

50:12 *The hindermost of the nations shall be a wilderness.*
That is, the least in the order of importance among the nations.
Rashi says: Ye Chaldeans once were very great. Now you will
end up as a wilderness.

50:13 *Shall . . . hiss at all her plagues.* A similar expression is
used in Jeremah 19:8. Hissing was an expression of astonishment
at a calamity.

14. Set yourselves in array against Babylon round
     about,
   All ye that bend the bow,
   Shoot at her, spare no arrows;
   For she hath sinned against the LORD.
15. Shout against her round about, she hath submitted
     herself;
   Her buttresses are fallen, her walls are thrown
     down;
   For it is the vengeance of the LORD, take vengeance
     upon her;
   As she hath done, do unto her.
16. Cut off the sower from Babylon,
   And him that handleth the sickle in the time of
     harvest;
   For fear of the oppressing sword, they shall turn
     every one to his people,
   And they shall flee every one to his own land.
17. Israel is a scattered sheep,
   The lions have driven him away;
   First the king of Assyria hath devoured him,
   And last this Nebuchadrezzar king of Babylon
     hath broken his bones.
18. Therefore thus saith the LORD of hosts, the God
     of Israel:
   Behold, I will punish the king of Babylon and his
     land,
   As I have punished the king of Assyria.
19. And I will bring Israel back to his pasture,
   And he shall feed on Carmel and Bashan,
   And his soul shall be satisfied upon the hills of
     Ephraim and in Gilead.
20. In those days, and in that time saith the LORD,

50 : 16 *Cut off the sower . . . flee every one to his own land.*
Most of the labor in Babylon was done by captive slaves. Now
that Babylon has fallen and the various slaves are escaping to their
homelands, there will be no more sowing or harvesting in Babylon.

50 : 20 *Iniquity . . . shall be sought for.*   In those blessed days

The iniquity of Israel shall be sought for, and there
shall be none,
And the sins of Judah, and they shall not be found;
For I will pardon them whom I leave as a remnant.

21. Go up against the land of ᵃMerathaim, even against
it,
And against the inhabitants of ᵇPekod;
Waste and utterly destroy after them, saith the
LORD,
And do according to all that I have commanded
thee.

22. Hark! battle is in the land,
And great destruction.

23. How is the hammer of the whole earth
Cut asunder and broken!
How is Babylon become
A desolation among the nations!

24. I have laid a snare for thee, and thou art also
taken, O Babylon,
And thou wast not aware;
Thou art found, and also caught,
Because thou hast striven against the LORD.

25. The LORD hath opened His armoury,
And hath brought forth the weapons of His in-
dignation;
For it is a work that the Lord GOD of hosts
Hath to do in the land of the Chaldeans.

26. Come against her from every quarter, open her
granaries,

Israel's sins will be forgiven; so if one wants to search for Israel's
sins, he will not find any: "there shall be none."

50 : 21   *Go up against . . . Merathaim . . . Pekod.*   Merathaim is
a symbolic name meaning "double rebellion." It may be a cipher
of Kasdim, i.e., Chaldeans, as Sheshach is for Babel (see note to
Jeremiah 25:26). Pekod is the name of a town in Babylon (see
Ezekiel 23:23).

50 : 23   *Hammer of the whole earth.*   Babylon, which had shattered all the nations (Rashi).

ᵃ That is, *Double rebellion.*
ᵇ That is, *Visitation.*

Cast her up as heaps, and destroy her utterly;
Let nothing of her be left.

27. Slay all her bullocks, let them go down to the
    slaughter;
    Woe unto them! for their day is come,
    The time of their visitation.

28. Hark! they flee and escape out of the land of
    Babylon,
    To declare in Zion the vengeance of the LORD
    our God,
    The vengeance of His temple.

29. Call together the archers against Babylon,
    All them that bend the bow;
    Encamp against her round about,
    Let none thereof escape;
    Recompense her according to her work,
    According to all that she hath done, do unto her:
    For she hath been arrogant against the LORD,
    Against the Holy One of Israel.

30. Therefore shall her young men fall in her broad
    places,
    And all her men of war shall be brought to silence
    in that day,
    Saith the LORD.

31. Behold, I am against thee, O thou most arrogant,
    Saith the Lord GOD of hosts;
    For thy day is come,
    The time that I will punish thee.

32. And the most arrogant shall stumble and fall,
    And none shall raise him up;
    And I will kindle a fire in his cities,
    And it shall devour all that are round about him.

33. Thus saith the LORD of hosts:
    The children of Israel and the children of Judah
    are oppressed together;
    And all that took them captives hold them fast;
    They refuse to let them go.

34. Their Redeemer is strong,

50 : 30   *Fall in her broad places.*   The same phrase is used in the
prophecy against Damascus (Jeremiah 49:26).

Jeremiah

50

The Lord of hosts is His name;
He will thoroughly plead their cause,
That He may give rest to the earth,
And disquiet the inhabitants of Babylon.

35. A sword is upon the Chaldeans, saith the Lord,
And upon the inhabitants of Babylon, and upon
her princes, and upon her wise men.

36. A sword is upon the boasters, and they shall become fools;
A sword is upon her mighty men, and they shall
be dismayed.

37. A sword is upon their horses, and upon their
chariots,
And upon all the mingled people that are in the
midst of her,
And they shall become as women;
A sword is upon her treasures, and they shall be
robbed.

38. A drought is upon her waters, and they shall be
dried up;
For it is a land of graven images,
And they are mad upon things of horror.

39. Therefore the wild-cats with the jackals shall dwell
there,
And the ostriches shall dwell therein;
And it shall be no more inhabited for ever,
Neither shall it be dwelt in from generation to
generation.

40. As when God overthrew Sodom and Gomorrah
And the neighbour cities thereof, saith the Lord;
So shall no man abide there,
Neither shall any son of man dwell therein.

50 : 38 *Mad upon things of horror.* They grow mad and wild
in their worship of their horrible idols (Kimchi).

50 : 39 *Wild-cats . . . jackals . . . ostriches.* A frequent description of a land which was once settled but now turned into a
desert. Virtually the same sentence appears in Isaiah 13:21, where

41. Behold, a people cometh from the north,
    And a great nation, and many kings
    Shall be roused from the uttermost parts of the
    earth.
42. They lay hold on bow and spear,
    They are cruel, and have no compassion;
    Their voice is like the roaring sea,
    And they ride upon horses;
    Set in array, as a man for war,
    Against thee, O daughter of Babylon.
43. The king of Babylon hath heard the fame of them.
    And his hands wax feeble;
    Anguish hath taken hold of him,
    And pain, as of a woman in travail.
44. Behold, he shall come up like a lion from the
    thickets of the Jordan
    Against the strong habitation;
    For I will suddenly make them run away from it,
    And whoso is chosen, him will I appoint over it;
    For who is like Me? and who will appoint Me a
    time?
    And who is that shepherd that will stand before
    Me?
45. Therefore hear ye the counsel of the LORD,
    That He hath taken against Babylon,
    And His purposes, that He hath purposed against
    the land of the Chaldeans:
    Surely the least of the flock shall drag them away,
    Surely their habitation shall be appalled at them.
46. At the noise of the taking of Babylon the earth
    quaketh,
    And the cry is heard among the nations.

it is used as a description of Babylon devastated and then forever
deserted.

50 : 44-45 *Whoso is chosen . . . the least of the flock shall drag
them.* The same two verses are in Jeremiah 49:19-20 in the
prophecy against Edom.

51

CHAPTER 51 continues the prophecy of doom against Babylon.

Jeremiah

51

1. Thus saith the LORD:
   Behold, I will raise up against Babylon,
   And against them that dwell in ªLeb-kamai, a destroying wind.
2. And I will send unto Babylon strangers, that shall fan her,
   And they shall empty her land;
   For in the day of trouble they shall be against her round about.
3. Let the archer bend his bow against her,
   And let him lift himself up against her in his coat of mail;
   And spare ye not her young men,
   Destroy ye utterly all her host.
4. And they shall fall down slain in the land of the Chaldeans,
   And thrust through in her streets.

51 : 1 *Leb-kamai.*   A cypher for "Kasdim," the Chaldeans. See note to Jeremiah 25:26.

51 : 2 *That shall fan her.*   "Fan" here means "to winnow." The thought is connected with the words "destroying wind" in the preceding sentence. It means that the wind which comes will blow them away like chaff.

ªThat is, *The heart of them that rise up against Me.* According to ancient tradition, a cypher for *Casdim*, that is, Chaldea.

5. For Israel is not widowed, nor Judah,
   Of his God, of the LORD of hosts;
   For their land is full of guilt
   Against the Holy One of Israel.
6. Flee out of the midst of Babylon
   And save every man his life,
   Be not cut off in her iniquity;
   For it is the time of the LORD's vengeance;
   He will render unto her a recompense.
7. Babylon hath been a golden cup in the LORD's
      hand,
   That made all the earth drunken;
   The nations have drunk of her wine,
   Therefore the nations are mad.
8. Babylon is suddenly fallen and destroyed,
   Wail for her;
   Take balm for her pain,
   If so be she may be healed.
9. We would have healed Babylon, but she is not
      healed;
   Forsake her, and let us go every one into his own
      country;
   For her judgment reacheth unto heaven,
   And is lifted up even to the skies.

51 : 5 *Israel is not widowed.*   The same metaphor is used frequently in the Second Isaiah, namely, God is the husband and Israel the wife. The phrase here therefore means: The God of Israel (the "husband") still lives (Kimchi).

Land is full of guilt against the Holy One.   This refers to the land of Babylon which is full of sins against God. Thus the following verse says: "Flee out of the midst of Babylon . . . Be not cut off in her iniquity."

51 : 7 *Babylon hath been a golden cup in the Lord's hand.*   Jeremiah 25:15 and 49:12 and Isaiah 51:17 speak of the cup of drunkenness, staggering, or madness as a metaphor for the punishment of sinful nations who will be made to drink the cup of destruction. The verse here means that Babylon had been God's instrument for this purpose.

51 : 9 *We would have healed Babylon.*   If we had *tried* to heal Babylon, we would have failed. She is incurable.

Jeremiah

51

10. The LORD hath brought forth our victory;
    Come, and let us declare in Zion
    The work of the LORD our God.
11. Make bright the arrows,
    Fill the quivers,
    The LORD hath roused the spirit of the kings of
        the Medes;
    Because His device is against Babylon, to destroy
        it;
    For it is the vengeance of the LORD,
    The vengeance of His temple.
12. Set up a standard against the walls of Babylon,
    Make the watch strong,
    Set the watchmen, prepare the ambushes;
    For the LORD hath both devised and done
    That which He spoke concerning the inhabitants
        of Babylon.
13. O thou that dwellest upon many waters,
    Abundant in treasures,
    Thine end is come,
    The measure of thy covetousness.
14. The LORD of hosts hath sworn by Himself:
    Surely I will fill thee with men, as with the canker-
        worm,
    And they shall lift up a shout against thee.
15. He that hath made the earth by His power,
    That hath established the world by His wisdom,
    And hath stretched out the heavens by His dis-
        cernment;
16. At the sound of His giving a multitude of waters
    in the heavens,

51 : 13 *Dwellest upon many waters.* The Tigris and Euphrates and the many connecting canals.

51 : 14 *The cankerworm.* A voracious caterpillar which destroys fruits. Thus the invading armies will shout the harvest-shout and consume all thy crops as a plague of caterpillars would. So Nahum 3:15: "It shall devour thee like the cankerworm."

51 : 15-19 This passage, contrasting the Creator's grandeur with the nothingness of the idols, is also found in Jeremiah 10:12-16.

282

He causeth the vapours to ascend from the ends of
  the earth;
He maketh lightnings at the time of the rain,
And bringeth forth the wind out of His treasuries;

17. Every man is proved to be brutish, for the knowl-
    edge—
Every goldsmith is put to shame by the graven
  image—
That his molten image is falsehood, and there is no
  breath in them.
18. They are vanity, a work of delusion;
In the time of their visitation they shall perish.
19. The portion of Jacob is not like these;
For He is the former of all things,
And [Israel] is the tribe of His inheritance;
The Lord of hosts is His name.
20. Thou art My maul and weapons of war,
And with thee will I shatter the nations,
And with thee will I destroy kingdoms;
21. And with thee will I shatter the horse and his rider,
And with thee will I shatter the chariot and him
  that rideth therein;
22. And with thee will I shatter man and woman,
And with thee will I shatter the old man and the
  youth,
And with thee will I shatter the young man and
  the maid;
23. And with thee will I shatter the shepherd and his
  flock,
And with thee will I shatter the husbandman and
  his yoke of oxen,

51 : 17 *Brutish, for the knowledge.*   The idol-maker, for all his
knowledge of his craft, is actually foolish ("brutish") since he is
an idolater.

51 : 19 *The portion of Jacob.*   God is Jacob's portion. So Psalm
73:26: "But God is my portion forever."

51 : 20-24   God says to Babylon: You were once My hammer to
destroy sinful nations, but now you will be destroyed (see also
50:23).

And with thee will I shatter governors and deputies.

24. And I will render unto Babylon and to all the
inhabitants of Chaldea
And their evil that they have done in Zion, in your
sight,
Saith the LORD.

25. Behold, I am against thee,
O destroying mountain, saith the LORD,
Which destroyest all the earth;
And I will stretch out My hand upon thee,
And roll thee down from the rocks,
And will make thee a burnt mountain.

26. And they shall not take of thee a stone for a corner,
Nor a stone for foundations;
But thou shalt be desolate for ever, saith the LORD.

27. Set ye up a standard in the land,
Blow the horn among the nations,
Prepare the nations against her,
Call together against her the kingdoms of Ararat,
Minni, and Ashkenaz;
Appoint a marshal against her;
Cause the horses to come up as the rough canker-
worm.

28. Prepare against her the nations, the kings of the
Medes,
The governors thereof, and all the deputies thereof,
And all the land of his dominion.

29. And the land quaketh and is in pain;
For the purposes of the LORD are performed
against Babylon,
To make the land of Babylon a desolation, without
inhabitant.

30. The mighty men of Babylon have forborne to fight,
They remain in their strongholds;

51 : 25 *O destroying mountain.*   Babylon was a flat plain, but
it is called a mountain here because it was built up in towering
fortresses (Kimchi).

51 : 25-26 *A burnt mountain . . . a stone for a corner.*   The
mountain (i.e., Babylon) will be so completely burned that even
its stones will be unusable for building.

Their might hath failed, they are become as women;
Her dwelling-places are set on fire,
Her bars are broken.

31. One post runneth to meet another,
And one messenger to meet another,
To tell the king of Babylon
That his city is taken on every quarter;

32. And the fords are seized,
And the castles they have burned with fire,
And the men of war are affrighted.

33. For thus saith the LORD of hosts,
The God of Israel:
The daughter of Babylon is like a threshing-floor
At the time when it is trodden;
Yet a little while, and the time of harvest
Shall come for her.

34. Nebuchadrezzar the king of Babylon hath devoured
me,
He hath crushed me,
He hath set me down as an empty vessel,
He hath swallowed me up like a dragon,
He hath filled his maw with my delicacies;
He hath washed me clean.

35. 'The violence done to me and to my flesh be upon
Babylon,'
Shall the inhabitant of Zion say;
And: 'My blood be upon the inhabitants of Chal-
dea,'
Shall Jerusalem say.

36. Therefore thus saith the LORD:
Behold, I will plead thy cause,
And take vengeance for thee;

Jeremiah 51

51 : 31 *One post . . . to . . . another . . . tell the king of Babylon.*
Presumably the king remained in his palace and was kept in-
formed of the progress of the siege by messengers. Now he is
told that the city has fallen.

51 : 33 *A threshing-floor . . . when . . . trodden.* The commentators take this to mean: At present Babylon is as prosperous
as a full threshing-floor ready to be trodden. But she will soon
be despoiled: "the time of harvest shall come for her."

285

And I will dry up her sea,
And make her fountain dry.

37. And Babylon shall become heaps,
A dwelling-place for jackals,
An astonishment, and a hissing,
Without inhabitant.

38. They shall roar together like young lions;
They shall growl as lions' whelps.

39. With their poison I will prepare their feast,
And I will make them drunken, that they may be
convulsed,
And sleep a perpetual sleep, and not wake,
Saith the LORD.

40. I will bring them down like lambs to the slaughter,
Like rams with he-goats.

41. How is Sheshach taken!
And the praise of the whole earth seized!
How is Babylon become an astonishment
Among the nations!

42. The sea is come up upon Babylon;
She is covered with the multitude of the waves
thereof.

43. Her cities are become a desolation,
A dry land, and a desert,
A land wherein no man dwelleth,
Neither doth any son of man pass thereby.

44. And I will punish Bel in Babylon,
And I will bring forth out of his mouth that which
he hath swallowed up,
And the nations shall not flow any more unto him;
Yea, the wall of Babylon shall fall.

45. My people, go ye out of the midst of her,
And save yourselves every man

51 : 42   *The sea is come up upon Babylon.*   A metaphor for the
invading army. Rashi: An army as vast as a sea.

51 : 44   *Nations shall not flow any more unto him.*   Crowds will
no longer stream toward Babylon. It will no longer be a magnet
for merchants and visitors. A similar phrase is used in Isaiah 2:2:
"And all nations shall flow into it."

From the fierce anger of the LORD.

46. And let not your heart faint, neither fear ye,
For the rumour that shall be heard in the land;
For a rumour shall come one year,
And after that in another year a rumour,
And violence in the land, ruler against ruler.

47. Therefore behold, the days come,
That I will do judgment upon the graven images of
Babylon,
And her whole land shall be ashamed;
And all her slain shall fall in the midst of her.
48. Then the heaven and the earth, and all that is
therein,
Shall sing for joy over Babylon;
For the spoilers shall come unto her
From the north, saith the LORD.
49. As Babylon hath caused the slain of Israel to fall,
So at Babylon shall fall the slain of all the land.
50. Ye that have escaped the sword,
Go ye, stand not still;
Remember the LORD from afar,
And let Jerusalem come into your mind.
51. 'We are ashamed, because we have heard reproach,
Confusion hath covered our faces;
For strangers are come
Into the sanctuaries of the LORD's house.'
52. Wherefore, behold, the days come, saith the LORD,
That I will do judgment upon her graven images;
And through all her land the wounded small groan.
53. Though Babylon should mount up to heaven,
And though she should fortify the height of her
strength,
Yet from Me shall spoilers come unto her, saith
the LORD.

51 : 46 *And after that in another year a rumour.* Kimchi explains this verse as addressed to the captives in Babylon. They will be hearing rumor after rumor that invading armies are marching against Babylon. Let them not be afraid. Babylon will indeed be destroyed, but they will be safe.

287

54. Hark! a cry from Babylon,
    And great destruction from the land of the Chaldeans!
55. For the LORD spoileth Babylon,
    And destroyeth out of her the great voice;
    And their waves roar like many waters,
    The noise of their voice is uttered;
56. For the spoiler is come upon her, even upon Babylon,
    And her mighty men are taken,
    Their bows are shattered;
    For the LORD is a God of recompenses,
    He will surely requite.
57. And I will make drunk her princes and her wise men,
    Her governors and her deputies, and her mighty men;
    And they shall sleep a perpetual sleep, and not wake,
    Saith the King, whose name is the LORD of hosts.
58. Thus saith the LORD of hosts:
    The broad walls of Babylon shall be utterly overthrown,
    And her high gates shall be burned with fire;
    And the peoples shall labour for vanity,
    And the nations for the fire;
    And they shall be weary.

59. The word which Jeremiah the prophet commanded Seraiah the son of Neriah, the son of Mahseiah, when he went with Zedekiah the king of Judah to Babylon in the fourth year of his reign. Now Seraiah was quartermaster. 60. And Jeremiah wrote in one book all the evil that should come upon Babylon, even all these words that are written concerning Babylon. 61. And Jeremiah said to Seraiah: 'When thou comest to Babylon, then see that thou read all these words, 62. and say: O LORD, Thou hast spoken concerning this place, to cut it off, that none shall dwell therein, neither man nor beast, but that it shall be desolate for ever. 63. And it shall be, when thou hast made an end of reading this book, that thou shalt bind a stone to it, and cast it into the midst of the Euphrates; 64. and thou shalt say: Thus shall Babylon sink, and shall not rise again because of the evil that I will bring upon her; and they shall be weary.'

Thus far are the words of Jeremiah.

51 : 59-64   An incident. When Zedekiah and the leaders of the people were carried off captive in Babylon, Jeremiah wrote out this prophecy of doom against Babylon and gave it to Seraiah, the quartermaster. He told him to read the prophecy when he arrived in Babylon, then tie it to a stone and sink it in the Euphrates. This would be a symbol: "Thus shall Babylon sink and shall not rise again" (verse 64).

52

THE BOOK OF Jeremiah actually closes with the last words of chapter 51: "Thus far are the words of Jeremiah." The narrative in chapter 52, an appendix giving an account of the fall of Jerusalem, is taken from II Kings 24:18-25:30.

Jeremiah
52

1. Zedekiah was one and twenty years old when he began to reign; and he reigned eleven years in Jerusalem; and his mother's name was Hamutal the daughter of Jeremiah of Libnah. 2. And he did that which was evil in the sight of the LORD, according to all that Jehoiakim had done. 3. For through the anger of the LORD did it come to pass in Jerusalem and Judah, until He had cast them out from His presence. And Zedekiah rebelled against the king of Babylon. 4. And it came to pass in the ninth year of his reign, in the tenth month, in the tenth day of the month, that Nebuchadrezzar king of Babylon came, he and all his army, against Jerusalem, and encamped against it; and they built forts against it round about. 5. So the city was besieged unto the eleventh year of king Zedekiah. 6. In the fourth month, in the ninth day of the month, the famine was sore in the city, so that there was no bread for the people of the land. 7. Then a breach was made in the city, and all the

men of war fled, and went forth out of the city by night by the way of the gate between the two walls, which was by the king's garden—now the Chaldeans were against the city round about—and they went by the way of the Arabah. 8. But the army of the Chaldeans pursued after the king, and overtook Zedekiah in the plains of Jericho; and all his army was scattered from him. 9. Then they took the king, and carried him up unto the king of Babylon to Riblah in the land of Hamath; and he gave judgment upon him. 10. And the king of Babylon slew the sons of Zedekiah before his eyes; he slew also all the princes of Judah in Riblah. 11. And he put out the eyes of Zedekiah; and the king of Babylon bound him in fetters, and carried him to Babylon, and put him in prison till the day of his death.

12. Now in the fifth month, in the tenth day of the month, which was the nineteenth year of king Nebuchadrezzar, king of Babylon, came Nebuzaradan the captain of the guard, who stood before the king of Babylon, into Jerusalem; 13. and he burned the house of the LORD, and the king's house; and all the houses of Jerusalem, even every great man's house, burned he with fire. 14. And all the army of the Chaldeans, that were with the captain of the guard, broke down all the walls of Jerusalem round about. 15. Then Nebuzaradan the captain of the guard carried away captive of the poorest sort of the people, and the residue of the people that remained in the city, and those that fell away, that fell to the king of Babylon, and the residue of the multitude. 16. But Nebuzaradan the captain of the guard left of the poorest of the land to the vinedressers and husbandmen. 17. And the pillars of brass that were in the house of the LORD, and the bases and the brazen sea that were in the house of the LORD, did the Chaldeans break in pieces, and carried all the brass of them to Babylon. 18. The pots also, and the shovels, and the snuffers, and the basins, and the pans, and all the vessels of

brass wherewith they ministered, took they away. 19. And the cups, and the fire-pans, and the basins, and the pots, and the candlesticks, and the pans, and the bowls—that which was of gold, in gold, and that which was of silver, in silver—the captain of the guard took away. 20. The two pillars, the one sea, and the twelve brazen bulls that were under the bases, which king Solomon had made for the house of the Lord—the brass of all these vessels was without weight. 21. And as for the pillars, the height of the one pillar was eighteen cubits; and a line of twelve cubits did compass it; and the thickness thereof was four fingers; it was hollow. 22. And a capital of brass was upon it; and the height of the one capital was five cubits, with network and pomegranates upon the capital round about, all of brass; and the second pillar also had like unto these, and pomegranates. 23. And there were ninety and six pomegranates on the outside; all the pomegranates were a hundred upon the network round about.

24. And the captain of the guard took Seraiah the chief priest, and Zephaniah the second priest, and the three keepers of the door; 25. and out of the city he took an officer that was set over the men of war; and seven men of them that saw the king's face, who were found in the city; and the scribe of the captain of the host, who mustered the people of the land; and threescore men of the people of the land, that were found in the midst of the city.

26. And Nebuzaradan the captain of the guard took them, and brought them to the king of Babylon to Riblah. 27. And the king of Babylon smote them, and put them to death at Riblah in the land of Hamath. So Judah was carried away captive out of his land.

28. This is the people whom Nebuchadrezzar carried away captive: in the seventh year three thousand Jews and three and twenty; 29. in the eighteenth year of Nebuchadrezzar, from Jerusalem, eight hundred thirty and two persons; 30. in the three and twentieth year of Nebuchadrezzar Nebuzaradan the captain of the guard carried away captive of the Jews seven hundred forty and five persons; all the persons were four thousand and six hundred.

31. And it came to pass in the seven and thirtieth year of the captivity of Jehoiachin king of Judah, in the twelfth month, in the five and twentieth day of the month, that Evilmerodach king of Babylon, in the first year of his reign, lifted up the head of Jehoiachin king of Judah, and brought him forth out of prison. 32. And he spoke kindly to him, and set his throne above the throne of the kings that were with him in Babylon. 33. And he changed his prison garments, and did eat bread before him continually all the days of his life. 34. And for his allowance, there was a continual allowance given him of the king of Babylon, every day a portion until the day of his death, all the days of his life.

Bibliography

Introductions

Cornill, Carl. *Introduction to the Canonical Books of the Old Testament*. New York, 1907.
Eissfeldt, Otto. *The Old Testament: An Introduction*. New York, 1965.
Pfeiffer, Robert H. *Introduction to the Old Testament*. New York, 1941.

Ancient and Medieval Commentaries

The Targum.
Rashi (Troyes, N. France), 1040-1105.
David Kimchi (Narbonne, S. France), ca. 1160-1235.
Adne Kesef. Joseph ibn Caspi (S. France), 1297-1340, ed. I. Last, London, 1912.
Jeremiah. Joseph b. Simon Kara (N. France), ca. 1060-1130, ed. Schlossberg, Paris, 1881.
Perush Neviim. Isaac of Trani the Elder (Bari, S. Italy), ca. 1180-1250, ed. Abraham Wertheimer, Jerusalem, 1959.
Jeremiah. Joseph ibn Nachmias (Toledo, Spain), 14th cent., ed. Moses Bamberger, Frankfurt a/M, 1854.
Jeremiah. Isaac Abravanel (b. Lisbon 1437, d. Venice 1508).

Modern Hebrew Commentaries

Luzzato, Samuel David. *Commentary on Jeremiah*. Lemburg, 1870.
Malbim, Meir Leb b. Jehiel Michel, 1809–79 (Kiev).
Ehrlich, Arnold. *Randglossen zur Hebräischen Bibel*, vol. 4. Leipzig, 1912.
Tur-Sinai (Torczyner), Napthali Herz. *Peshuto shel Mikra*, vol. 3. Jerusalem, 1967.
Segal, Moses. "Jeremiah." In *Encyclopedia Mikrait*, Jerusalem, 1950–68.

Modern Critical Studies

Blank, Sheldon H. *Jeremiah: Man and Prophet*. Cincinnati, 1961.
Bright, John. *Jeremiah*. Anchor Bible, New York, 1965.
Buttenwieser, M. *The Prophets of Israel*. New York, 1914.
Duhm, B. *Das Buch Jeremia erklärt*. Tübingen, 1901.